AF594260

THE BRITISH SURREALISTS

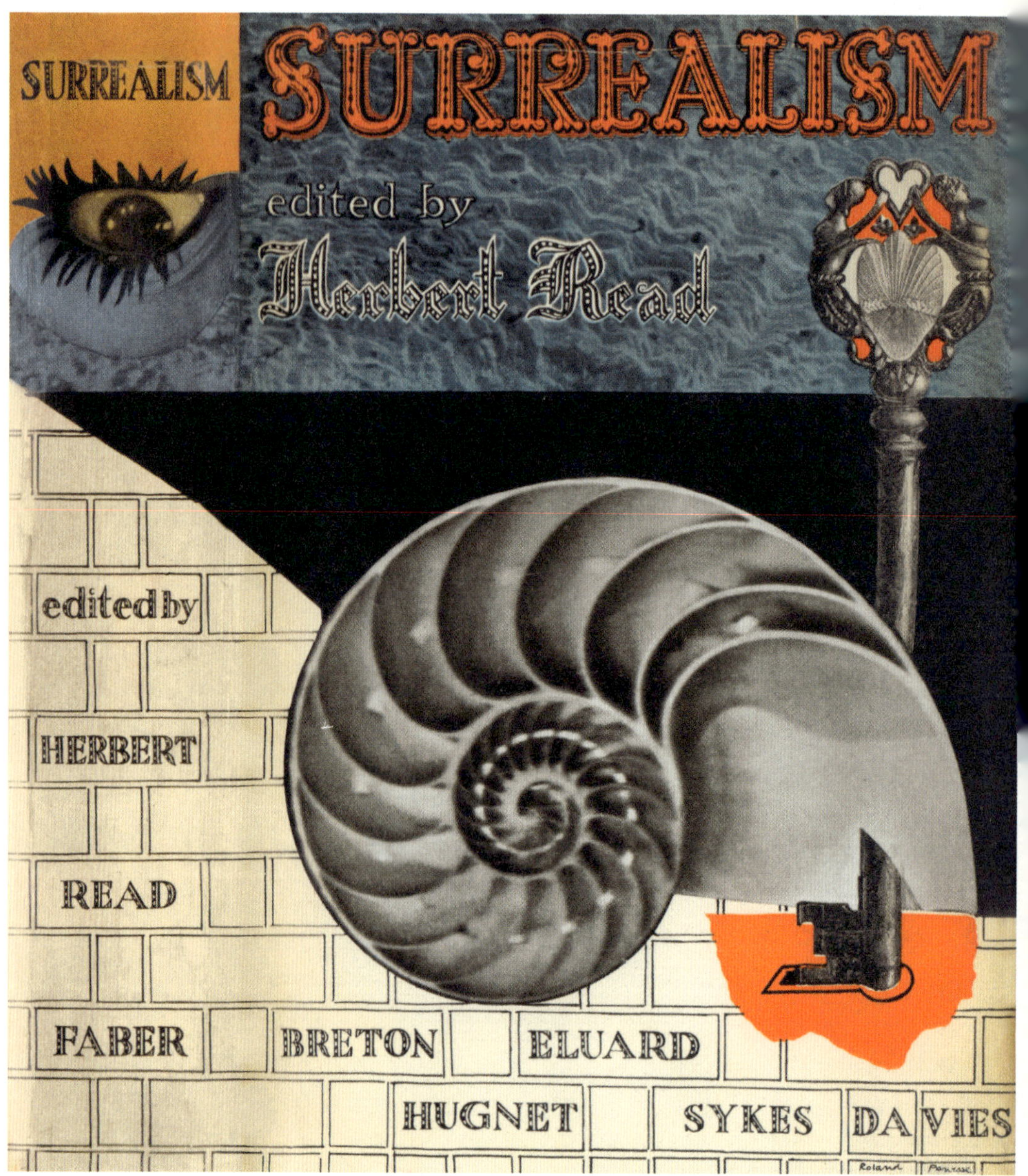

Front cover of Herbert Read's 1936 book *Surrealism*, with a collage by Roland Penrose.

THE BRITISH SURREALISTS

DESMOND MORRIS

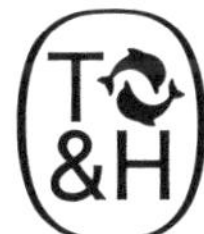

CONTENTS

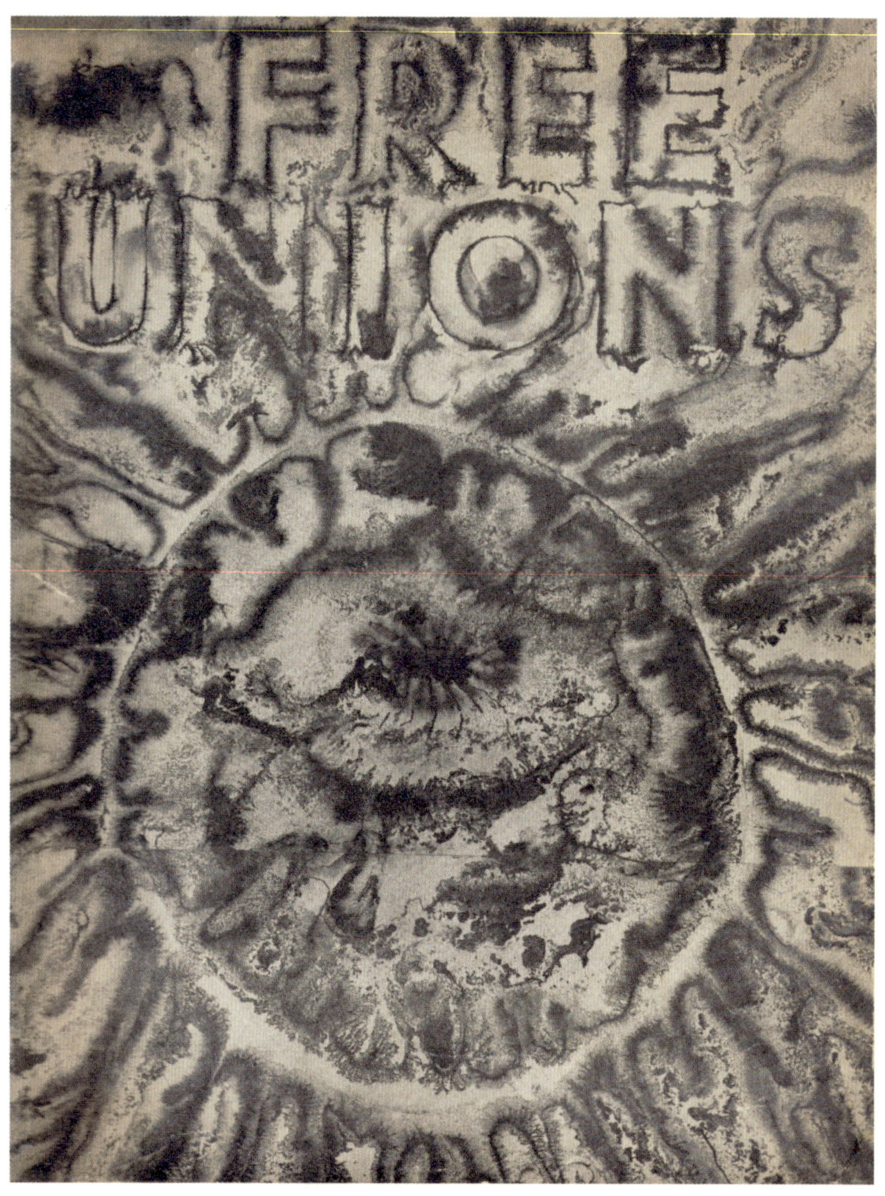

Free Unions, published by The Surrealist Group in England and edited by Simon Watson Taylor, July 1946, front cover design by Conroy Maddox.

PREFACE

In 2014 I began work on a book that was designed to present short biographies of all the better-known surrealists. I wanted to find out as much as I could about the personalities of the artists involved in the surrealist movement. My library was full of monographs about their work, but I wished to know more about what sort of lives they lived and how their backgrounds had influenced their creativity. I became so absorbed in this project that it soon started to get out of hand. I kept finding more and more artists who were either fully committed but less well-known surrealists, or who were major figures that were in some way related to the movement but without being fully involved with it. I went on adding more and more artists until, to my surprise, I had assembled biographies of 100 of them – at which point I reluctantly called a halt.

My text was now far too long for a single volume, and it was decided to select just those artists who had been most prominent in the movement or who had become most renowned on an international scale. This meant removing about two-thirds of the 100 biographies, including most of the British surrealists. The resulting book, *The Lives of the Surrealists*, was published in 2018. It was soon joined by editions in Spanish, Italian, German, Danish, Czech, Russian and Chinese. The only British figures that 'made the cut' were Eileen Agar, Francis Bacon, Leonora Carrington, Conroy Maddox, Henry Moore and Roland Penrose. There were many more who, although serious artists deserving recognition, were not familiar on the international scene. The same is true elsewhere. There are surrealist artists who are well known in, say, Denmark, Hungary or Portugal, but who are virtually unknown outside their own countries. In the case of the British surrealists, there is a particularly fascinating range of eccentric, idiosyncratic artists who may not be feted abroad, but who have played an important role in the history of modern art in Britain.

LONDON BULLETIN

JUNE 1940

FIVE SHILLINGS

EILEEN AGAR
JOHN BANTING
VICTOR BRAUNER
ANDRE BRETON
J. B. BRUNIUS
J. BUCKLAND-WRIGHT
PAUL DELVAUX
MATTA ECHAURREN
PAUL ELUARD
MAX ERNST
ESTEBAN FRANCES
S. W. HAYTER
LEN LYE
PIERRE MABILLE

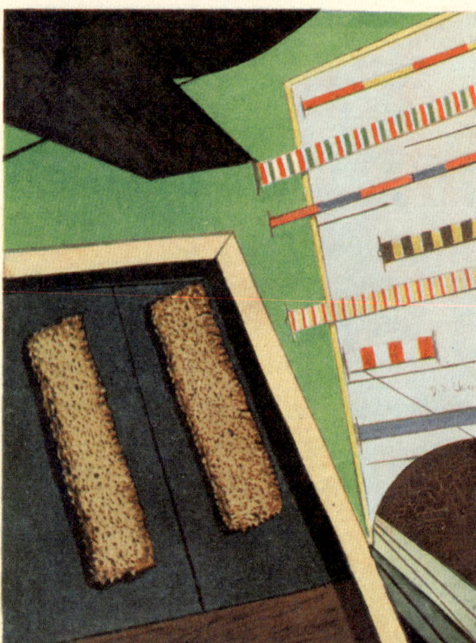

GIORGIO DE CHIRICO THE WAR

F. E. McWILLIAM
CONROY MADDOX
JOHN MELVILLE
ROBERT MELVILLE
E. L. T. MESENS
LEE MILLER
HENRY MOORE
G. ONSLOW-FORD
ROLAND PENROSE
BENJAMIN PERET
E. RIMMINGTON
BRIERY RUSSELL
YVES TANGUY
JOHN TUNNARD

18-20

PUBLISHED BY THE SURREALIST GROUP IN ENGLAND
SOLE AGENT: A. ZWEMMER
76-80 CHARING CROSS ROAD, LONDON, W.C.2

Front cover of the last edition of the surrealist *London Bulletin*, published in June 1940 by The Surrealist Group in England, with a work by Giorgio de Chirico on the cover.

So I am delighted that it is now possible to gather in this new volume all the British surrealists who were numbered among my original 100 artists, plus a few more. The six who did appear in *The Lives of the Surrealists* could not be omitted here, of course, and I apologize for the slight repetition that this involves.

Thanks largely to Roland Penrose, who was the main driving force behind the great surrealist exhibition in London in 1936, the British surrealist movement has been a vigorous presence for many years. For the purposes of this book, however, I have confined myself to those artists who were active when the movement was in its heyday – in the inter-war period. As an organized art movement, with group meetings, discussions and exhibitions, British surrealism went into decline shortly after the end of World War II. For me personally this was a disaster because no sooner had I joined the movement the 1940s than I found it collapsing around me. Its effective end came with the closure in 1951 of the London Gallery, which had been its headquarters and its focal point for exhibitions, publications and meetings. I was no longer able to enjoy the noisy debates of the group meetings and the endless arguments about the finer points of surrealist philosophy.

On an international scale, however, surrealism was far from dead, with most of the leading surrealists – although now widely scattered in Europe and the Americas – continuing to produce work for many years. In addition, a new generation of younger surrealists appeared and, even today in the twenty-first century, surrealism remains an active force, having outlived all the other specialized art movements that flowered in the aesthetic rebellions of the early twentieth century. The group meetings, the Bretonesque rules and regulations, and the infamous expulsions may have faded into history, but the spirit of surrealist rebellion has managed to survive. Like me, many of the other British surrealist artists also remained active long after the official disbanding of the London group. We may no longer have been a close-knit, organized circle, but separately we each continued to create new work.

In addition to restricting my text to the British artists who were working before World War II, I have also limited it in another way, by including only those surrealists who were visual artists and who created paintings, sculptures or surrealist constructions. I have omitted the surrealists who solely wrote books, poems or pamphlets, or who confined themselves to making films or

INTERNATIONAL SURREALIST EXHIBITION
London, 1936

English Committee :
HUGH SYKES DAVIES, DAVID GASCOYNE, HUMPHREY JENNINGS, McKNIGHT KAUFFER, RUPERT LEE (*Chairman*), HENRY MOORE, PAUL NASH, ROLAND PENROSE (*Hon. Treasurer*), HERBERT READ.
Secretary : DIANA BRINTON LEE.

France :
ANDRÉ BRETON, PAUL ELUARD, GEORGE HUGNET, MAN RAY.

Belgium :
E. L. T. MESENS.

Scandinavia :
VILH. BJERKE-PETERSEN.

Spain :
SALVADOR DALI

Artists Exhibiting :

Eileen Agar
Hans Arp
Jacqueline B.
John Banting
Hans Bellmer
John Selby Bigge
Constantin Brancusi
Victor Brauner
Edward Burra
Alexander Calder
Giorgio de Chirico
Cecil Collins
Salvador Dali
P. Norman Dawson
Oscar Dominguez
Marcel Duchamp
Max Ernst
Mervyn Evans
Leonor Fini
Freddie
David Gascoyne
Alberto Giacometti
S. W. Hayter
Charles Howard
Marcel Jean
Humphrey Jennings
Paul Klee
Rupert Lee
Len Lye
Dora Maar
René Magritte
Maruga Mallo
André Masson
Robert Medley
Reuben Mednikoff
E. L. T Mesens
Joan Miró
Henry Moore
Stellan Mörner
Paul Nash
Richard Oelze
Erik Olson
Meret Oppenheim
Wolfgang Paalen
G. W. Pailthorpe
Roland Penrose
Francis Picabia
Pablo Picasso
Angel Planells
Man Ray
Pierre Sanders
Max Servais
Styrsky
Graham Sutherland
Yves Tanguy
S. H. Tauber-arp
Julian Trevelyan
Toyen

Also Objects by :

André Breton
Gala Dali
Hugh Sykes Davies
Rouge Dragon (Eric Geijer)
Geoffrey Grigson
Diana Brinton Lee
Sheila Legge
Margaret Nash
Herbert Read
Roger Roughton
Jean Varda

Nations Represented :

America
Austria
Belgium
Czecho-Slovakia
Denmark
France
Germany
Great Britain
Greece
Italy
Roumania
Spain
Sweden
Switzerland

List of artists included in the 1936 'International Surrealist Exhibition', taken from the exhibition catalogue.

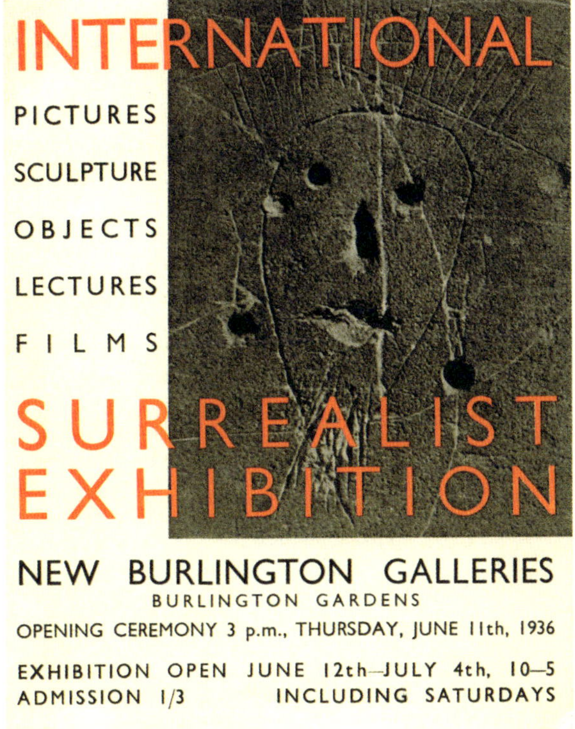

photographs. For an in-depth discussion of the wider surrealist movement in Britain, see Michel Remy's landmark study *Surrealism in Britain* (1999).

Finally, I should mention that, when I was a young surrealist in the 1940s, I was fiercely doctrinaire and totally intolerant of all artists who were not 'party members'. In those days there was such strong opposition to surrealism from society at large that we had to band together as a besieged little group. Later, when I was developing my public career as a zoologist, I continued to produce surrealist paintings, but I could no longer be called a doctrinaire party member. In retrospect I do not think that that reduced the surrealist validity of my works of art. In fact, I think my separation from any surrealist group helped me to develop and mature my own form of art.

Poster for the 'International Surrealist Exhibition' at the New Burlington Galleries in London, June–July 1936.

INTRODUCTION

This is a book about the British painters and sculptors who were producing surrealist works of art in the 1930s. It is not an analysis of their work – surrealists dislike having their work analysed – but rather a series of pen-portraits of the men and women who rebelled against traditional, representational art in the period between the two great wars. What kind of people were they, so bent on exploring new visual freedoms and rejecting the strict rules of the established art world?

The answer is that they were of two kinds. There were the total surrealists, who followed the dictates of André Breton, the founder of the movement who, in 1924, had published a manifesto in Paris in which he gave a precise definition of surrealism. And there were those who, although they produced surrealist works of art, were not interested in attending surrealist meetings or being part of an organized group. It has to be said that there was often an uneasy relationship between the two. The doctrinaire surrealists were critical of those whose lifestyle did not toe the party line. And the others either actively disliked Breton's regulations or simply ignored them.

Matters came to a head in 1936 when Roland Penrose, after spending more than a decade in Paris with the original surrealist group there, returned to England to mount a major surrealist exhibition in London. The rich son of a Quaker banking family, he had become totally devoted to the surrealist ideals and wanted to see them promoted in his home country. He bought a house in Hampstead and formed a committee to start organizing the exhibition. The idea was to import works by the major Parisian surrealists and show them alongside British works – thereby elevating the status of the British contingent. His problem was that there were only a few artists working in Britain who considered themselves to be out-and-out surrealists. All the others, who may have been producing strange, rebellious, imaginative works, were not calling themselves surrealists and, in some cases, were not even aware of the movement.

In order to present a strong British showing at his exhibition, it was Roland's task to round them up and label all of them as true surrealists. He toured the studios and assembled his British contingent. Some of them were happy to exhibit, but, when the show was over, had little more to do with organized surrealism. Others became active in the movement and, in the late 1930s, a serious group was formed whose members, like their Paris counterparts, started to have official meetings, electing members and expelling those who did not obey the party rules. A Belgian surrealist, E. L. T. Mesens, saw his chance of becoming the London version of André Breton and moved to England to take control. In 1937 Penrose set him up in an art gallery – the London Gallery on Cork Street – and this would soon become the surrealist headquarters in England, not only mounting regular surrealist exhibitions but also producing a string of surrealist publications.

In 1939 the outbreak of World War II meant that the London Gallery had to be closed. The British Surrealist Group lost it momentum, and there were fierce squabbles concerning its future. It did manage to reassemble briefly after the war, and the gallery was reopened and operated again from 1946 to 1951. Then, owing to lack of sales and high running costs, Roland shut it down and the reign of Mesens as surrealist supremo came to an end. The group scattered, but many of them did continue, individually, to produce good surrealist work until, one by one, they began to die off. Today, a new generation of British surrealists has arisen, and the tradition of creating rebellious, irrational works of art continues. The key concept of surrealism – allowing the unconscious to control the creation of imagery – will probably survive forever in one form or another.

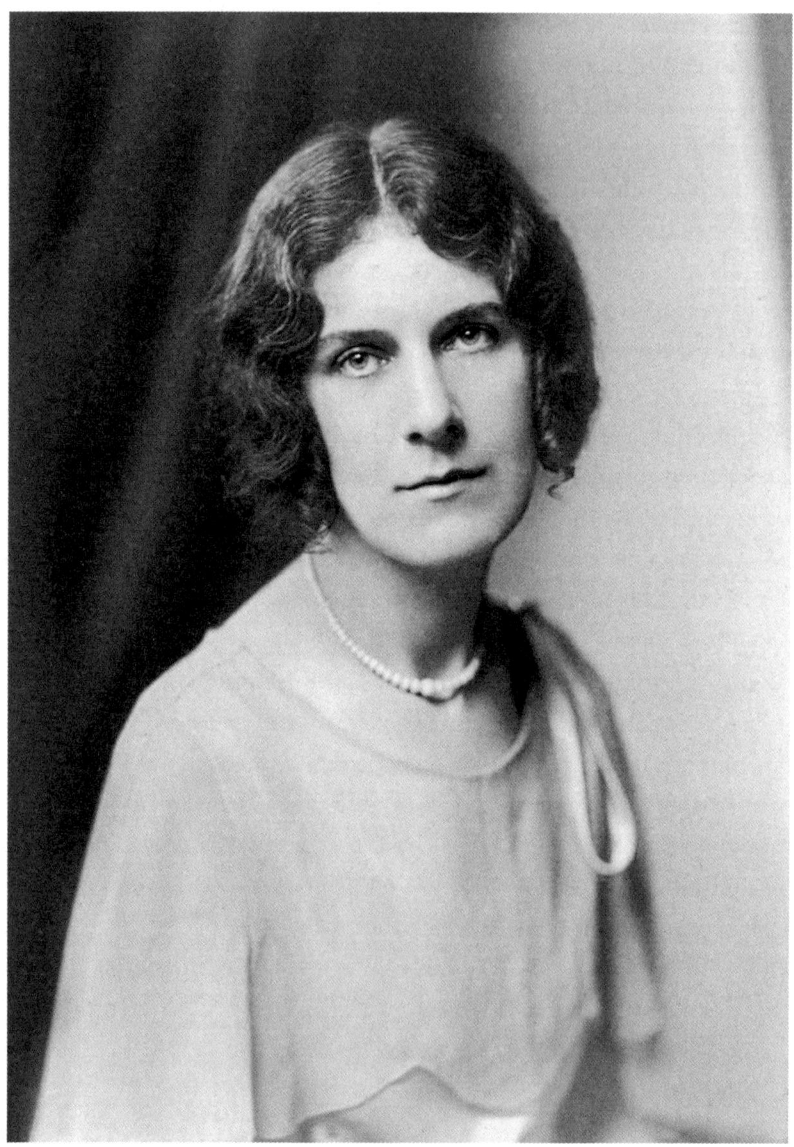

Marion Adnams, c. 1919.

MARION ADNAMS

Produced surrealist paintings but was outside the surrealist group

BORN: 3 December 1898 in Derby

PARENTS: Father a woodwork teacher at Derby School

LIVED: Derby 1898 to 1995; second home in France in the 1960s

PARTNERS: None recorded

DIED: 24 October 1995 in Derby, aged 96

Marion Adnams is a classic example of an artist who produced highly accomplished surrealist paintings but was neither involved in the surrealist movement nor a member of the British Surrealist Group. Although she liked to socialize, and travelled when she could, she lived her whole life in the city of Derby, where she was born and where she pursued a lengthy career as an art teacher. She died in the house in which she was born, and her funeral was held in Derby Cathedral. The nearest she ever came to the surrealist movement was when, from time to time, she exhibited her paintings in London galleries alongside those of, for example, Max Ernst, Henry Moore and Eileen Agar. As a result of living a comparatively quiet life in a provincial city, she became one of the 'forgotten surrealists', rarely mentioned in books or articles despite having been better known in her early years. There was nothing remotely surrealist about her lifestyle or her philosophy of life. She became a surrealist only when she was sitting in front of her easel.

Marion was essentially a teacher, and a greatly appreciated one. From an early age she expressed the desire to study art but was diverted from this by her family, who persuaded her to attend college in nearby Nottingham to study modern languages. Dutifully she obtained her degree in 1919. After graduating, she set off on art trips to Belgium, France and Italy in the 1920s. The artwork she created during these trips was exhibited at the Derby Art Gallery. Then, in the 1930s, she attended evening art classes in Derby, where her teacher was an artist called Alfred Bladen who aroused her interest in surrealist paintings. The two masters of surrealism who had the strongest

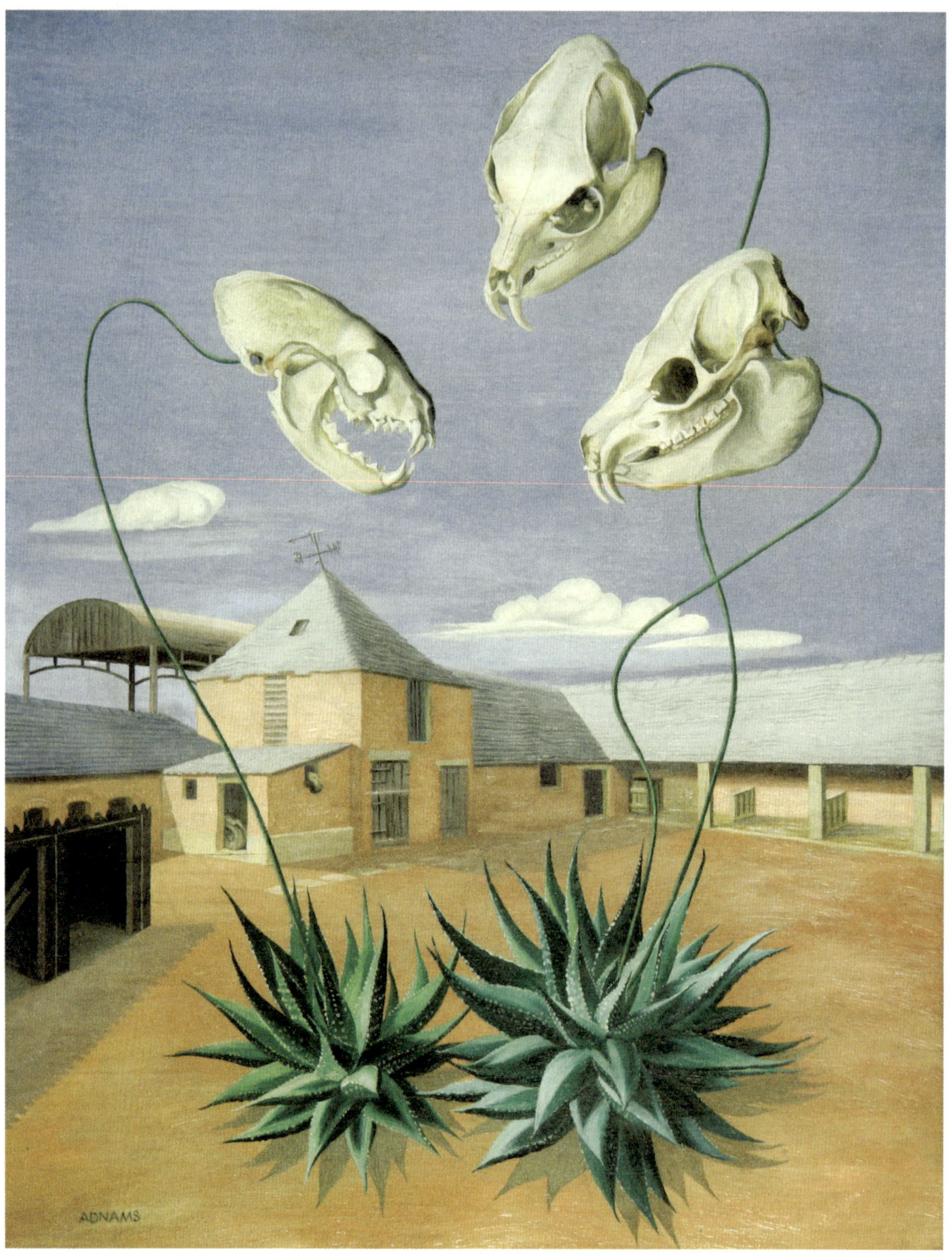

Marion Adnams, *Nightmare at Noon*, c. 1945.

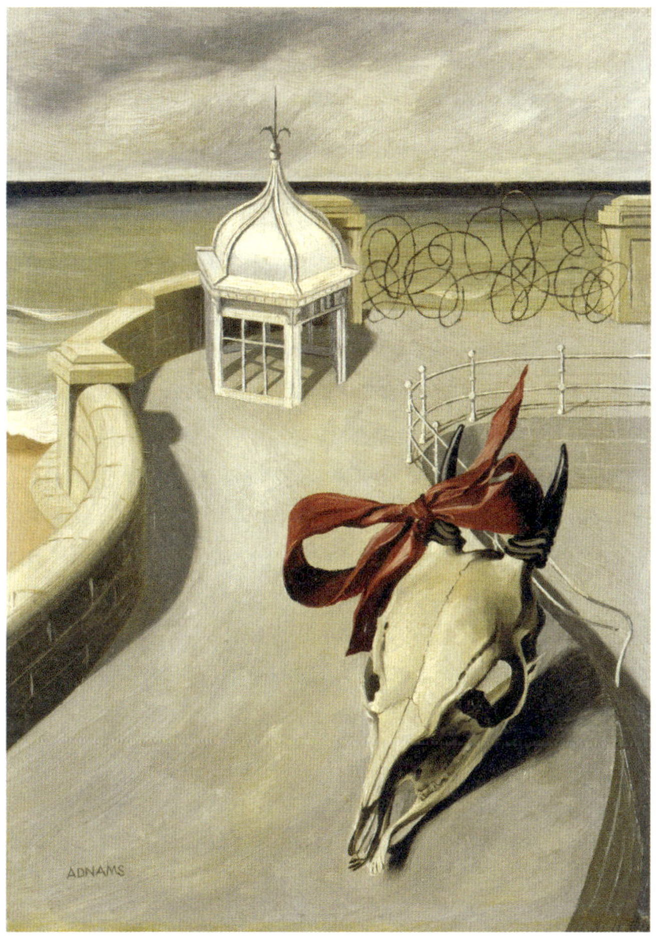

influence on her work were René Magritte and Salvador Dalí. She began to make meticulous landscapes in which familiar objects appeared in irrational relationships to one another. She would go out to explore local landscapes, often collecting natural objects, as Paul Nash was doing, and bringing them back to her studio. There, she would start painting and enter what she called 'the enchanted country' – her personal dream world. Asked about her themes, she replied that she had a special interest in 'death and resurrection – life coming out of death in varied and curious ways'.

Marion Adnams, *Aftermath*, 1946.

Towards the end of the 1930s she began her teaching career, not in languages but as an art teacher at a girls' school in Derby. It was at this point that, in her spare time, she started to devote herself more and more to her surrealist paintings, exhibiting at Manchester City Art Gallery in the 1940s. She moved on to teach at a grammar school in Derby and eventually ended up as head of art at a Derby training college – pursuing a lifelong career as a dedicated and accomplished art teacher in middle England, well away from the surrealist activities in the capital.

Adnams retired from teaching in 1960, at the age of sixty-one, and was then able to concentrate even more on her painting. After visiting Provence, she acquired a second home in Burgundy and, when painting there, was strongly influenced by the French countryside. However, her life as a painter ended tragically: macular degeneration caused her eyesight to fail over a period of many years. Her blindness became so severe that, for the last quarter of a century of her life, from the age of seventy-one to ninety-six, she could not see well enough to paint, although she still travelled and talked about art.

Retrospective exhibitions of her work were held in Nottingham in 1971 and at the Derby Museum and Art Gallery in 2017.

EILEEN AGAR

Joined the surrealist group in 1936

BORN: 1 December 1899 in Buenos Aires, as Eileen Forrester Agar

PARENTS: Father Scottish businessman (windmills); mother Anglo-American

LIVED: Buenos Aires 1899; London 1911; Paris 1927; London 1930

PARTNERS: Married fellow art student Robin Bartlett 1925; divorced 1929 • Hungarian author Joseph Bard 1926 onwards • Paul Nash 1935–44 • Paul Éluard 1937 • Married Joseph Bard 1940 (until his death in 1975)

DIED: 17 November 1991 in London, aged 91

I first met Eileen Agar when she was ninety years old, and even then she retained the beauty and the charm that must have enchanted the surrealists she had known when she was young. Her figure was still slim, her posture upright and her face mischievous. She gave off an aura of imaginative playfulness that is rare in the very old. She herself would probably have put this down to the fact that she never had children. As a teenager she had read about a possible human population explosion and recalled the huge relief she felt at having found a justification for not wanting to breed.

Although there was nothing especially erotic about her paintings, in life she seems to have been more sexually adventurous than many women of her generation. According to her husband she was always 'trying to do something in a way that cannot be done, such as making love standing up in a hammock'. She was a hedonist, but in a cheerfully childlike way. She once remarked gleefully that she slept in Picasso's bed, but not when he was in it – setting up a wicked thought only to demolish it. A wicked innocence is a contradictory idea, but it somehow fits Agar's appealing personality as well as her work as an artist.

She was born in Argentina of an Anglo-American mother and a Scottish father who was selling windmills to the local population. The family was wealthy and sociable, so the children usually saw their parents only briefly, once a day, to say goodnight. Eileen admitted to having a temper and to rule-breaking that, on one occasion, led to her being struck with a hairbrush by her mother – a punishment that made her very angry and that she still remembered vividly eight decades later. A young rebel was being formed. She was happiest when playing out of doors, reacting strongly to the colours and shapes of the Argentine landscape. Even as an old lady she could still see, in her mind's eye, such details as the glinting bridles of the black horses that drew her green carriage.

When she was ten, the family left Argentina and her father retired to England. On the journey, they were accompanied by a cow and an orchestra to provide them with fresh milk and music. In London they lived in a large mansion in Belgrave Square complete with a ballroom. Her mother became a society hostess with lavish parties, a butler, housemaids, footmen and a chauffeur-driven Rolls Royce. The relaxed splendour of Agar's childhood, during which time she had become passionate about drawing, came to a sudden, jarring halt with the outbreak of World War I. The Rolls was given to the Red Cross, and Eileen's eccentric mother sent a telegram to her boarding school forbidding them to teach her German. After the war, the Agar family resumed their lavish lifestyle at a new house in Mayfair, where Eileen recalled playing musical chairs with ex-Prime Minister Herbert Asquith – she was told she had to let him win. Her home life was full of formalities; even when there were no guests, she had to appear in evening dress for dinner, summoned by the gong.

Despite her mother's repeated attempts at matchmaking, Eileen rejected all offers of a husband. Art had become increasingly important to her, and she now saw it as her future way of life. Her mother, on the other hand, viewed it as an elegant pastime and enlisted the help of a friend of Auguste Rodin's to teach her daughter watercolour painting. When an acquaintance of Pierre-Auguste Renoir's said that Eileen should take art more seriously and attend art school, her mother was outraged but lost the struggle and, in 1920, Eileen started attending art classes in London. Even so, that autumn, her mother managed to disrupt this by whisking the family away to Argentina, where she organized a lavish all-night ball for 600 people in Buenos Aires to celebrate Eileen's twenty-first birthday. When the family returned to London she was, at last, allowed to attend the Slade School of Fine Art, but only if she was ferried there and back each day in the family Rolls. To avoid embarrassment, she arranged with the chauffeur that he should drop her off and collect her around the corner.

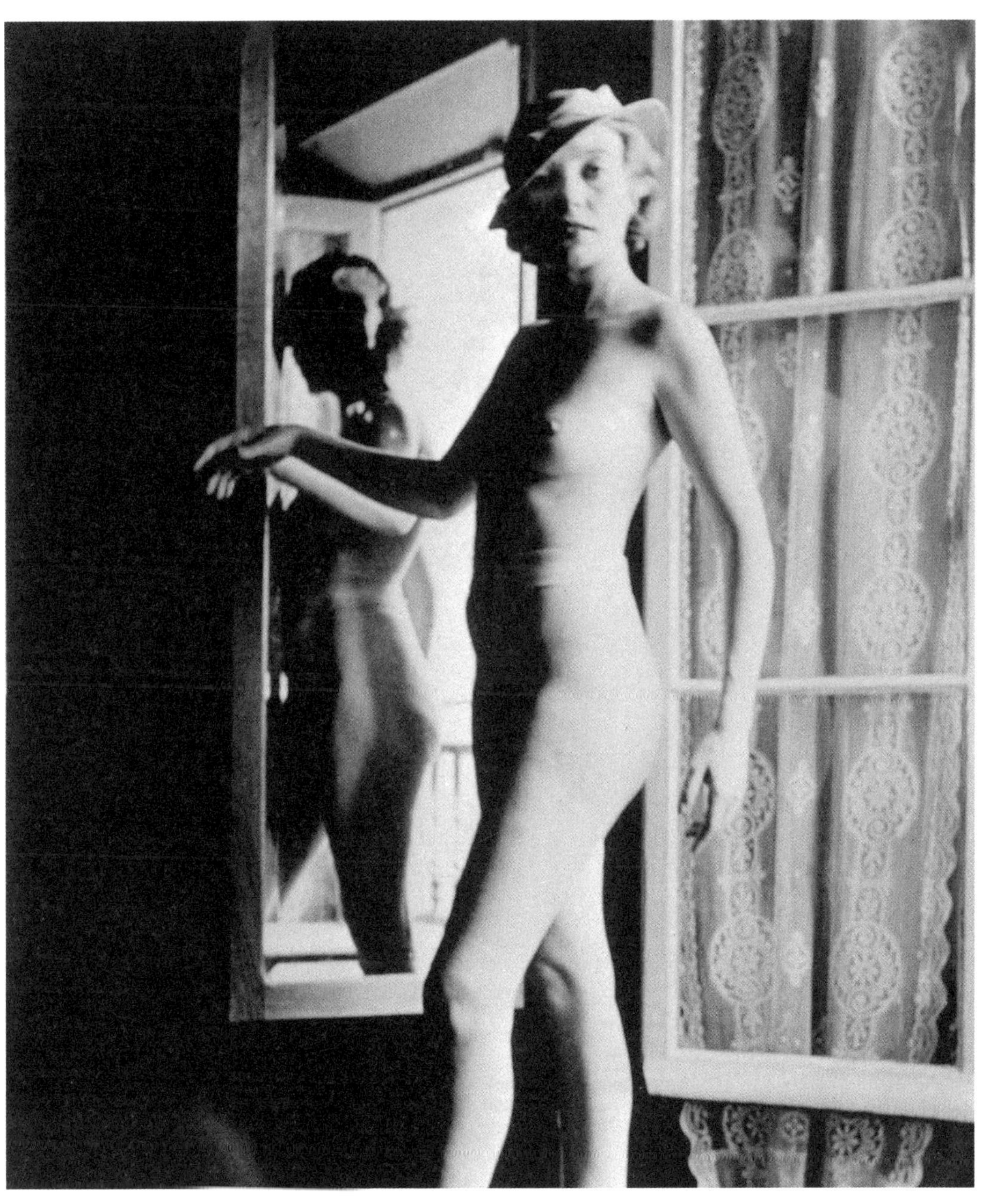

Eileen Agar, undated.

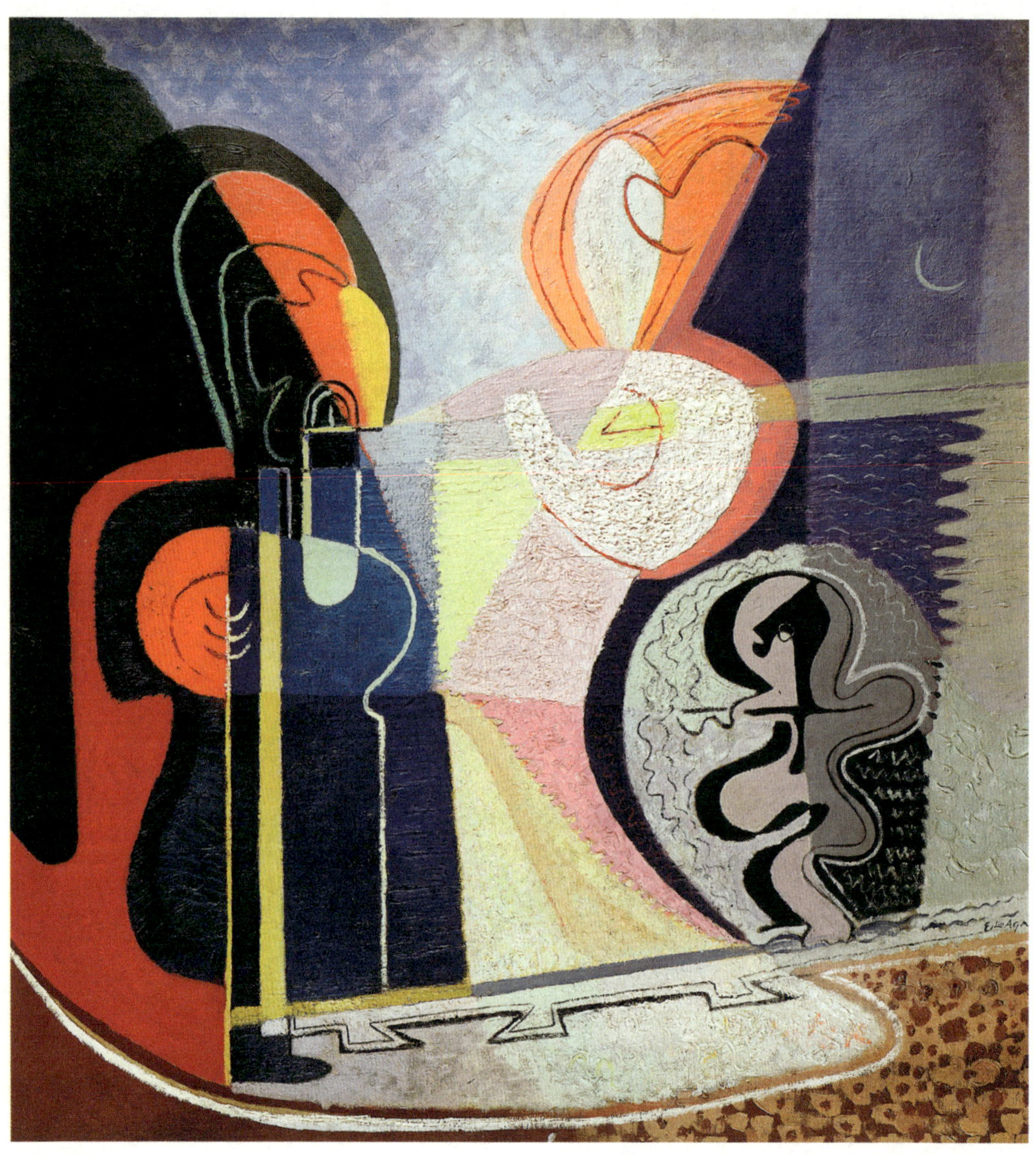

Eileen Agar, *Family Trio*, c. 1934.

Shortly after this, following a family row in which her mother had slapped her, the twenty-one-year-old Eileen packed her bags and left home for good. She found a small studio in Chelsea and began painting seriously. Having determinedly lost her virginity in a leafy glade on the Isle of Wight to a fellow Slade student, Robin Bartlett, she went on to marry him in 1925, and they moved to a small mud-floored cottage in rural France. She soon tired of him, however, and left him for the man who would become the love of her life, a handsome Hungarian writer called Joseph Bard.

Eileen and Bard moved to Italy and later to Paris where, in the late 1920s, she met the avant-garde artists and poets and revelled in her rebellious freedom. She visited Constantin Brancusi's studio and encountered André Breton at the very peak of the surrealist revolution. Her father had died and left her a generous annual allowance, so that she never had to face the prospect of working for a living. This meant that she could satisfy every intellectual whim and spend time with many of the major figures of the day, including Evelyn Waugh, Ezra Pound, Cecil Beaton, Aldous Huxley, W. B. Yeats, Osbert Sitwell, Ernest Hemingway and F. Scott Fitzgerald.

Back in London in the early 1930s, Agar received encouragement as an artist from Henry Moore and they became close friends, though he never forgot that she beat him at tennis. He introduced her to Jacob Epstein and the American Alexander Calder. In 1935, while passing the summer on the south coast of England, Eileen met the artist Paul Nash and his wife, Margaret Odeh. Nash excited Agar and encouraged her to search for strange items on the beach and elsewhere that could be modified to make surrealist objects. Eileen and Nash fell in love and after a while became lovers, causing much heartache for their still actively involved partners. Eventually Eileen decided to end the relationship, but neither she nor Nash could bear to lose the excitement they felt when they were together, and they took to arranging secret meetings to avoid causing more distress. Having two lovers at the same time was something that Eileen could not resist, although she admitted it involved considerable pain for all concerned.

When Roland Penrose and David Gascoyne decided to arrange a major exhibition in London to introduce surrealism to the British public, they invited Paul Nash and Henry Moore to join the organizing committee. Both Nash and Moore knew about the strangely powerful paintings that Agar had been producing since her time in Paris, and she was visited in her studio by Penrose and Herbert Read, who selected three of her oils and five of her surrealist objects for the show. Agar was initially startled to find that she was now an official member of the surrealist movement. She had always fought to be a free spirit, working on her own, but now she found herself co-opted into a fervently rebellious group. After she had experienced the intense excitement of the opening night of the exhibition, however, she commented: 'I was proud to be among them.' She was fascinated by her new surrealist friends. She found Max Ernst bird-like, Paul Éluard romantically classic-looking, André Breton leonine, Yves Tanguy bizarre, nervous and excitable, Salvador Dalí conspicuous and with an explosive temper, and Joan Miró childlike and poetic. She made the interesting point that the surrealist women were all elegantly, quietly dressed – in complete contrast with the female bohemian artists, who showed off in deliberately scruffy, paint-splattered clothes. She added that this was not an act of compliance or 'pandering to masculine demands', but that the juxtaposition of elegant dress with outrageous behaviour was 'carrying the beliefs of surrealism into public existence'.

The following year, while staying with Roland Penrose in Cornwall, Agar found her love life becoming even more complicated. Roland, as she put it, was always 'ready to turn the slightest encounter into an orgy'. The atmosphere was sexually loaded, and Eileen quickly succumbed to the charms of the French surrealist poet Paul Éluard. She described him as a living Eros and was soon in his arms and in his bed, despite the presence of his second wife, Nusch, an ex-circus performer. Eileen's other lovers, Joseph Bard and Paul Nash, were also on hand. Nash became insanely jealous of Éluard, but Bard minded less, consoling himself in the arms of Nusch. It was around this time that Lee Miller, by now coupled with Penrose, having split from Man Ray, was told by mischief-maker Édouard Mesens that Eileen had sexual designs on Roland. Lee's forthright reaction was to throw a glass of water over Eileen before she discovered that the story was untrue. Such were the complexities and intricacies of the relations within the surrealist group that Agar was now a part of but, far from being upset by it all, she took to it with a twinkle in her eye and a joyous sense of release from the formal restrictions of her earlier family existence.

Following the house party in Cornwall, most of the group moved on to the south of France to join up with Man Ray, Picasso and Dora Maar. It is rumoured that, during this gathering, Eileen and Picasso had a brief sexual

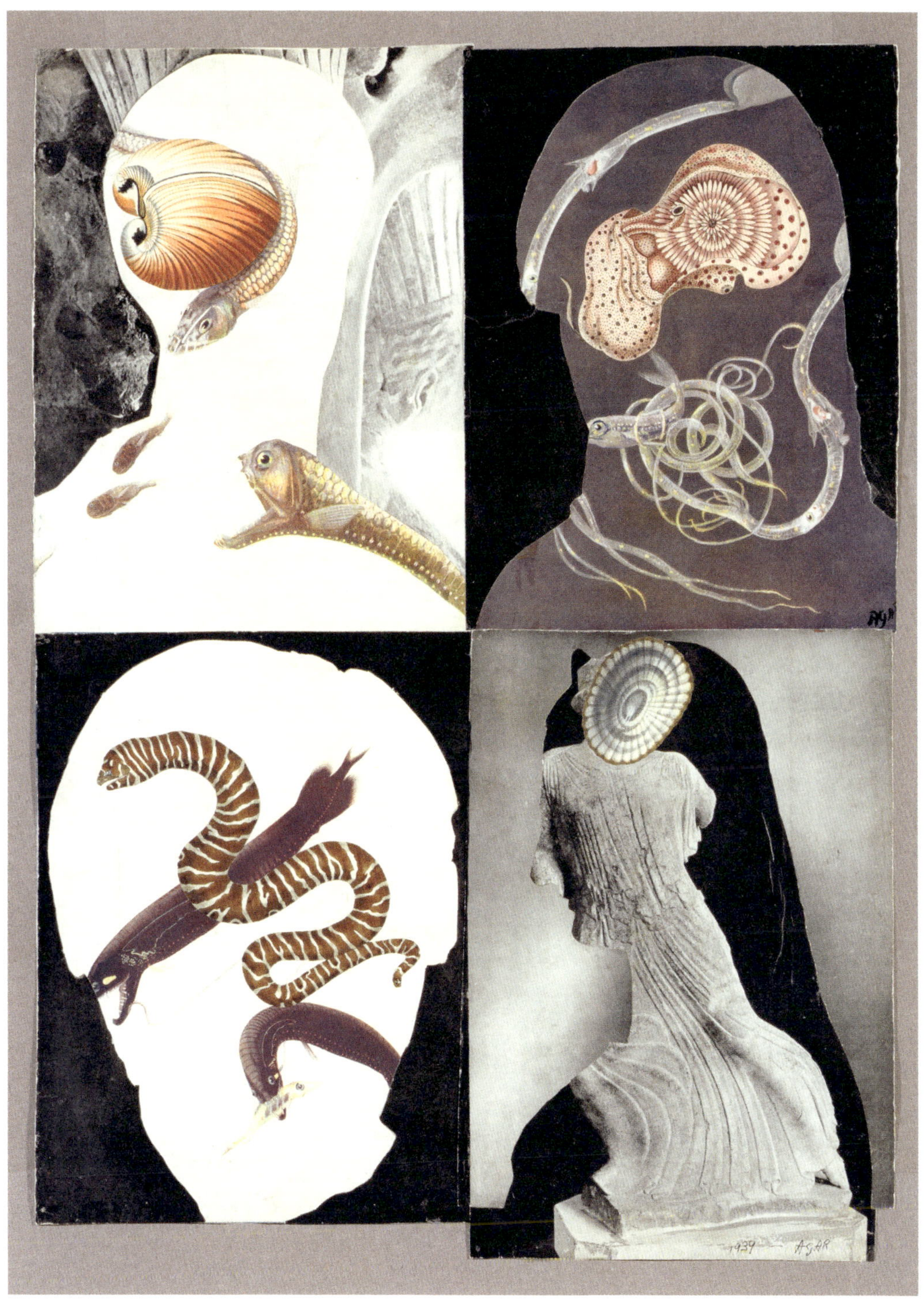

Eileen Agar, *Marine Collage*, 1939.

encounter, but she herself never admitted to this. Despite the social pleasures of the time, war was on the horizon. In an oddly prophetic gesture at table one day, Picasso pulled the cork out of a bottle, handed it to Eileen and told her to put it between her teeth to stop them chattering when the bombs started falling. And fall they did.

Back in London, with the war raging in earnest, Agar and Bard decided to get married after a night of heavy bombing that left them feeling lucky to be alive. Henry Moore, still a good friend, was one of the guests at a party to celebrate their marriage in 1940. Agar found it hard to concentrate on painting while the war was going on around her. Instead, she poured herself into war work. When the conflict was over, she returned to painting 'as if I were renewing a belief in life itself'. For the next thirty years she lived happily with Joseph Bard, and her wild days were over. She worked hard on her paintings and her surrealist constructions, exhibited frequently and successfully, and travelled abroad with the man she described as 'the warmth of my life'. When he died in 1975, she faced the last sixteen years of her long life alone with her memories and, in 1988, nearing her ninetieth year, she recorded them for posterity in her autobiography *A Look at My Life*. And she never stopped working in her studio.

Eileen Agar described her work as a blend of abstraction and surrealism rather than pure surrealism, but the words she used to sum up her life suggest that she was more of a surrealist than she liked to admit: 'I have spent my life in revolt against convention, trying to bring colour and light and a sense of the mysterious to daily existence.'

JOHN ARMSTRONG

Said that some of his work was surrealist but that he did not belong in the surrealist group

BORN: 14 November 1893 in Hastings, Sussex, as John Rutherford Armstrong

PARENTS: Father a parson

LIVED: Hastings 1893; West Dean, Sussex 1895; London 1913; Dunmow, Essex 1939; Lamorna, Cornwall 1945–55; London 1955

PARTNERS: Elsa Lanchester 1932
• Married Benita Jaeger 1936–38; divorced (two children)
• Elizabeth Smart 1939 • Married Veronica Sibthorp 1939–55; divorced
• Married Annette Heaton 1956–73 (one child)

DIED: 19 May 1973 in London, from Parkinson's disease, aged 79

As an artist, John Armstrong was a loner, an independent spirit who had no links to the surrealist group but many of whose paintings were undeniably surrealist in character. The reason for this is simple. He described his mode of working as follows: 'These things come to me as complete images, often when I am half asleep.... Afterwards I may have ideas about what they mean, but I suppose only a conference of psychologists could really analyse them.' In other words, he was painting from the unconscious mind, in keeping with the central surrealist tradition. Many of his paintings, however, would have had the true surrealists running for the exits, or worse.

Armstrong was the delicate son of a strict Victorian parson in the south of England. He grew up in a country vicarage where he and his siblings were tutored at home by their parents. He soon rebelled against his rigorously imposed religious upbringing, seeing his art as a way of escape. At art school, however, he was rarely in attendance, preferring to spend his time at museums, galleries and the ballet. During World War I he was fortunate to be posted to the Middle East, where he was able to study the art of the ancient civilizations at first hand. After the war, he enjoyed further encounters with early cultures when he was employed as a travel guide escorting a rich elderly lady who was touring the Mediterranean and North Africa. Back in London, he devoted himself to his painting but was so poor that he often went hungry and, on one occasion, was so starved that he subsided into a coma and had to be rushed to hospital to save his life. A friend described him as tall, thin and round-shouldered, with a sensitive face and a vulnerable expression.

He escaped from this period of poverty by painting set designs and murals; but he did not give up his easel work and was rewarded with his first solo show in London in 1928. It was a success, with half the works sold, but the great depression of the 1930s was soon to throw a dark shadow over the art world. A compensation for Armstrong was his friendship with the actor Charles Laughton and his wife, Elsa Lanchester. He had been a witness at their wedding in 1929 and in the 1930s moved into the world of the cinema with them, working on various design projects.

Armstrong's relationship with Elsa Lanchester was strangely intimate. She described him as a lifelong friend but also commented that 'here and there a friend was a lover'. She admitted that she possessed some limericks he had written for her that were too obscene to include in her memoirs. The only verse she quoted was: 'Christmas comes but once a year; not like you and me I fear.' While her husband Charles Laughton was away filming *Mutiny on the Bounty* (1935), Elsa made three short amateur films starring John Armstrong and his new girlfriend, Benita Jaeger, who later became his wife. Elsa seemed to be obsessed with him, calling him 'brilliant, adoring, tall, wispy', and described him as pursuing models like a lepidopterist. Armstrong's marriage to Benita lasted only two years: when she, reclining in her bath, told him she was having an affair, he leant across, kissed her hand and it was all over. He soon had more lovers, always needing a woman in his life. One of these was the Canadian writer Elizabeth Smart.

It is tempting to see Armstrong's emotional upheavals as the source of some of the images in his paintings at this time. His work in 1938 became more richly surrealist and bizarre, with a review in the *Telegraph* describing him as 'our foremost surrealist painter'. The critic was at pains to point out that Armstrong was not slavishly copying a foreign fashion, rather that he derived his strange, dreamlike landscapes from a much earlier, purely English visual tradition. Another important critic, the artist Wyndham Lewis, declared that there were only two British surrealists: Paul Nash and John Armstrong. He wrote this in the late 1930s, some time after the infamous International Surrealist Exhibition of 1936, when London had been introduced to a whole

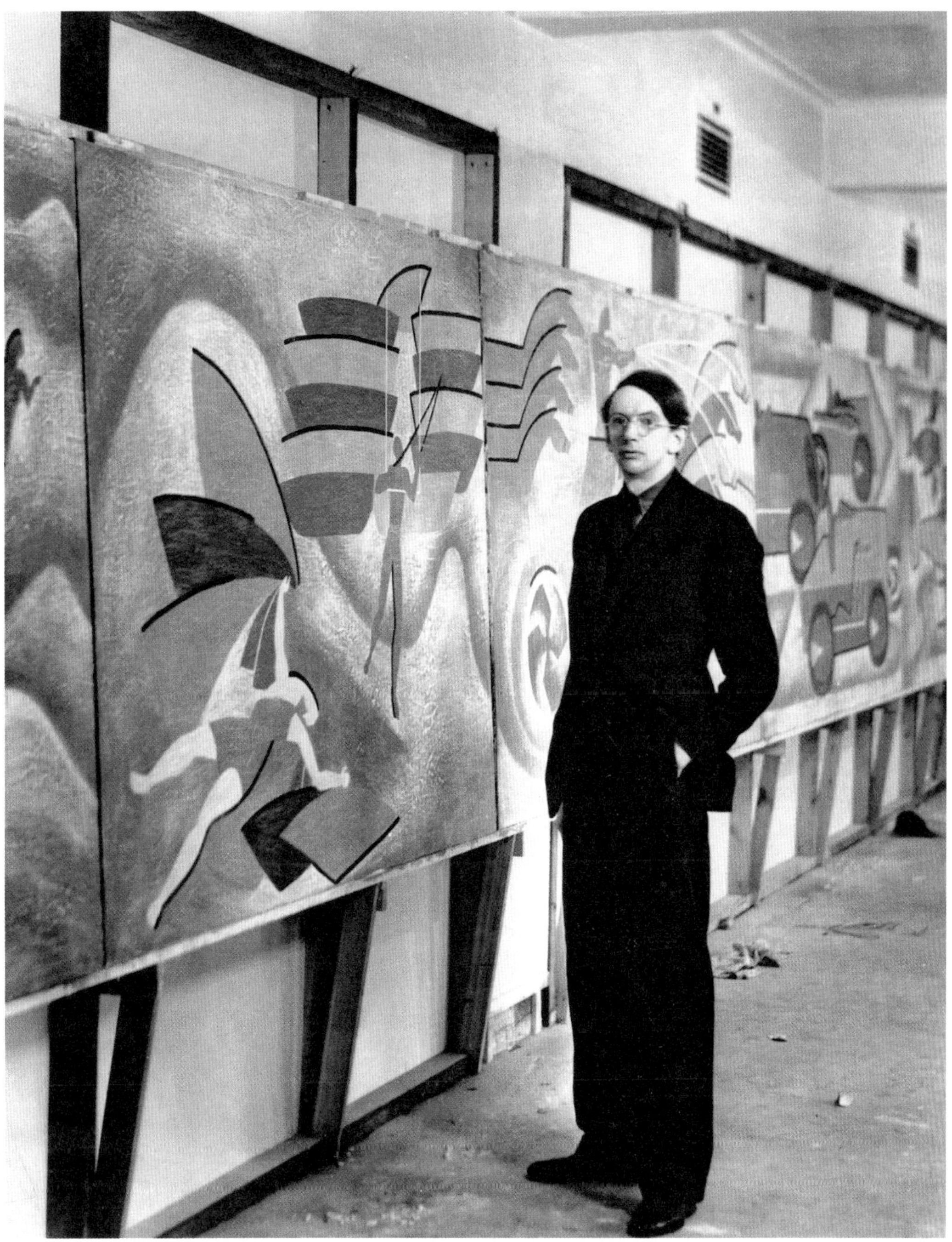

John Armstrong standing beside his mural panels at Shell-Mex House, London, 1933.

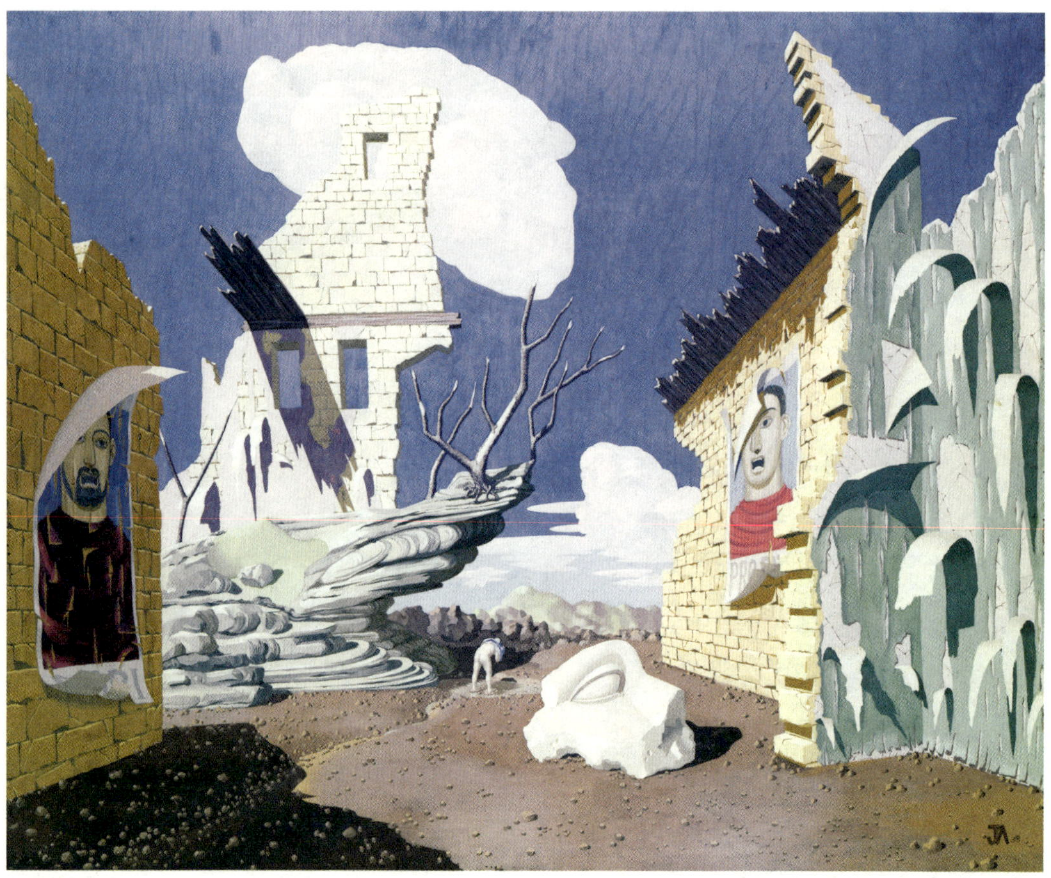

range of British surrealists. This makes Lewis's comment sound like a deliberate insult, saying in effect that the other British surrealists were not worth considering and perhaps, at the same time, castigating the organizers of the exhibition for omitting Armstrong's work.

Armstrong's friend Paul Nash had been on the organizing committee for the surrealist exhibition, which must have taken the view that John would not fit in with that rebellious group. When he was being interviewed many years later, Armstrong himself made his position clear, saying that he did not feel he belonged with the surrealists. He made the important distinction that he himself was not a true surrealist, but that some of his paintings

John Armstrong, *Pro Patria 1938*, 1938.

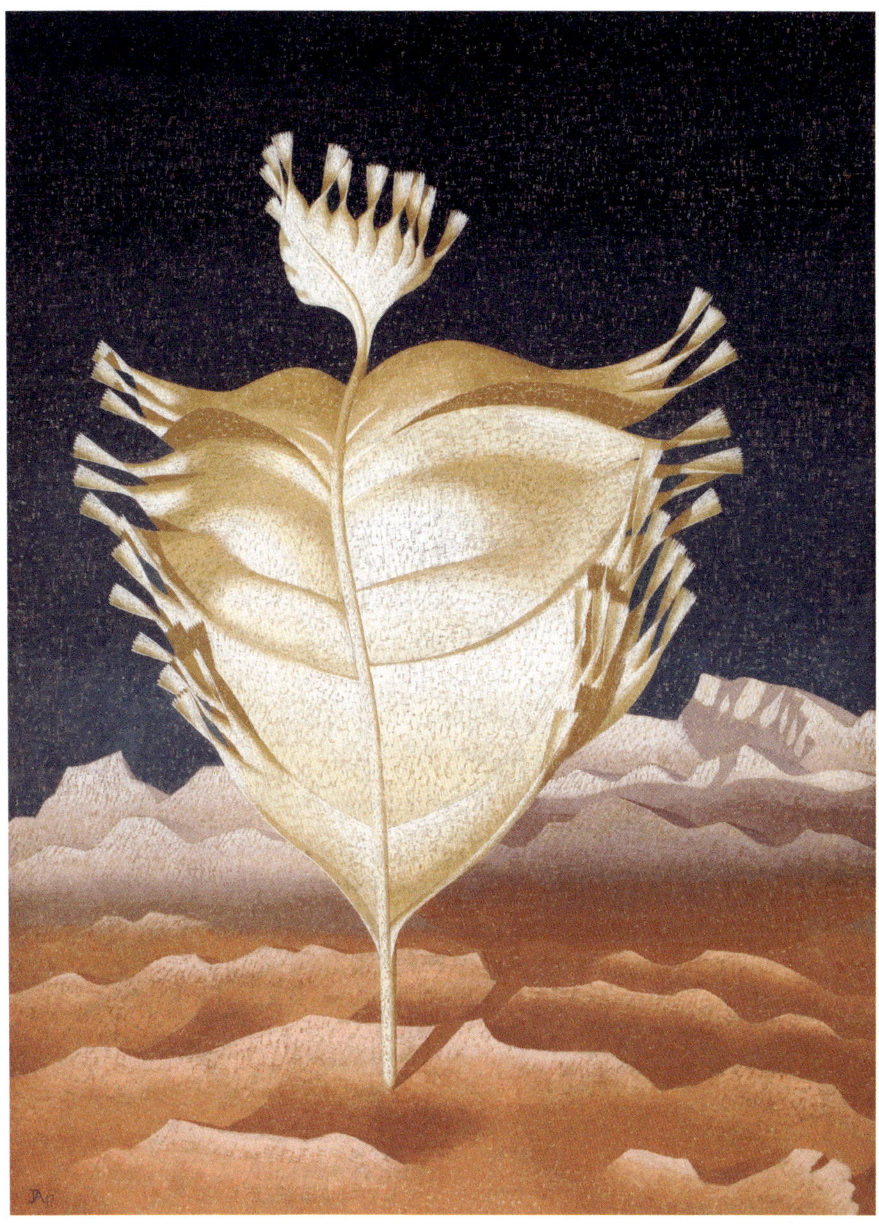

John Armstrong, *The Passion of the Inanimate*, 1947.

were surrealist works. This is not as contradictory as it sounds. There were other artists who painted surrealist pictures but knew nothing at all about the surrealist movement itself or its manifestos and theories. They arrived at surrealist images via a strange, private, individual obsession. Some, like the Renaissance artist Giuseppe Arcimboldo, lived long before the surrealist era. Others were largely outside the professional art world and ignorant of its modern movements. These, like Armstrong, were natural surrealist artists, but strictly on their own terms.

In 1939 Armstrong met Veronica Sibthorp, a rich, one-legged artist, whose artificial leg was called Gilbert and who had recently had an affair with Dylan Thomas. Described, rather unkindly, as a sharp-tongued, articulate, amusing, self-centred, middle-class snob, she and Armstrong were soon married and would endure a long, turbulent relationship. For a decade they lived together in a cottage in Cornwall until eventually it became too much for John. In a revealing poem he described the end of their relationship. The poem began: 'I saw her devil in her face / Immediately mine went out / And in the intervening space / Attempted to put hers to rout.' Finally, in 1955, he left her and moved back to London. There, in 1956, he met Annette Heaton, who had recently graduated from the Courtauld Institute of Art. He painted her portrait and she found him 'witty, ironic, kind and gentle'. They soon became a couple, marrying when his divorce from Veronica came through, and in 1959 a daughter was born.

A few years later, in 1962, Annette was distraught to discover that Armstrong had the early signs of Parkinson's disease. He refused to give in to the disease and kept painting energetically, day in and day out, knowing that time was against him. Fortunately, although he was suffering from the shakes that come with the illness, he was still able to control a brush efficiently. In 1970 he suffered a stroke, but even then he still insisted on painting. Finally, after a second stroke in 1972, he was no longer able to paint and he died the following year.

FRANCIS BACON

Considered himself a surrealist and wished to join the London group but was rejected by them in 1935–36

BORN: 28 October 1909, in Dublin

PARENTS: Father an English racehorse trainer; mother a socialite and heiress

LIVED: Dublin 1909; rented homes in England (childhood); Ireland 1918; Gloucester 1924; Ireland 1926; London 1926; Berlin & Paris 1927; London 1928; Monte Carlo 1946; London 1948

PARTNERS: Eric Hall 1929–50 • George Dyer 1964–71 (died of an overdose) • John Edwards 1974–92

DIED: 28 April 1992 in Madrid, of a heart attack, aged 82

I once made Francis Bacon laugh when I told him that he was the only artist whose work had made me physically sick. I hastened to explain that it was not the content of his paintings that disturbed me, but their weight. One night, at a drunken party, my host, who had bought a number of Bacon's screaming Popes, asked me to rearrange them, in order of increasing disintegration. In some, the pope was more realistically depicted; in others the pontiff was unravelling, as if his scream was tearing him physically to pieces. It was my job to shift the pictures around so that the disintegration process increased from left to right. The pictures were massive – taller than me – and had been encased in heavy gold frames and covered in glass to protect their unvarnished surfaces. This made them immensely heavy – almost unmovable – but my drunken, youthful bravado spurred me on, and I was soon heaving and shoving them this way and that until, at last, they were displayed in the desired sequence. That was the moment when I realized that my exertions had brought on a state of acute nausea and I had to make a frantic dash for the nearest bathroom.

That was in the 1940s, when Bacon was virtually unknown and my friend was the only person who collected him on a large scale. When I got to know Francis in the 1960s, he was now famous but, to my surprise, was very modest about his work. He wanted my opinion on whether the figure of a screaming

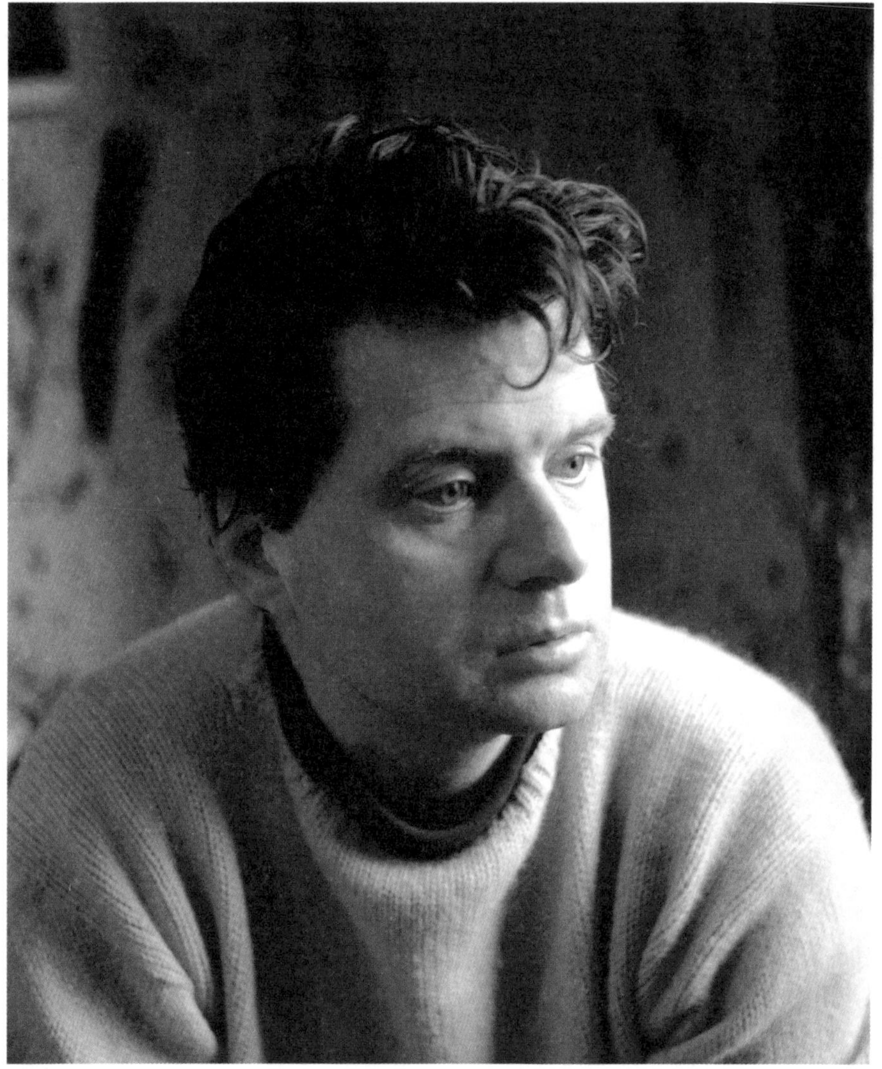

baboon that he had painted was convincing. I assured him that it was, but this was a white lie. I had been told that Francis often copied photographs rather than studying the real thing and, in this instance, I knew the particular photograph from which he had taken the baboon image. It was not of a screaming baboon but of one that was yawning widely. I did not dare tell him

Francis Bacon in his studio, c. 1960.

this because he was notorious for taking a Stanley knife to any canvas that dissatisfied him, and his baboon may well have suffered this fate had I told him the truth. He is known to have slashed to pieces over one hundred of his paintings and I did not wish to be responsible for yet another one. Instead, I changed the subject to other facial expressions, and he amused me by saying, 'I think I've got the scream, but I am having terrible trouble with the smile.'

It may seem strange to include Francis Bacon in a volume on the surrealists, but I have done so for the simple reason that he considered himself to be a surrealist and wanted to be a member of the British Surrealist Group and to be included in their great 1936 exhibition. Herbert Read and Roland Penrose visited his studio in London to decide whether to include him or not, but were dismayed by what they thought were religious elements in his work. They rejected him on these grounds, to his great disappointment. This rejection was based on a misunderstanding: there was nothing faintly religious about Bacon's art. His interest in crucifixions was based not on Christian iconography but on his own, private sexual fantasies. For Francis was deeply involved in sado-masochistic practices and the crucified figures were, in essence, self-portraits. His early life helps to explain this.

Francis's father was a racehorse trainer at the Curragh in County Kildare in Ireland, and Francis was a great disappointment to him. Living in an intensely masculine world, Bacon senior was horrified to discover that his son was less than manly. His reaction to this discovery rebounded on him in spectacular fashion. His first mistake was to have the young Francis whipped by his stable grooms for being effeminate. To his dismay, Francis loved this and even had sex with his tormentors. His second mistake was to send Francis away to boarding school. There, Francis had an affair with another boy and was promptly expelled. His father's third mistake was to throw Francis out of the house for trying on his mother's underwear, whereupon Francis immediately departed for the homosexual underworld of London. When he discovered what his son was up to, the father made his fourth mistake, sending him packing again, this time to Berlin, little knowing that this was the sexual capital of pre-war Europe, where anything went. Francis was in his element. His father had lost every round in their family feud, and the young man was at last free to do as he wished.

From Berlin Francis moved to Paris, where he enjoyed the company of artists and started to paint. His first major influence was Pablo Picasso,

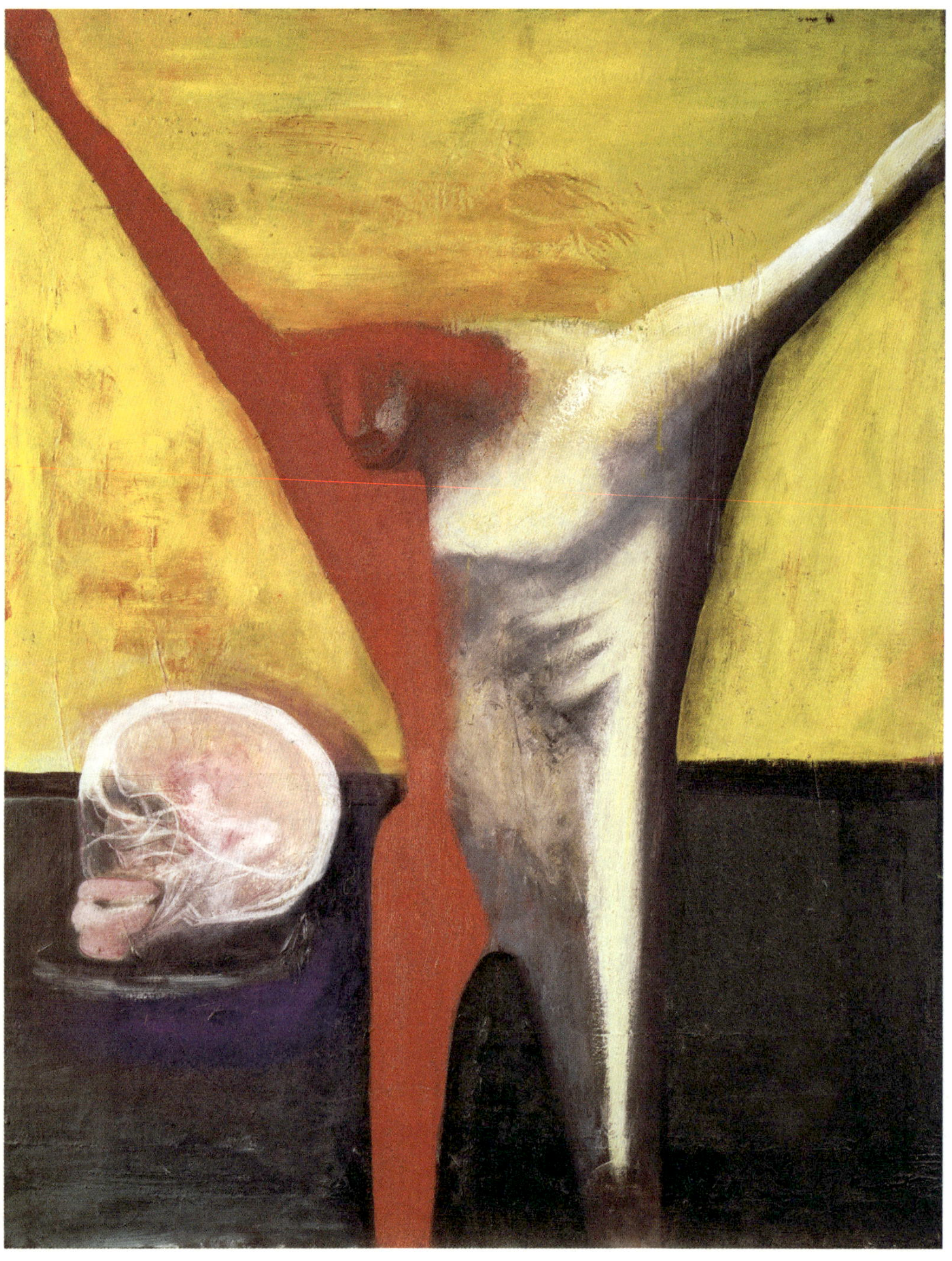

Francis Bacon, *The Crucifixion*, 1933.

whose work he saw in 1928. After a while he returned to London, continued to paint and earned his keep by acting as a homosexual male prostitute, advertising his services discreetly in the columns of *The Times* newspaper as a 'gentleman's companion'. During the London blitz, he volunteered to help in the grisly task of pulling mangled bodies from bombed buildings as the bombing took an increasingly heavy toll. This experience gave him unforgettable visual images of tormented flesh that he would later incorporate into his paintings. When the war ended, his serious work as an artist was soon to begin, although his sexual excesses continued to the end of his life.

Francis's sexual preferences were always of a dangerous nature. He was exclusively homosexual at a time when it was totally illegal to be so. However, he took no pride in it, saying bluntly that 'being homosexual is a defect ... like having a limp'. And he strongly opposed the idea of making homosexuality legal because it would take away some of the spice of engaging in it. When it was finally legalized in 1967, Francis voiced his disapproval, insisting that it was 'so much more interesting when it was illegal'. Bacon also enjoyed being beaten and was said to have had an astonishing ability to withstand physical pain. He told the American poet Allen Ginsberg that he once obtained gambling money by allowing himself to be whipped, with a bonus for every stroke that drew blood. Deliberately selecting brutal partners, he was often injured, but this never weakened his lifelong quest for erotic extremes. Even as an elderly man in his eighties, he was successfully seeking new young lovers.

Though this knowledge of Bacon's private life might make it easier to understand the tortured images in his paintings, it does not explain their greatness. It might be easy to imagine a homosexual masochist producing embarrassingly lurid images with no artistic merit whatever. In contrast, with Bacon, it is the restraint and the ambiguity of his images that make them so powerful and so haunting. The secret of his success lies in the way in which he was able to absorb the intensity of his sexual indulgences and transform them into his uniquely ambiguous paintings. We know we are looking at something that is horribly disturbing, but we are never quite sure what it is or why we react to it so strongly.

One of his favourite motifs was that of a solitary figure, apparently unable to move, trapped inside a kind of box-like structure. The origin of this obsession can be found in an acute trauma from his own childhood. As he told the story, when his hated parents were away, he was left in the care of an Irish servant who enjoyed sexual visits from her boyfriend. Francis was jealous of this male visitor and repeatedly interrupted the couple's lovemaking. The woman's solution was to lock the little boy in a dark cupboard at the top of the stairs, where he would scream and scream until the sex was over and he would be let out again.

Only six of Bacon's oil paintings survived from his pre-war days. It has been claimed that he destroyed around 700 early works, forever dissatisfied with his achievements. All his life he was savagely dismissive of his work, despite the praise it was receiving worldwide. So the biggest surprise in talking to Francis was to discover how gentle his manner was. It simply didn't match the powerful, brutal imagery of his paintings. It was as though all his agony and his intense emotional turmoil went onto his canvases, so that after the act of painting he was left drained and effete.

Outside his studio, Bacon's other obsessions – his boozing, gossiping and gambling – played little or no part in his art. The only possible connection is that he took great risks in his gambling and great risks in his images. Nor is his sharp sense of humour to be found in his typically tense and sombre canvases. None of his painted figures share the twinkle in the eye, the ready smile or the joyous laughter for which he was renowned in his social circle. In his art he 'made heavy' of everything. In life, by contrast, he made light of everything. When, in his later years, as an elderly, world-famous artist, he was offered various honours, including a knighthood, he even laughed at those, refusing them 'because they're so ageing!' It is doubtful if anyone other than Francis would have come up with such a delightful reason for declining such accolades.

Bacon was a creative genius who was also, at times, a thief, a prostitute, a compulsive gambler, a drunkard and a liar. He repeatedly broke the law by organizing illegal gambling sessions. He was mischievous, sarcastic, vain, abusive, arrogant, disloyal and unreliable. Even his published statements, on his own admission, are unreliable: 'I often say anything, you know, to pass the time.' He polished his teeth with Vim, coloured his hair with brown boot-polish, had beady eyes and a slack mouth, and lived in cramped squalor even when he became rich. When people gave him flowers on his birthday, he pointed out that he was not 'the sort of person who has vases'. He loathed nature, the countryside, and all forms of convention and authority. He despised religion and, when someone mentioned the soul to him, he replied 'Ah! Soul!' Then,

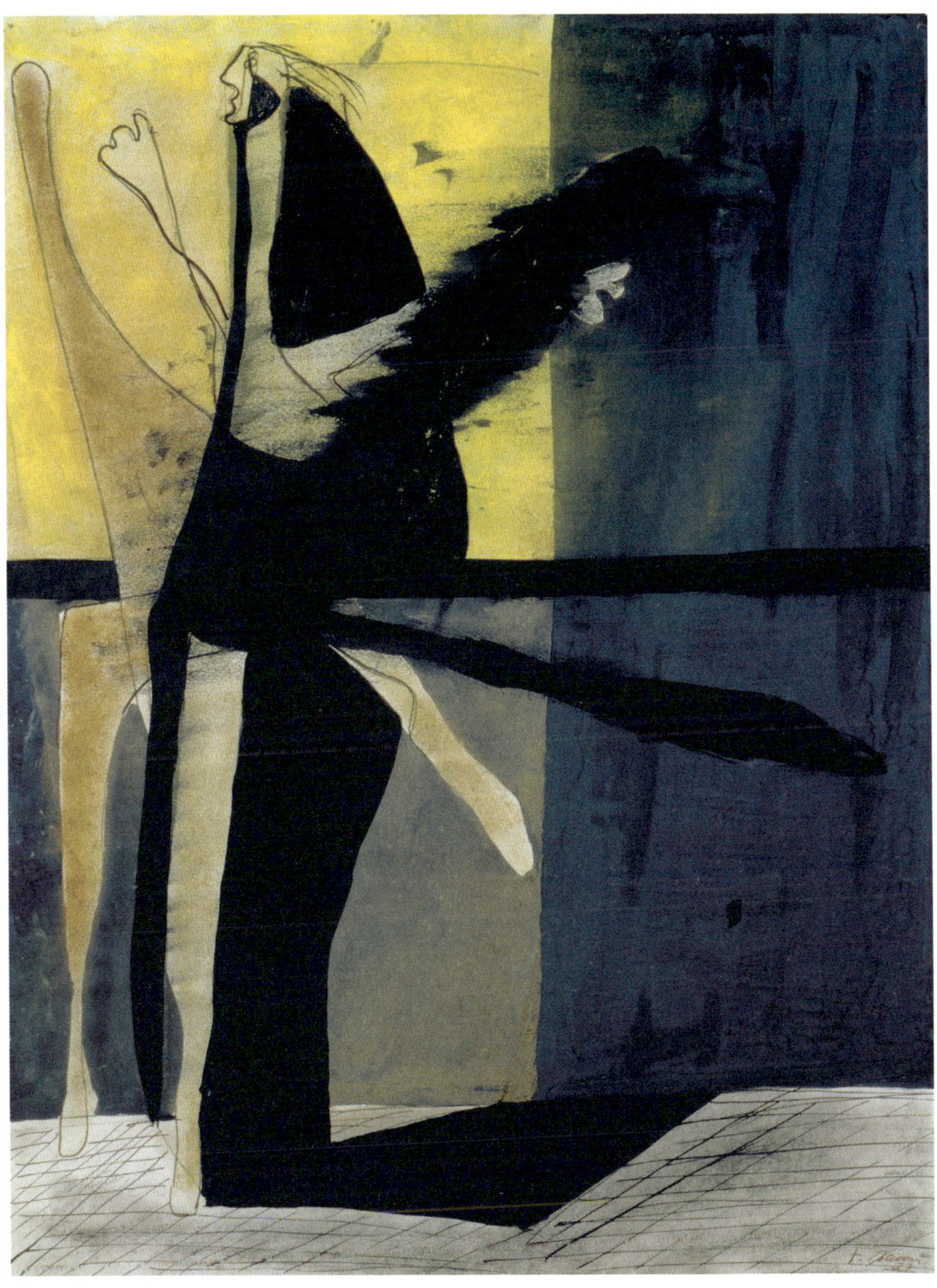

Francis Bacon, *Composition (Figure)*, 1933.

as if having contemplated the subject deeply, repeated his comment with a slightly different emphasis: 'Arsehole!' As for death, he said: 'When I'm dead, put me in a plastic bag and throw me in the gutter.' He was often vicious in his criticism of other artists, once comparing Picasso to Walt Disney, and saying that Jackson Pollock's paintings looked like 'old lace' and were, to him, completely meaningless. He railed against the decorative vacuity of abstract art and the 'inanities of academic art'.

Finally, although there were many flaws in Bacon's character, it must be said that he was also a great conversationalist, with a caustic wit and a wanton generosity towards those he liked. He radiated charisma when he entered a room and was endowed with great charm when he wished to exercise it. As with many shy people, when he did manage to shake off his natural timidity, he over-compensated wildly and became an expansively entertaining social companion, with an exuberant, vivacious sense of fun. What an asset he would have been to the British Surrealist Group if only they had not so foolishly rejected him. He would certainly have added a great deal of colour to their social gatherings and formal meetings, and his great surrealist art would certainly have enhanced their movement.

JOHN BANTING

Member of the British Surrealist Group

BORN: 12 May 1902 in Chelsea, London

PARENTS: Father a bookbinder; mother a teacher

LIVED: London 1902; Ireland 1947; Rye, East Sussex in the 1950s; Hastings 1965

PARTNERS: Close friendship with NANCY CUNARD

DIED: 30 January 1972 in Hastings, aged 70

JOHN BANTING WAS ONE OF THE JOKERS who frequented surrealist circles. Painting surrealist pictures was not enough for him – life itself had to become a surrealist event. He was once seen dancing at a club in a smart business suit but wearing shoes on which he had made a realistic painting of his toes, complete with nail varnish, his personal tribute to Magritte's iconic work *The Red Model* (1934–35). On another occasion he went round a London art exhibition signing all the works on show 'Marcel Duchamp'. Presumably Banting argued that, if Duchamp could sign a print of the *Mona Lisa*, then why not other works of art as well.

He was also involved in a famous art world hoax, the so-called Bruno Hat affair of 1929. An imaginary avant-garde artist called Bruno Hat was said to be holding an exhibition of his work in London. Smart invitations were sent out to all the London art critics, who flocked along to the private view and were impressed by what they saw. The spoof catalogue had been written by Evelyn Waugh, and the role of Bruno Hat was played by one of the famous Mitford family. 'Bruno' was brought into the exhibition in a wheelchair, muffled in scarves, but as he was a foreigner it was impossible to interview him, although he did manage to mumble a few words. The paintings themselves, done on cork bathmats and framed in rope, were the work of Banting and his friend the poet Brian Howard. Ironically, those pictures that have managed to survive have become highly sought after.

Banting was born in Chelsea and grew up in Edwardian London. His first influence was the work of Wyndham Lewis and the vorticists, but he had to earn his living working as a bank clerk and could only attend art classes in his spare time. At the age of twenty-three he was able to set up his first studio, working on book illustrations and making set designs for ballet companies. Banting had met some important members of the avant-garde on a visit to Paris in 1922, including Man Ray, Peggy Guggenheim and Constantin Brancusi. But it was a later visit, in 1930, when he encountered André Breton, Alberto Giacometti and Marcel Duchamp, that made a major impact on him. Under their influence he became a serious convert to the surrealist cause and remained devoted to the movement for the rest of his life. He had a close relationship with the Anglo-American writer and activist Nancy Cunard – the black sheep of the famous Cunard family – and helped her with her anti-racist campaign in the 1930s, staying with her in Harlem in New York. He also spent three months with her in Spain during the civil war there.

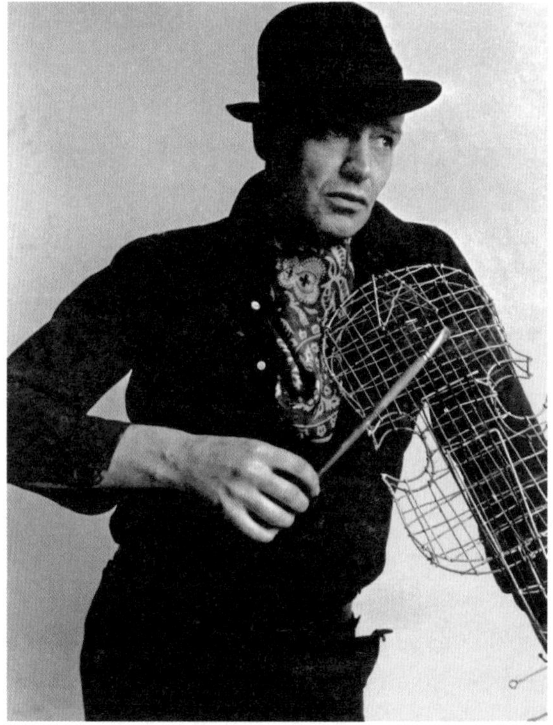

John Banting, photographed by Humphrey Spender, 1930s.

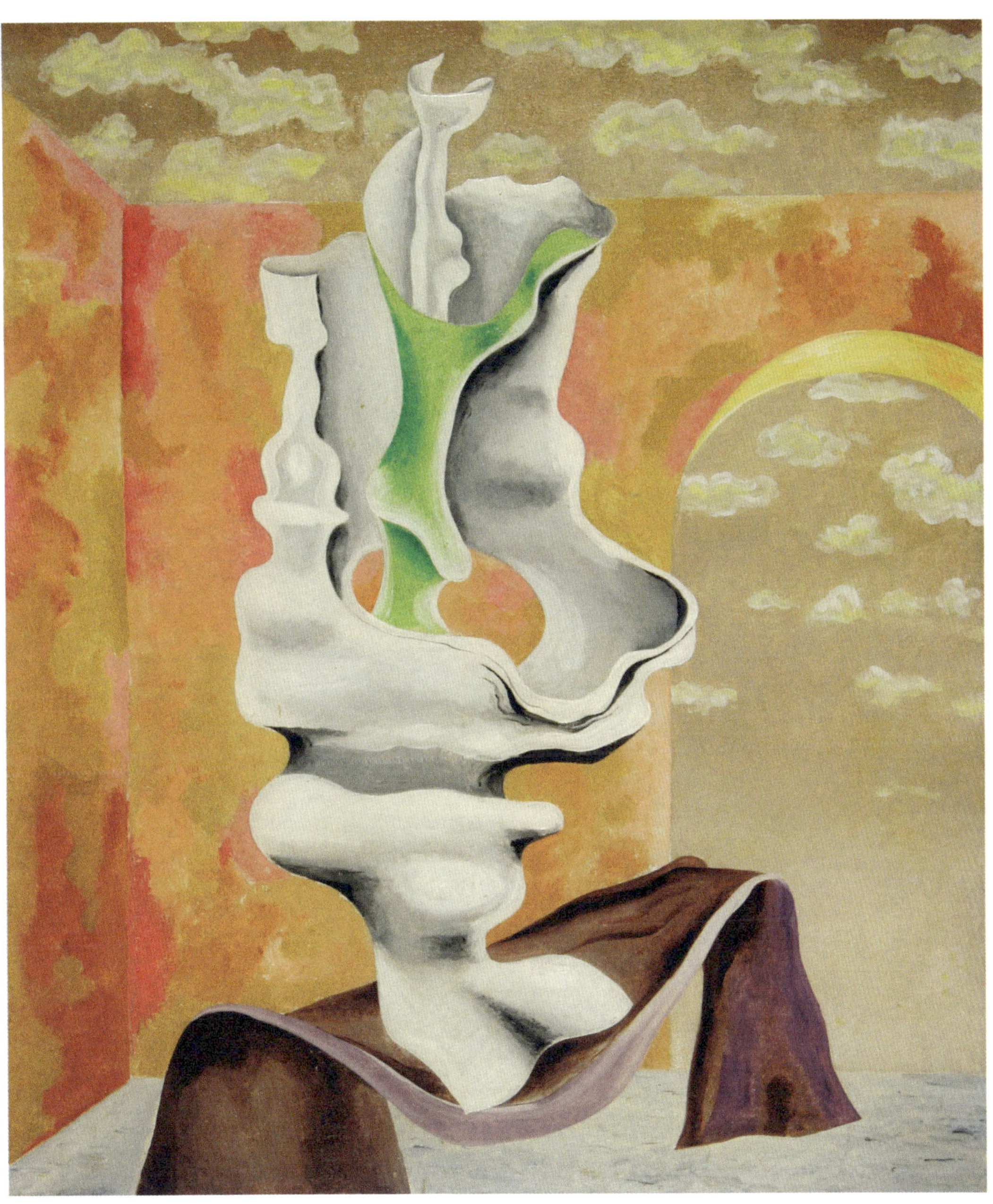

John Banting, *Guardian Bust*, 1936.

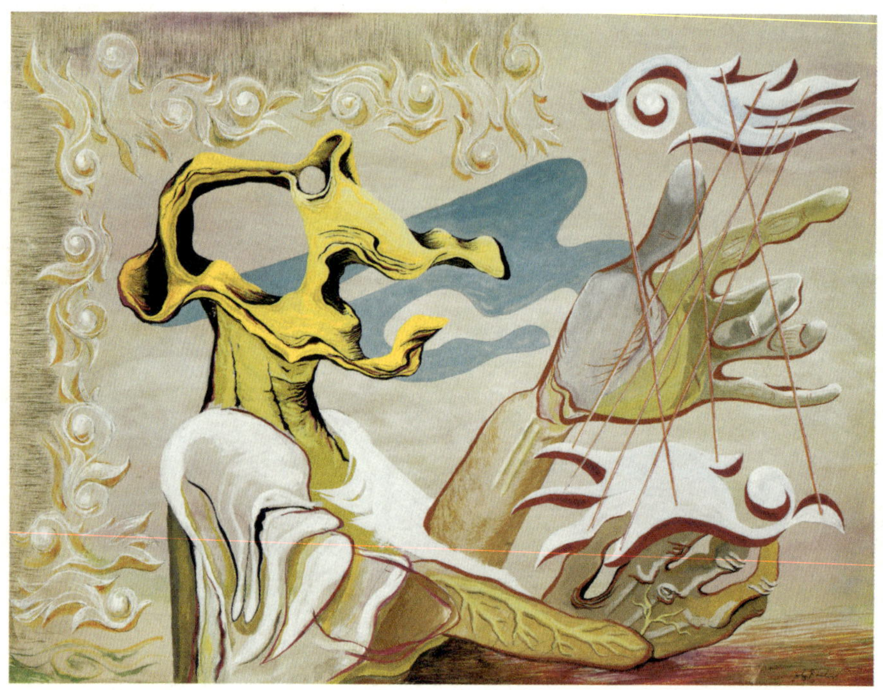

In 1936 he took part in the International Surrealist Exhibition in London, showing five works: two oils, two watercolours and a surrealist object. He strongly supported the communist leanings of the early surrealists and throughout his life was intensely left wing. His images were accused of being misogynistic because of the bizarre way in which he portrayed the female form, but Marcel Duchamp was impressed by his work and invited him to show in the next major surrealist exhibition, in Paris in 1938.

At the start of World War II, Banting failed his medical for the military and spent the war years as an air-raid warden and working for the Ministry of Information, making propaganda films with Dylan Thomas. In London after World War II, he created a remarkable surrealist publication, his *Blue Book of Conversation* (1946), for which he provided both the text and the illustrations. It amounted to a vitriolic attack on English high society, whose representatives appeared as formally dressed carcasses and were given hideous names

John Banting, *The Yellow Harpist*, 1946.

such as Lady Crevice Raikes-Bagge or Mrs Fuchsia Stingwing. During this period he was desperately poor, but Julian Trevelyan managed to secure a grant for him from the Artists' Benevolent Fund.

In 1956 Banting moved to Rye in Sussex to become a neighbour of his friend the eccentric artist Edward Burra. In his later years he produced little work but kept busy writing, also exhibiting his early works in surrealist exhibitions. The published letters of Edward Burra have many references to Banting, nearly always in relation to heavy drinking sessions in the 1960s. At this stage in his life Banting was plagued not only by alcoholism but also by ill heath and poverty. It is thought that he was surviving on an annual allowance from a rich boyfriend of his youth. According to Burra, when Banting left Rye and transferred to nearby Hastings in 1965, the move was prompted by the need to save money, the new flat that he would share with his equally alcoholic male lover 'Jimbo', a Devonshire fisherman, being £30 a year cheaper than the one in Rye.

In his sixties, Banting, who seems never to have enjoyed robust health, was always complaining to Burra about his ailments – a stiff hip, swollen ankles, swollen knees. There is a poignant letter, written by Burra ten days before Banting's death, in which he describes a visit to see his old friend in hospital in Hastings, awaiting an operation to 'rehabilitate' his pelvic region. Banting describes his forthcoming surgical procedure as 'distinctly Picasso cum Heath Robinson'. Burra adds that Banting 'has been having trouble at that end for 18 months or more'. His body ruined by years of alcohol abuse, he never recovered from the operation. In one of his final letters, written to Burra, he described his old friend as 'my consolation in this wilderness'. It was a sad end to a life that, in its early days, had promised so much more.

It was especially sad since, even when his body had given up the struggle, Banting's brain was still as sharp as ever. Eleven weeks before he died, he wrote to me from Hastings asking me to arrange a meeting with him at the Natural History Museum in London. He described the museum as his 'resort' and wanted to discuss the subject of biomorphs with me. 'You search to invent – the only thing to do,' he wrote, adding that 'Duchamp said this to me when I was about 27 and it has been a hang-up ever since.' His letter was full of ideas and comments and gave no hint that he was nearing his death. Unhappily for me the meeting never took place.

JOHN SELBY BIGGE

Involved with the British surrealists in the 1930s

BORN: 20 June 1892 in Oxford

PARENTS: Father Sir Amherst Selby-Bigge, permanent secretary to the Board of Education

LIVED: Oxford 1892; Kings Sutton 1900; London 1913; war service in Greece 1915; London 1923; Austria, France, Portugal, Spain 1936; London 1941; Austria 1945; London 1946; Le Bugue, Dordogne 1950s to 1973

PARTNERS: Married Rachel Humphries 1914; divorced 1944 (four children) • Married Marija Bacik from Vienna 1946 (until her death in 1955)

DIED: 3 October 1973 in Le Bugue, Dordogne, aged 81

John Selby Bigge was not a typical surrealist. He held the hereditary rank of baronet, and his full title was Sir John Amherst Selby-Bigge, Bart. His father, Sir Amherst Selby-Bigge, who had been permanent secretary to the Board of Education in England between 1911 and 1925, had been awarded a baronetcy in 1919. On the death of his father in 1951, John inherited this title, but when he himself died in 1973, the title became extinct as he had no heir.

Bigge can best be described as a 'gentleman surrealist' – a contradiction in terms. He certainly had a period when he painted surrealist pictures, but he would never have considered joining any formal group or signing any manifestos or declarations. Nor did he have a surrealist lifestyle. Indeed, in his history of British surrealism, Michel Remy states bluntly that 'Bigge could in no way be seen as belonging to the ranks of surrealism'. Instead, he suggests the term 'magic realism' both for Bigge and for his friend Edward Wadsworth. Remy does however admit that, in his work, Bigge was 'stepping into a world of unidentifiable shapes, vaguely reminiscent of vegetal or sometimes human organs'. He goes on to say that Bigge's use of 'bright, glazed colours ... blunts their disquieting and disruptive quality'.

The fact was that Bigge painted for pleasure, and his surrealist landscapes reflected this. They were expertly painted but they lacked any sense of

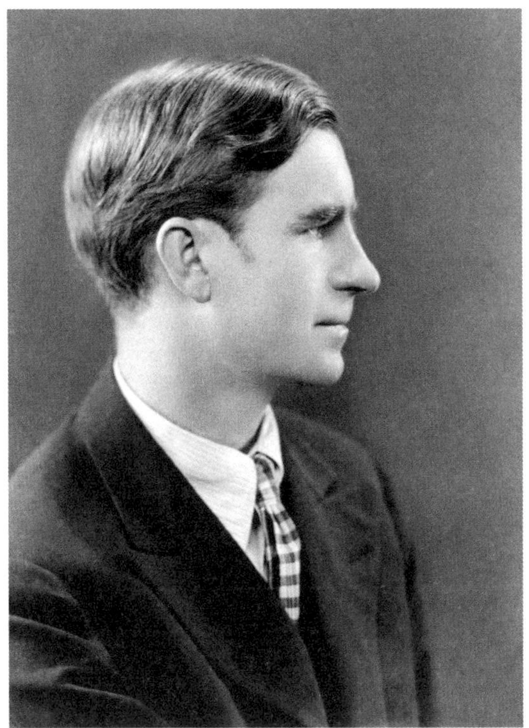

surrealist passion or rebellion. He took natural forms, modified them slightly and then presented them in an unnatural setting, making them seem novel and intriguing. The result was an appealing, dreamlike landscape that lacked any sort of threat or sinister undercurrent. It was surrealism for country ramblers, but remarkably attractive and easy on the eye, nevertheless.

Born in Oxford towards the end of the nineteenth century, Bigge was educated at Winchester College, an independent boys' boarding school, and at Christ Church, Oxford. In 1912, at the age of twenty, he abandoned formal education and adopted a gypsy lifestyle, declaring his rejection of 'the banalities of the sophisticated world'. The following year, however, he changed his mind and was admitted to the Slade School of Fine Art in London. There, he met a fellow art student called Rachel Ruth Humphries, whose family ran the major publishing company Lund Humphries. They were married in

John Selby Bigge, photographed by Bassano Ltd., London, 1933.

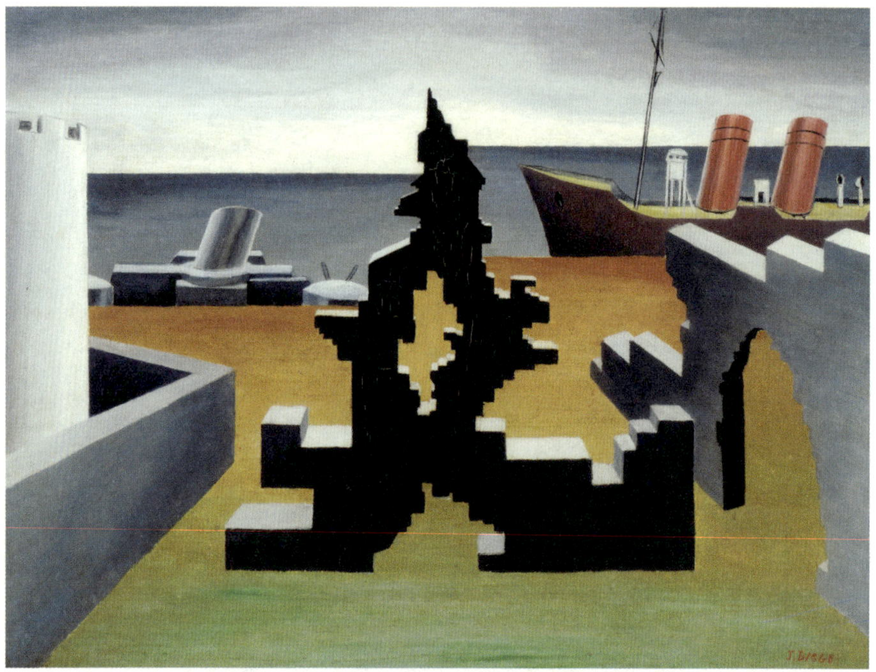

1914 and would have four daughters, but sadly no son and heir to carry on the Bigge family title.

At this crucial point in his career, John's studies were cut short by the start of World War I. He was called up for military duty and served with the Macedonian Mule Corps in Greece, where mules were used in place of mechanized vehicles as a method of transport for bringing supplies to the front or for field ambulance work, taking the wounded away. With the unusual title of Inspector of Muleteers, he managed to survive the war. When it ended, he worked in intelligence in Athens before being repatriated. At home, his wife had made many connections in the world of art and literature and enjoyed giving dinner parties. The writer and founder of the Bloomsbury Group, Lytton Strachey, after dining with the Bigges, wrote of John: 'He had evidently been crushed flat by the war – not its worst horrors but the stupidity of everyone he was with, and the appalling dullness of existence.... I thought he was really one of the most truly good people I had ever met.'

John Selby Bigge, *Dieppe*, 1931.

John's reaction to civilian life was to move to the countryside and become a chicken farmer. He later took a job at the Ashmolean Museum in Oxford, where he was employed to illustrate by hand the new acquisitions in the museum catalogue. During this period, he painted as much as he could in his spare time. At the start of the 1920s, he and his wife moved south to Eastbourne, where he once again became a chicken farmer, this time on a grand scale, with 3,000 laying hens. Tiring of this task, in 1923 he moved to London where he became an estate agent, but whatever job he was doing he never stopped painting, working on his canvases whenever there was a free moment.

Like several other surrealists, Bigge had a dramatic moment of 'conversion' when he saw the early work of the Italian painter Giorgio de Chirico.

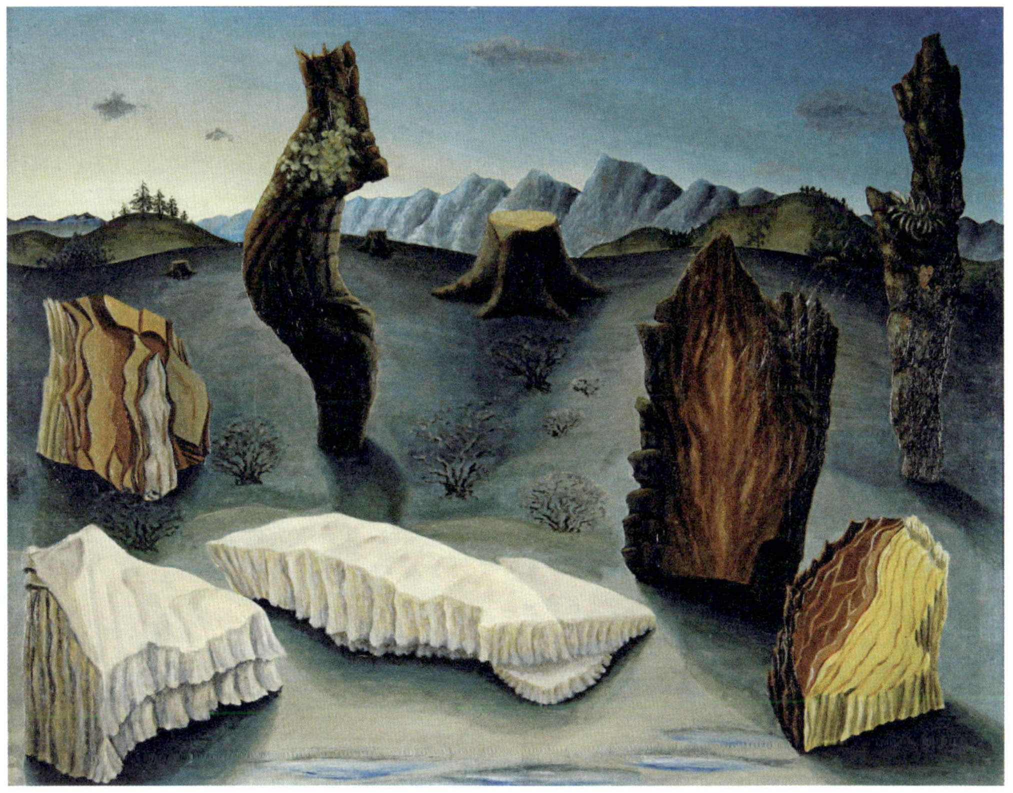

John Selby Bigge, *Surrealist Landscape*, 1942.

The encounter took place at Tooth's Gallery in London, where de Chirico was having an exhibition in 1928. It was at this point that Bigge decided he must become part of the surrealist movement. Bigge became friendly with the artist Edward Wadsworth, who was in touch with the latest developments in art that had been taking place across the English Channel in Paris since the 1920s, and this friendship had a considerable influence on his work. As time passed, Bigge became more and more serious about his painting and, in 1931, he was afforded his first solo exhibition at the Wertheim Gallery in London. The following year he had his first solo show in Paris and, in 1936, was included in the major International Surrealist Exhibition in London. He was quoted as saying that he preferred the surrealist movement because 'Its sur-realities ... are more real than the conventional realities of the modern world.' After 1936 Bigge began travelling across Europe, living for brief periods in Austria, France, Portugal and Spain. His marriage to Ruth began to collapse during this period and they eventually divorced in 1944. He then remarried in 1946, this time to a judge's daughter from Vienna called Marija Bacik.

During World War II Bigge worked for the BBC in the European News Service, from 1942 to 1943, and then, from 1943 to 1945, for the British Red Cross. At the end of the war, in Austria, he saved the lives of some 6,000 anti-communist Slovenian civilians who were destined to be repatriated to Yugoslavia, where they would have been slaughtered by the communist regime. He refused to carry out the order to repatriate them and persuaded his superiors to have it stopped. For his actions, John Bigge was awarded the OBE in 1946. Had he not already left the surrealist movement, accepting this honour would, of course, have seen him immediately expelled by André Breton. When Bigge's father died in 1951, he inherited the title of baronet – which would have proved another shock for Breton, had he heard of it. After the war John moved to France and lived in the Dordorgne until his death in 1973.

Writing in the 1930s, he said that a picture, 'whether it makes use of material or imaginary forms ... must keep its content pure; there must be no association of the forms either with function or symbol. It must be logical in construction, but with its own self-imposed logic. Its forms must appear solid within space.... Its colour must be integral with its form, colour-form becoming a single concept, and tone-values being merged within colour. It must be illuminated, but have its own internal illumination. It must retain an air of spontaneity and yet have the completeness of inevitability.'

EMMY BRIDGWATER

Joined the British surrealist group in 1940

BORN: 10 November 1906 in Edgbaston, Birmingham

PARENTS: Father a chartered accountant

LIVED: Birmingham 1906; Oxford 1926; Birmingham 1937; London 1948; Birmingham 1986

PARTNER: Toni del Renzio 1942

DIED: 13 March 1999 in Birmingham, aged 92

Emmy Bridgwater was a British surrealist whose career was cut short by family responsibilities. She did not discover surrealism until she was thirty and, just over a decade later, she had to abandon it. Out of the kindness of her heart, she devoted the rest of her active life to caring for relatives who could not look after themselves. The result is that her body of work is small and she is little known, but what works of hers do remain reveal a remarkable surrealist imagination. There is a primitive feeling to them, and no concession is made to aesthetic refinement or good taste.

Bridgwater was born into a middle-class family in Birmingham towards the end of the Edwardian period. At the age of sixteen she attended Birmingham Art School and, four years later in 1926, she moved to Oxford to continue her studies there. Being short of funds, she worked as a secretary to pay her way. Her visit to the International Surrealist Exhibition in London in 1936 was a life-changing experience. From this point onwards she knew that she had to devote herself to working in the surrealist tradition. For a further year of study, she enrolled at the Grosvenor School of Modern Art in London, again supporting herself by moonlighting as a secretary.

In 1937 she returned to Birmingham, where she joined the local surrealist group led by Conroy Maddox, and in 1940 she also joined the London surrealist group that had gathered around the Belgian E. L. T. Mesens. In 1942 she had a brief but passionate affair with the Russian surrealist Toni del Renzio, who unsuccessfully challenged Mesens for the leadership of the British Surrealist Group. She also had her first solo exhibition, at Jack

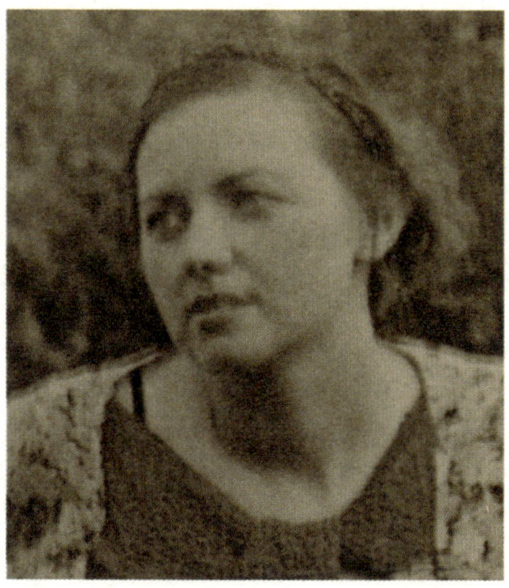

Bilbo's Modern Art Gallery in London. After the war, in 1947, Bridgwater was one of the signatories of the formal declaration of the British Surrealist Group, still led by Mesens. In the same year, André Breton was sufficiently impressed by her work to invite her to participate in the International Surrealist Exhibition in Paris.

Bridgwater's paintings are difficult to describe but they had a powerful impact on those who encountered them. Toni del Renzio said of them: 'We do not see these pictures. We hear their cries and are moved by them. Our own entrails are drawn painfully from us and twisted into the pictures whose significance we did not want to realize.' The critic Robert Melville commented that 'although they [her paintings] are dreamlike in their ambiguity they are realistic documents from a region of phantasmal hopes and murky desires'. More recently, Michel Remy described her as an 'explorer of the sulfurous lavas and springtimes of the unconscious', while fellow art historian Richard Warren, impressed by the intensity of her work, wrote that 'her tense, quirky spikiness is worth a dozen of the dutiful pastiches churned out by her Birmingham collaborator, the hugely overrated Conroy Maddox'. This comment is unfair to Maddox, but it does reveal the strength of the response

Emmy Bridgwater, 1940.

that Bridgwater's paintings elicit. The emotionally charged dream world she created was full of violence and disturbing black humour. It has been recorded that she was variously an admirer of Emily Brontë, King Kong and the Marx Brothers. In 1946, when asked what she hated most, Bridgwater replied: 'I hate being brushed by the black vestments of a nun.' Asked what she loved most, she said, 'I love looking through windows – outside as well as inside.' And asked what she feared most, she answered, 'I fear hubbub, tiny insects ... and the next war.'

In the late 1940s, Bridgwater's career as a surrealist came to an unexpected halt owing to family emergencies. Her elderly mother, who had been looking after Emmy's disabled sister, now needed care herself, and Emmy took on the responsibility of caring for them both. These duties occupied the majority of her time, and she was unable to devote herself to her painting. She did continue to exhibit, however, and to paint whenever she could find a spare moment; but eventually, in 1950, she finally had to admit defeat and

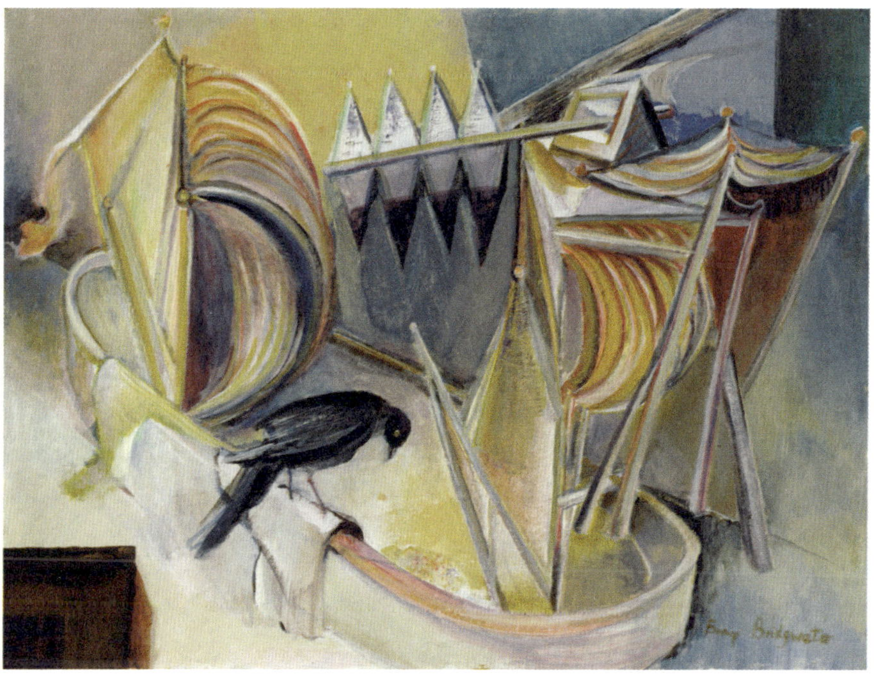

Emmy Bridgwater, *Night Work is about to Commence*, 1940–43.

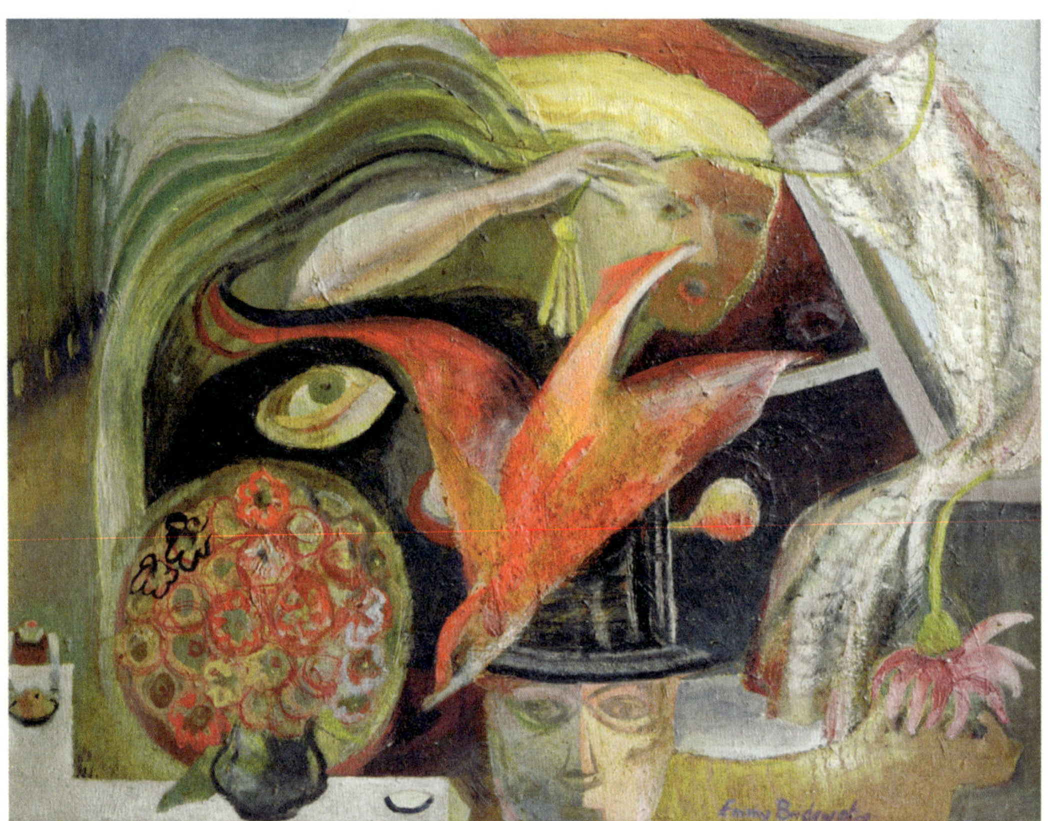

gave up painting altogether. In 1953 she moved to Stratford-upon-Avon to take up her role as a full-time carer. This state of affairs would continue for the next twenty years until, in 1970, she became active once more and started to make collages. After this, she began exhibiting again in a variety of surrealist group shows and in 1990 had a solo exhibition in London.

Sadly, after 1986, Bridgwater was incapable of painting or drawing and had to suffer this inactivity for many years until she died in a nursing home in 1999 at the age of ninety-two.

Emmy Bridgwater, *Brave Morning*, c. 1942.

EDWARD BURRA

Exhibited in the International Surrealist Exhibitions in 1936 and 1938

BORN: 29 March 1905 in South Kensington, London

PARENTS: Father a barrister; inherited wealth

LIVED: Rye, East Sussex – all his life (but travelled extensively)

PARTNERS: None (he was a lifelong invalid)

DIED: 22 October 1976 in Hastings, aged 71

Edward Burra was one of the rich surrealists. With his inherited wealth he never had to experience the indignities of poverty suffered by many of the other surrealist artists. He did, however, have his own cross to bear in the shape of crippling, lifelong rheumatoid arthritis that began at the tender age of five and stayed with him until he died many years later aged seventy-one. In addition, he suffered from hereditary anaemia, and his body was so frail that he had to be taken out of the prep school where he was a boarder and, instead of going on to Eton, was given private tuition at home. The son of a rich lawyer, Burra was born in Rye on the south coast of England. Even as a child he loved drawing and was encouraged in this by his family. When he was a little older, they sent him to art school, and he was eventually enrolled at the Royal College of Art in London. When he was twenty, he wrote to a friend saying, 'I should like to draw all day without stopping.'

Apart from his art, Burra's other great passion was travelling. This seems strange because it must have required considerable physical mobility, which would have been at odds with the weakness of his body. He once said, 'I must sit down most of the time; if I could work lying down I would do so.' It is true that his trips did involve a great deal of sitting down, drinking and observing in bars, cafés and music halls, but he still had to get there somehow to do this. His travels began when, as a child, his mother took him to Switzerland and, later, to Italy. When he was twenty, he made the first of many trips to Paris, and in the 1920s he also visited Florence, Marseilles and Toulon. This was an optimistic period, when the old Victorian restrictions were being discarded by

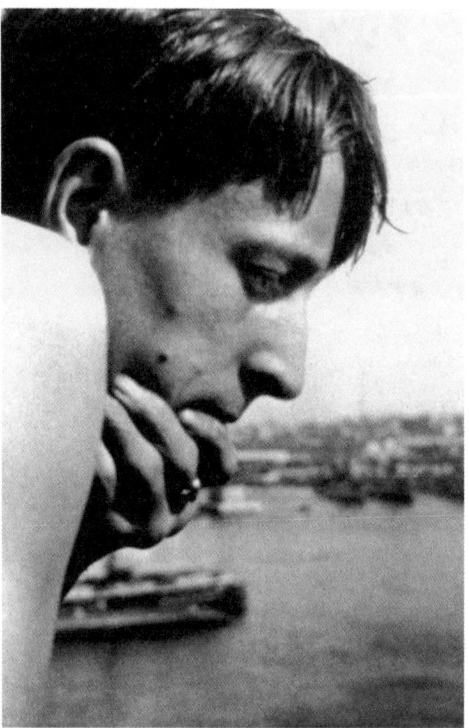

a new generation intent on pursuing forbidden pleasures. Burra continued his wanderings in the 1930s, visiting Mexico and the United States, where he was particularly taken with the notorious district of Harlem in New York.

For Burra, it was a time for discovering jazz, music halls, dance clubs, foreign cinemas, circuses, striptease clubs, burlesque theatres, bars and street cafés. His sheltered background and his semi-invalid status meant that, for him, it was a great adventure to explore the low life of Europe and America and to observe its excesses and decadence. He would frequent the old maritime quarters of Marseilles, the night life of Paris and the jazz clubs of Harlem, making endless satirical drawings of the people he encountered there – the sailors, the prostitutes, the hustlers, the street traders, the barflies, the dancers and the musicians. It was said that he was preoccupied with the macabre and the meretricious, the tawdry and the theatrical, the dodgy and

Edward Burra in London, undated.

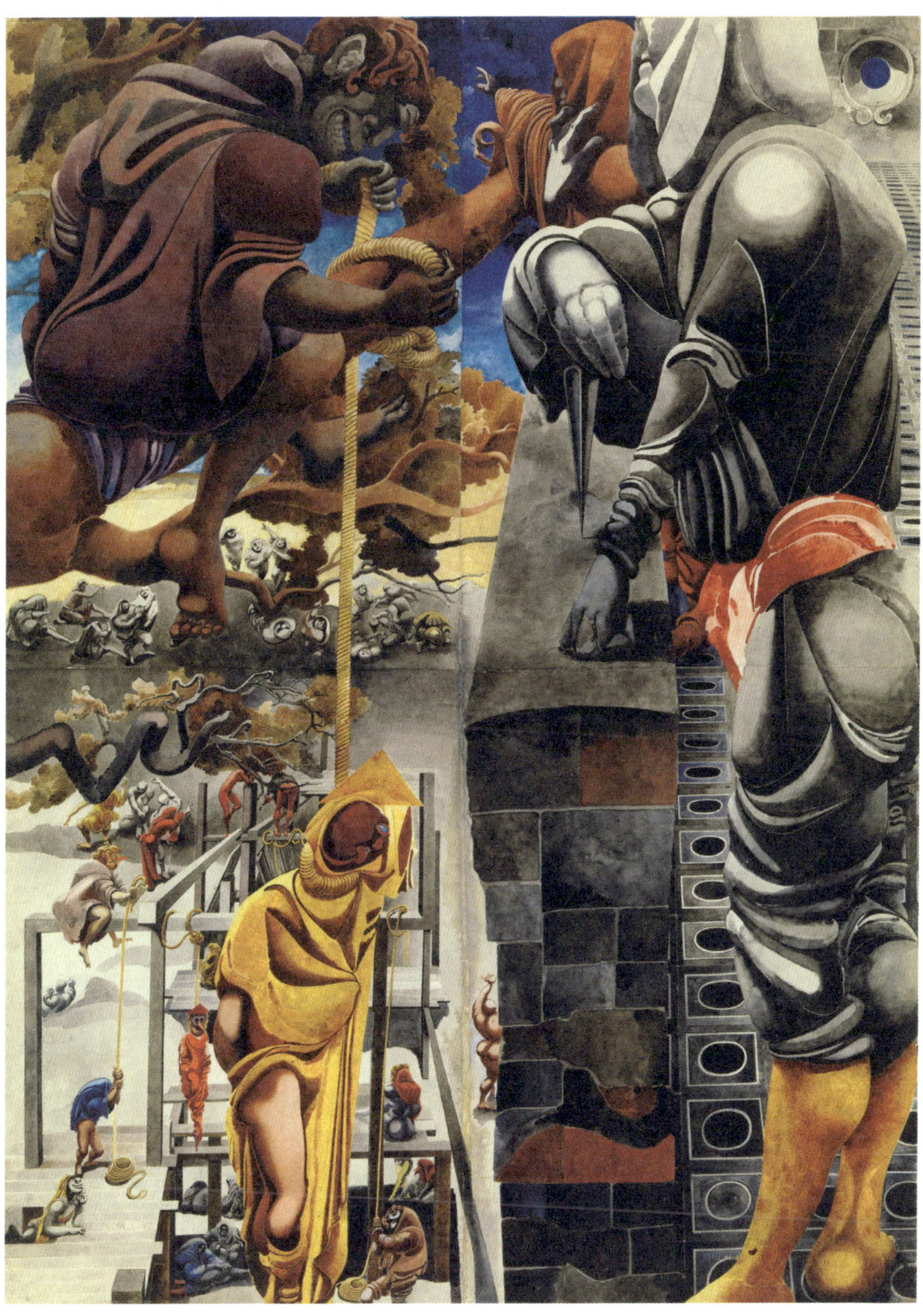

Edward Burra, *Bal des Pendus*, 1937.

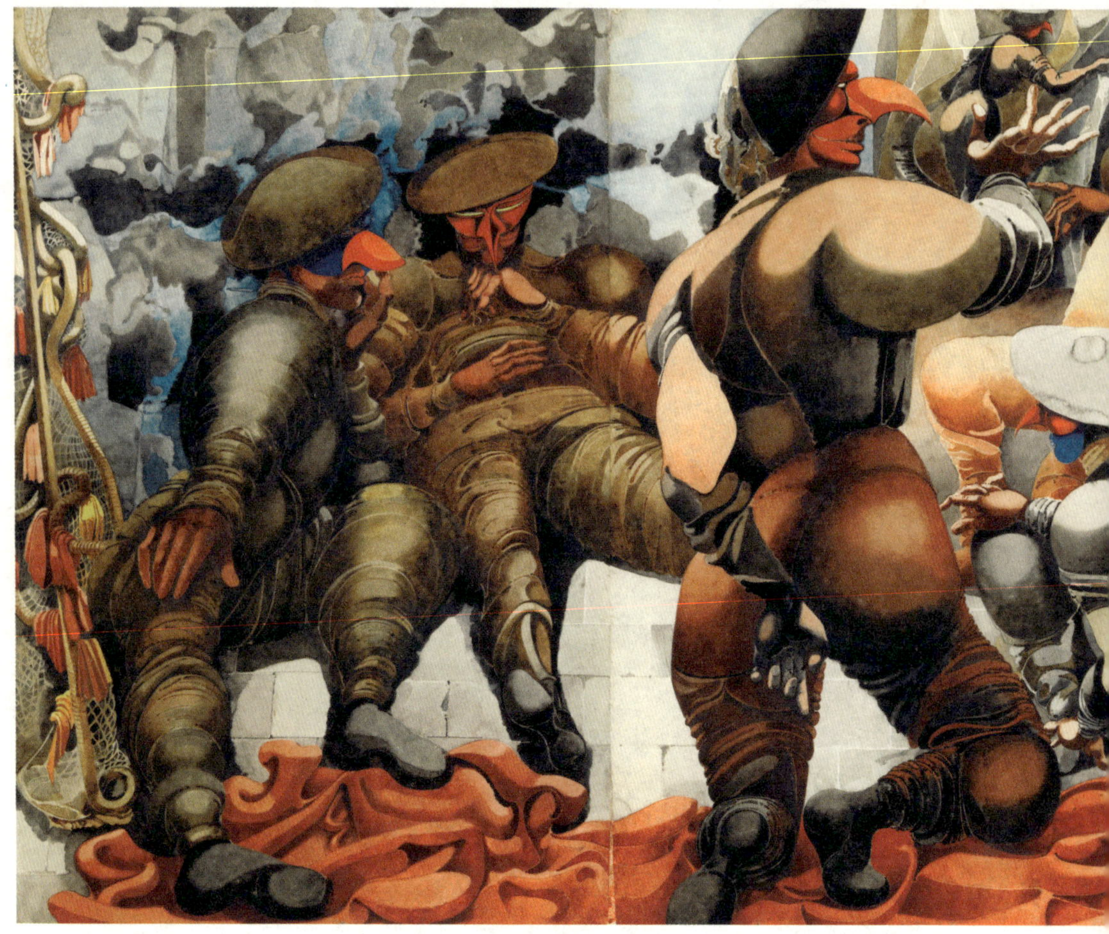

the shoddy. When portraying this world in his art, he described himself as often suffering from 'paroxysms of impotent venom'.

During this phase of his development, he came into contact with the avant-garde of the art world in Paris, but surrealism had not yet found its way into his art. His pictures of the 1920s are either conventional scenes or satirical cartoon-like compositions depicting the shady characters he was so keen to observe in their natural habitat. His first surrealist work did not appear until 1930. From this point onwards he would repeatedly abandon his satirical works and plunge into the darker world of surrealist imagery, but it cannot be said that he had a marked 'surrealist phase'. Other artists who painted both surrealist and non-surrealist works during their lifetime

Edward Burra, *Soldiers at Rye*, 1941.

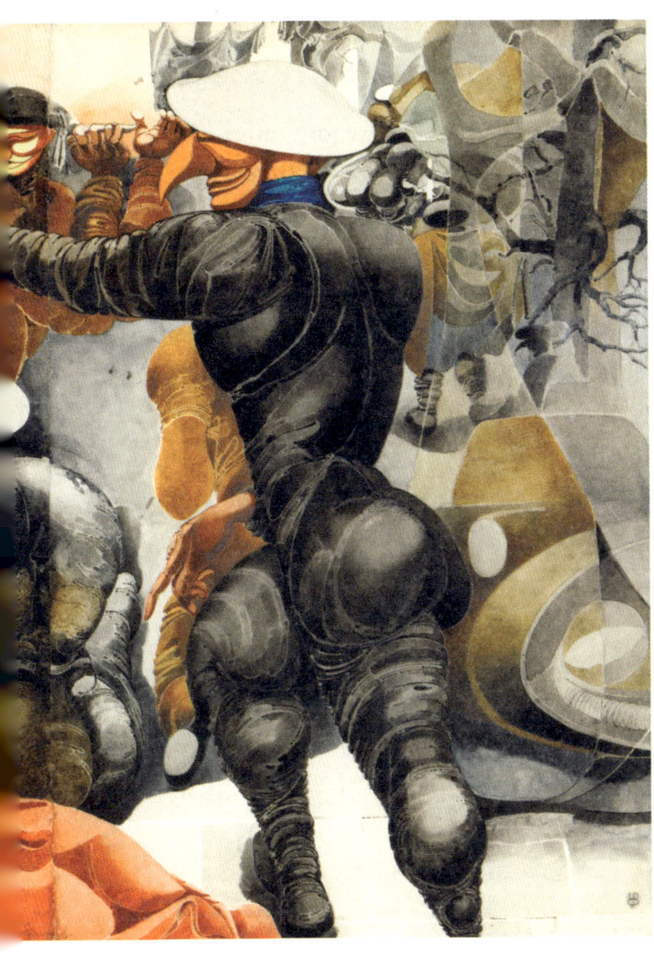

all had a specific period when they switched from one type of work to the other. Burra did not do this. His surrealism was spasmodic, interspersed with his more usual satirical observations or his landscapes. It was as if he could not make up his mind what he wanted to be – a sardonic commentator on the seedier, sleazier aspects of urban living, or a darkly sinister surrealist.

Burra's meticulous style of working, as well as his physical frailty and frequent travelling, meant that his total output was small. In the half-century when he was active, he produced only 413 paintings, an average of about 8 a year. Of these a total of no more than 60 were surrealist works. They were, however, of great intensity and complexity, and three of them were included in the International Surrealist Exhibition of 1936. He also participated in the International Surrealist Exhibition at the Galerie des Beaux-Arts in Paris in 1938, and again at the 'Surrealism Today' show at the Zwemmer Gallery in London in 1940. The paintings he sent to these exhibitions were truly surrealist, with imagery dredged directly from his unconscious mind. They differed markedly from his more usual satires on urban lowlife. Indeed, they made the latter look rather shallow and little more than sarcastic, comical kitsch. When he achieved such powerful images with his surrealist works, it is hard to see why he did not pursue this genre and abandon his other style.

Burra's biographers have suggested that the factor limiting his surrealist output was his dislike of certain aspects of the surrealist movement. André Breton had emphasized that the movement was essentially a collective, with strict group allegiance, and that it was also at the extreme end of the left wing of politics. Burra, a devoted individualist and non-joiner, had no interest in politics, and his wealthy background did not sit well with Breton's dictates. He found Breton's passion for trying to control his followers irksome. He said to one surrealist: 'I didn't like being told what to think, dearie.' Burra's insistence on 'non-joining' was not limited to surrealism. Typically, when he was telephoned and offered the honour of becoming a Royal Academician, he instructed his manservant, 'Tell them to eff off, I'm busy.' His biographer Jane Stevenson sums him up with the telling phrase: 'He spent his life jumping off bandwagons.'

What he did like about the surrealist movement was the way it released him to explore the recesses of his unconscious and the fact that it was essentially a rebel group opposed to the establishment. For these reasons he kept going back to surrealist imagery and was happy to exhibit with them when invited to do so. Also, it has to be said that his true surrealist works are among the most striking ever seen in that genre.

In personality, Burra was often difficult and acid-tongued. He hated being interviewed and, on the rare occasions when he permitted this intrusion into his private life, his responses were typically brief. When asked what really mattered to him, his reply consisted of a single word: 'Nothing.' When asked about art, he pronounced it 'fart'. He called an artist a 'fartist', saying 'there's no fartist like a dead one'. Needless to say, during his travels, he hated being quizzed by customs officials and on one famous occasion, during the prohibition era, when an American customs man spotted a large bulge on his hip caused by a bottle of whiskey hidden in his pocket and demanded to know what it was, Burra escaped by exploiting his misshapen body, snarling at the man, 'It's a growth.'

LEONORA CARRINGTON

Member of the surrealist circle from 1937

BORN: 6 April 1917 in Clayton Green, Chorley, Lancashire

PARENTS: Father a textile magnate; mother Irish

LIVED: Lancashire 1917; London 1935; Saint-Martin-d'Ardèche, France 1938; Spain 1940; Portugal 1941; New York 1941; Mexico 1943

PARTNERS: Max Ernst 1937–39 • Married Renato Leduc, Mexican poet, writer and consul 1941–44; divorced • Emerico Weisz, photographer 1946–2007 (two children)

DIED: 25 May 2011 in Mexico City, from pneumonia, aged 94

Leonora Carrington was one of those rebellious young women who were drawn to the surrealist circle in Paris in the 1920s and 1930s. They found the atmosphere of social freedoms, heated intellectual debates and deliberately improper behaviour irresistible. Carrington was relatively late arriving on the scene, joining the circle in 1937 when she was only twenty and newly out of art school. Although she was British-born and had been an art student in London for two years, it was not until she moved to Paris that her work as a surrealist artist really began. So, although she must be classified as a British surrealist, it is true to say that none of her surrealist paintings were actually created on British soil. She had the advantage of being fluent in French and found the surrealist gatherings in Parisian cafés and bars exhilarating. After her stifled childhood, this was not surprising.

Carrington was born in northern England, the daughter of a Lancashire textile tycoon, and grew up in a mansion with ten servants, a chauffeur, a nanny, a French governess and a religious tutor. Every moment of her young life was supervised, and she was allowed to visit her mother in her sitting room only on set occasions. Despite the grandeur of her existence, she saw her family home as little more than a huge prison. Architecturally she described it as 'lavatory gothic'. Her escape was into a world of private fantasy, aided by the fact that her Irish nanny told her wild folk tales that fired her imagination.

At school Carrington was soon in trouble because she could write with both hands and even backwards. (It was said that in later life she could paint with both hands at the same time, surely a unique accomplishment.) The nuns who taught her told her that, instead of possessing a remarkable skill, this strange ability of hers was a disease. She was informed that she was abnormal and punished for not conforming. This was the moment when her distrust of religion began, a feature of her life that would grow stronger in later years. In one of her earliest acts of rebellion, when she was only fourteen, she pulled up her dress in front of a Catholic priest. She was wearing no underclothes and she asked him, 'What do you think of that?'

She was expelled twice for not collaborating with her teachers and was eventually packed off to a boarding school in Florence to prepare her for being presented at court. The year she spent in that beautiful city allowed her to study the great art of the past, an experience that would have a lasting impact on her as an artist. After Florence she was sent to a finishing school in Paris, where she was again expelled for refusing to conform. Her family, undefeated by her wayward behaviour, had her presented at court wearing a tiara, gave her a debutante's ball at the Ritz in London and took her to the Royal Enclosure at Ascot races where, because she was not allowed to bet on the horses, she spent the day sitting in a corner, reading *Eyeless in Gaza* by Aldous Huxley.

In her family's eyes she was now primed for a high society marriage or, as she herself put it, to be 'sold to the highest bidder'. For her, this was the moment of truth. She announced her rebellion and in 1935, at the age of only eighteen, left home permanently for the life of an art student in London. Her parents were so furious that they gave her little financial support, but she was free at last. Her uncooperative behaviour ceased, and she applied herself obediently to instruction in painting and drawing.

Ironically, her introduction to the surrealists came in the form of a gift from her mother. It was Herbert Read's new book on the subject, called simply *Surrealism*, published in 1936. Carrington found it fascinating, especially the art of Max Ernst. She said that seeing his work was 'like burning inside'. In 1937 Ernst had a show in London, and the young Carrington met him at a dinner party in his honour. Ernst had the reputation of being irresistible to women and she certainly found this to be true. It was, she said later, love at first sight and, although he was a married man, she was very

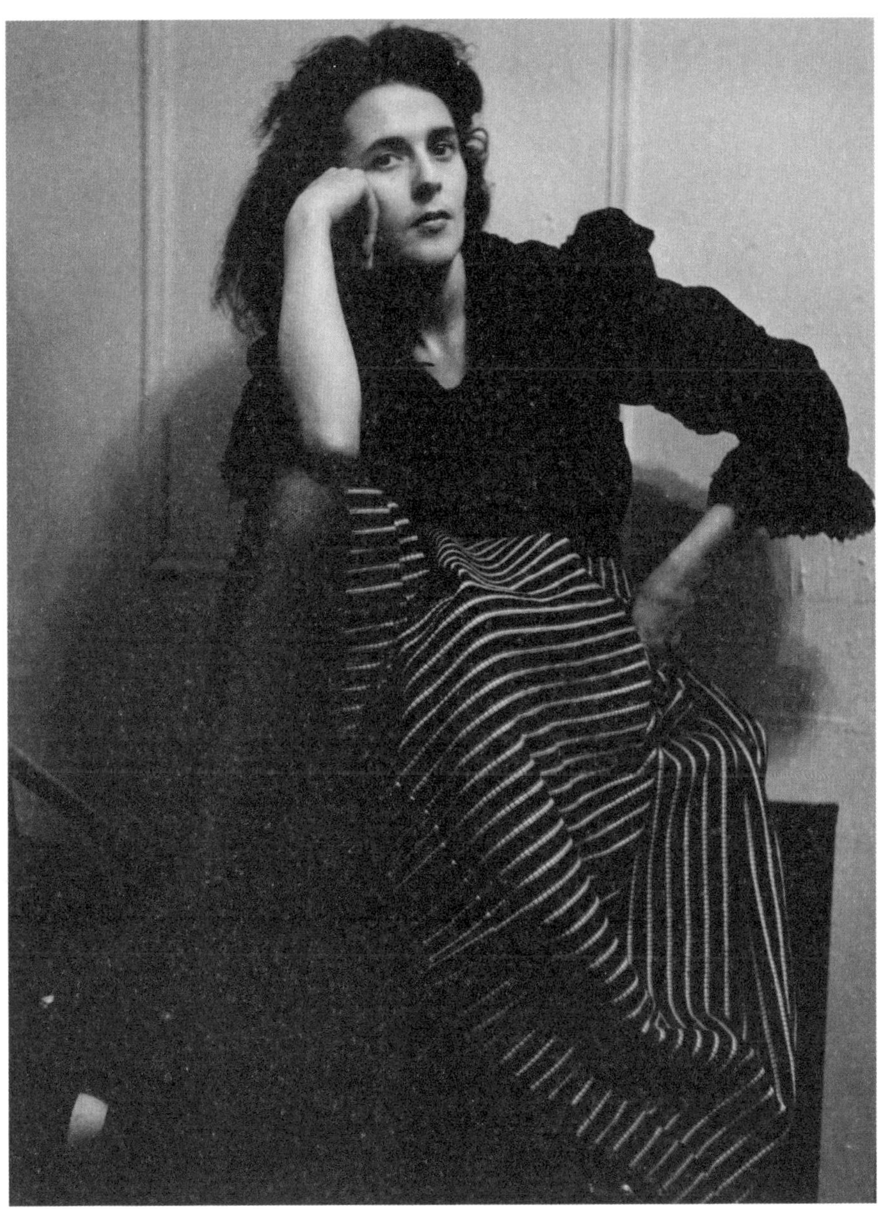

Leonora Carrington in her Greenwich Village apartment, photographed by Hermann Landshoff, c. 1942.

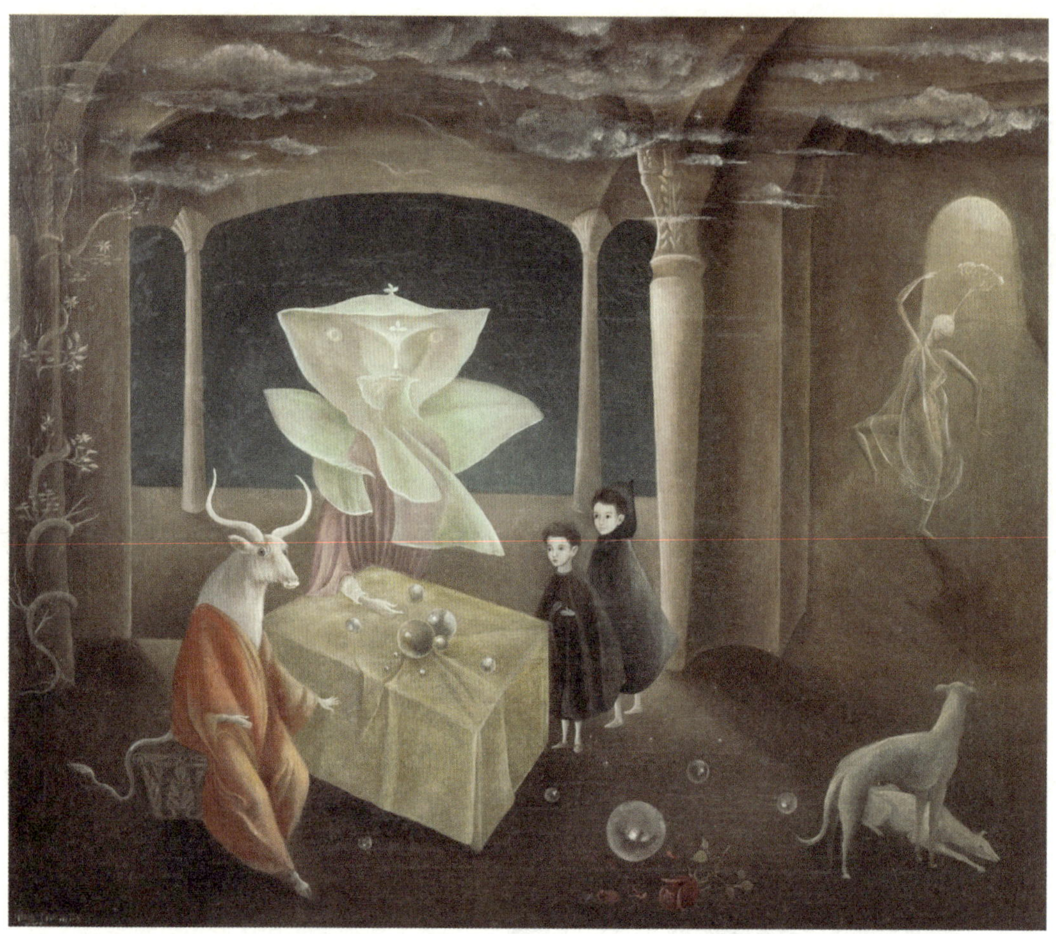

soon his lover and his protégée. When he left for Paris Carrington followed him there, telling her outraged family that she was going abroad to live in sin with a married German artist, twenty-five years her senior. Her father responded by telling her that she could never enter the family home again. She said she was glad to be leaving behind the English, 'whose souls have the consistency of pork brawn'.

In Paris in 1937 Carrington became an active member of André Breton's circle. The self-confidence she had acquired during her childhood meant that she was no compliant groupie, but a force to be reckoned with. At one party,

Leonora Carrington, *And Then We Saw the Daughter of the Minotaur*, 1953.

for instance, she arrived wearing nothing but a white sheet that she later allowed to drop, leaving her stark naked. She and Ernst were thrown out of the party. This period in the late 1930s was a productive time for Carrington, who found the atmosphere in Paris provocative and stimulating. In 1938, however, both she and Ernst started to tire of Breton's interminable squabbling with his group of followers, and they left Paris to spend over a year in an old farmhouse in a French village. It was, said Carrington, a time of paradise. Sadly, this would soon come to a juddering halt with the outbreak of World War II in 1939. Ernst, being German, was immediately interned in a French concentration camp. While he was a prisoner, Carrington's attitude towards him started to change. She saw their relationship in a different light and, when he was eventually released and was able to return to their farmhouse, he found that she had disappeared.

When Ernst had been arrested, Carrington suddenly found herself isolated in a foreign country with war approaching and all her family ties broken. She was only twenty-three and it was all too much for her. She stopped eating, started drinking and began to suffer from hallucinations. She sold their house to a local farmer for a bottle of brandy, and friends drove her south to Madrid, where her erratic behaviour became extreme. One day, she was discovered outside the British Embassy, screaming that she wanted to kill Hitler. Her father had her committed to a Spanish asylum, where she was classed as incurably insane. While she was there, she was treated with chemical shock therapy. The drug she was given induced convulsive spasms, and she spent her days tied to her bed with leather straps, fed through tubes in her nose. She nearly died.

Her worried parents arranged for her to be transferred to an institution in South Africa, and her father sent her old nanny over by submarine to escort her. Their journey began in Madrid, from where they travelled on to Lisbon. Once in the Portuguese capital, Carrington persuaded her guardian to let her go to a shop to buy some gloves. Ducking out of the back door, she made her way to the Mexican Embassy where the ambassador, Renato Leduc, was an old friend. She pleaded with him to get her out of the country, but this was not easy. The only way he could manage it was if he were to marry her, which he did. It was some months before they could sail off across the Atlantic, and those were difficult times for Carrington because Ernst arrived in Lisbon, also on his way to America. Although he was now in a relationship with Peggy

Guggenheim, he was still desperately in love with Carrington and they spent a great deal of time together in Lisbon cafés, deep in conversation. He repeatedly tried to persuade her to return to him, but she blamed him for not rescuing her from the nightmare of the asylum and was no longer prepared to live with him.

After the crossings to America had been made and they were all living in New York, Ernst and Carrington continued seeing one another, causing Peggy Guggenheim, who was by now married to Ernst, sharp pangs of jealousy. To her credit, she never allowed this to interfere with her assessment of Carrington's work, which she was happy to exhibit in her new art gallery. Carrington's behaviour while she was in New York was decidedly odd. On one occasion, when dining in a restaurant, she covered her feet in mustard, and on another she took a shower fully clothed when visiting a friend's house. It was not clear whether her eccentricities were surrealist events or moments of madness. Perhaps they were both.

In 1943 Carrington's Mexican husband-of-convenience moved back to his homeland and took her with him. Their special relationship ended a year later and they were amicably divorced. In Mexico City she met Emerico Weisz, a Hungarian Jew who was a photojournalist, and, after a brief courtship, they were married in 1946. They set up home together in Mexico and remained there as husband and wife for over sixty years, during which time she bore two sons and continued to paint well into her nineties. Her husband, known to everyone as Chiki, was something of a saint. He stayed with her to the bitter end, despite the fact that he was the victim of her sometimes raging temper and, on one occasion at least, was physically attacked by her. She took a number of lovers and left Chiki several times, but always returned to him.

Carrington's paintings, always skilfully crafted in a traditional manner, take the viewer into a fantastic private world full of monsters and arcane rituals. Some are like demented fairy tales, others like elegant nightmares. As with many surrealist works, they make their impact felt on the viewer even though their precise meaning is obscure. Octavio Paz, the Mexican poet, described Carrington as 'the bewitched witch, insensitive to social morality, to aesthetics and to price'.

When she was ninety years old, Carrington was asked by an interviewer whether certain strange animals in one particular scene were acting as guardians. The question clearly made her uncomfortable, and she replied, 'I

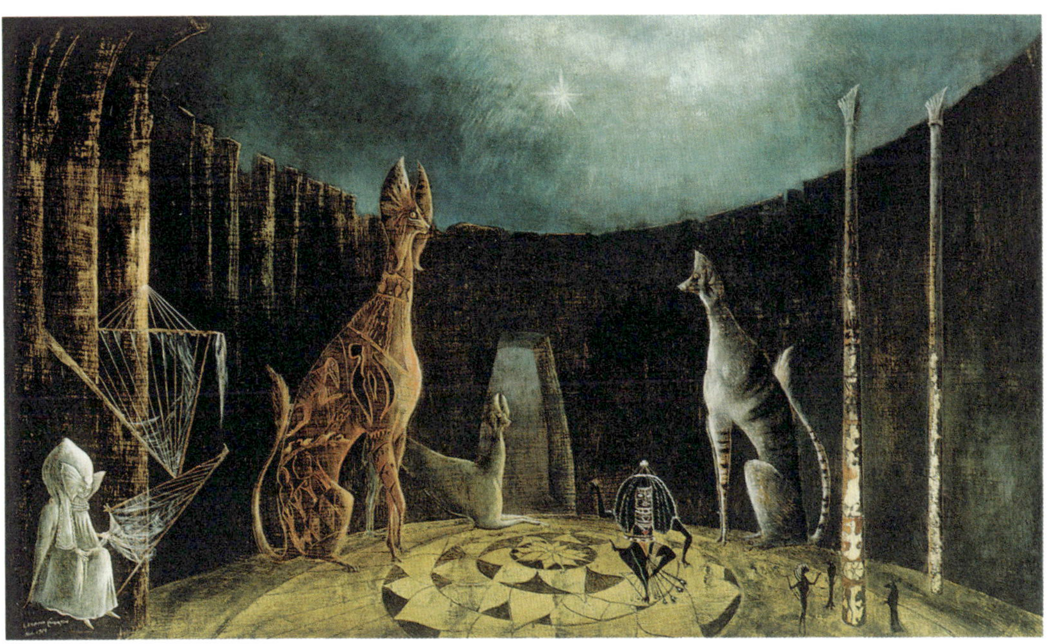

don't really think in terms of explanations.' When another interviewer asked her about the meaning of a painting of hers, she retorted sharply, 'This is not an intellectual game. It is a visual world. Use your feelings.'

In 2006, a relative, Joanna Moorhead, visited Carrington in Mexico, eager to find out the truth about the 'black sheep' of the family. To Joanna, she was known by her gloriously inappropriate family nickname of 'Prim', though Carrington soon found herself rejecting that title. Joanna had been told by her family that her cousin 'was deficient, disloyal and dangerous ... an impossible creature, a wild child, an unfathomable puzzle of a girl; a young woman who refused to be tamed and who eventually ... simply flounced off into the sunset.' But what she found, in the flesh, was 'not the [family] ghost, but the brilliant and complicated and talented artist she had become in the world: the renowned Leonora Carrington'.

Leonora Carrington, *Are You Really Syrious?*, 1953.

CECIL COLLINS

Exhibited with the surrealists in London in 1936

BORN: 23 March 1908 in Plymouth

PARENTS: Father an engineer opposed to art as a career

LIVED: Plymouth 1908; London 1927; Devon 1936; London 1944; Cambridge 1948; Chelsea, London 1970

PARTNER: Married ELIZABETH RAMSDEN, a sculptor, 1931

DIED: 4 June 1989, aged 79

CECIL COLLINS HAS TO BE INCLUDED IN A LIST OF SURREALIST ARTISTS because his work was shown in the landmark International Surrealist Exhibition at the New Burlington Galleries in London in 1936. It was Herbert Read who decided that he should be represented, and nobody appears to have objected. Superficially his work does appear to be in the surrealist mould, but a closer examination reveals that it is deeply religious and therefore breaks one of the basic rules of the surrealist movement. In 1928 André Breton had summed up the surrealist attitude to religion in his famous statement: 'Everything that is doddering, squint-eyed, vile, polluted and grotesque is summoned up for me in that one word: God!' It is little wonder that, once he was found out, Collins and surrealism went their separate ways.

What is surprising is the choice of the two works by Collins that were hung in the great 1936 exhibition, surrounded by surrealist masterworks. One of them depicts a host of angels and has the word 'resurrection' actually written on the painting eleven times. The other one is an ink and pencil drawing entitled *Angel Images and Negative Spectres in Conflict* (1933, Tate, London). One would have thought that there were enough clues there to alert the exhibition committee to the fact that Collins was not, perhaps, an ideal contributor to this revolutionary, anti-religious exhibition.

There are only two possible explanations for the acceptance of Collins as a member of the surrealist club. The first is that they viewed his depiction of mystical, religious themes as a satirical attack on the subject. His unusual

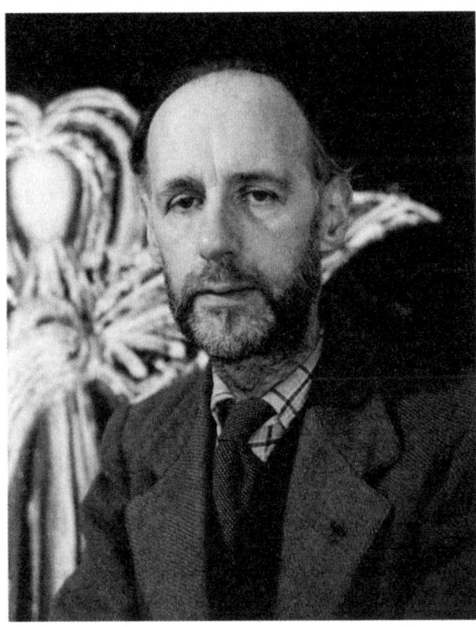

combination of a surrealist style of painting with the portrayal of religious images could have been seen as a way of belittling religion and laughing at angels and other sacred figures. It was nothing of the sort, but perhaps the organizers did not realize this until much later. A second possibility is that the surrealist committee and others involved were all so busy with other matters that they did not look too closely at the paintings by Collins. It is also possible that Édouard Mesens, the one person who must have studied them closely since it was he who hung the exhibition, was drunk at the time – a not uncommon event. Whatever the truth of the matter, the laughable fact remains that, at the very heart of an exhibition that vigorously opposed religion and all it stood for, there was a large painting about the resurrection.

Collins is one of those idiosyncratic, isolated, individualistic British artists whose work is immediately recognizable and who has no close parallels in modern art. He was born in middle-class Edwardian Plymouth, son of an engineer and a mother who taught her only child to read from the Bible. The estuarine landscape of his youth – the wild sea and the romantic

Cecil Collins, photographed by Tony Evans, c. 1965.

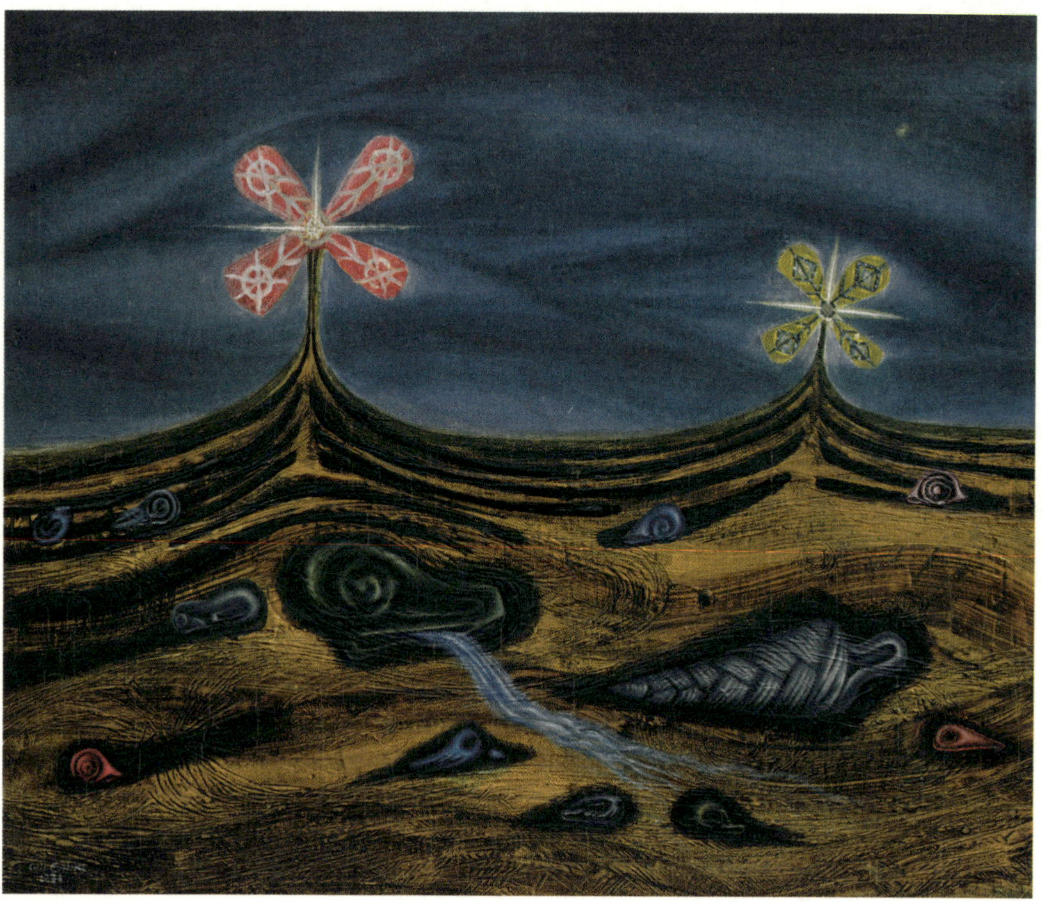

landscape of hills and valleys – made a powerful visual impact on his young imagination. He was a sickly, delicate boy, often away from school and spending many hours on his own, convalescing from illness. The solitude he experienced helped him to develop his visionary imaginings. In his mind, he occupied another, magical, spiritual world where the often-dark Cornish legends made him feel like someone who walked in another place, a realm far from the everyday practicalities of an English schoolboy. His adult art would owe a great deal to those childhood fantasies.

Cecil Collins, *The Promise*, 1936.

Despite his illnesses, he described his childhood as a happy period in his life. All this was changed in the hard times of the 1920s, when his father lost his engineering job and had to scrape a living as a labourer, working on road repairs. The family was forced to live in a single rented room to survive. He and his father soon began to clash. Collins senior wanted his son to take an engineering job and took him out of school at fifteen to put him into an engineering apprenticeship. The boy hated this and already had his mind firmly fixed on becoming an artist. Eventually, much to his father's fury, he walked out of the engineering firm and vowed never to go back. Fortunately, a Roman Catholic priest had seen his youthful drawings and arranged for him to have free lessons at the local art school. There he learnt painting techniques, began to study art history and read a great deal of poetry. Religious music entered his life, and he gave piano recitals in concerts at the Plymouth School of Art. He also started taking long night-time walks onto the nearby hills, where he would stand and absorb the patterns of lights in the gas-lit city streets below and the marine lights of the harbour. On one of his wanderings he came across a tramp who, bizarrely, taught him Shakespeare.

Even as a student, Collins was beginning to show personal eccentricities. He wore his hair very long, which was not an acceptable thing to do at the time. When he refused to have it cut, other students laid siege to the art school, attacking it with water hoses. As a result, the principal of the school had to ask Collins to cut his hair as nobody could enter or leave the building. Reluctantly he had to agree, but this incident reveals how already, as a teenager, Cecil Collins had become his own man, a person apart from the mainstream, relishing differences that most other boys would go to great lengths to avoid.

He was nineteen when his father died. His mother, who had always been sympathetic to his interest in drawing and painting, was delighted when he won a scholarship to the Royal College of Art in London. There, he became the 'golden boy' of his year and, strangely, went through an anti-religious phase during which he made a watercolour entitled *There is no God*. But, at the same time, he became fascinated by mystical painting and spent a great deal of time studying the works on display in the Victoria and Albert Museum, the National Galley and the British Museum. By the early 1930s his brief atheist period was over, and he was in love with a fellow student, the lively, intelligent and beautiful Elizabeth Ramsden. She seemed happy to share his eccentricities. Once, when he decided to pay a visit to his mother in Cornwall, he and Elizabeth turned it into a pilgrimage, walking the nearly 200 miles from London, stopping at vicarages along the way to ask for help in finding shelter. They made a habit of pilgrimages of this kind, and it is not surprising to find that pilgrims sometimes put in an appearance in his visionary paintings.

Cecil and Elizabeth were married in 1931, and she inspired him to start work on some huge religious pictures that are, to my mind, so badly painted that one cannot help thinking that, smitten as he was, his mind was elsewhere. With titles such as *Scene in Paradise* (1932) and *The Fall of Lucifer* (1933), these ungainly, amateurish, mystical compositions give no hint of the exciting work yet to come. When calling these works religious, it should be stressed that serious theology is not involved. These are visionary works full of clouds and angels, paradises and pilgrims. This is the religious world of the Sunday school or a small child's bedtime story, and it is a world that haunted Collins's work throughout his life. Even much later, when he had arrived at a more mature stage in which he was painting in a fascinating, highly individualistic style that was unmistakably his own, he still felt the urge to depict sentimental little angel figures.

His other obsession was with a character he called simply 'The Fool'. The Fool is a sad but slightly comical figure, a universal clown, an innocent abroad. He is usually depicted wearing a dunce's cap, as if he were being punished for being stupid. Fools are seen dancing, in a stately procession, sleeping under a tree, picking a flower or running from a storm. The artist himself called the Fool a symbol of 'purity of consciousness', whatever that may mean.

The type of modern art for which Collins had a passionate dislike was the school of hard-edge abstraction, and he complained bitterly about 'sterile geometric art with its tyrannical cultural snobbery'. This view, expressed in 1935, may explain why he was attracted to the surrealists and they to him. For they were also strongly opposed to the abstract school that was popular in avant-garde art circles at the time. And there was something else. Up to this point I have stressed the visionary paintings of Collins, the vaguely religious works full of angels. But when he omitted all forms of humanoid figures from his paintings – all the angels, fools, Christs, pilgrims and poets – he did create some wonderfully imaginative surrealist landscapes, with no hint of sacred

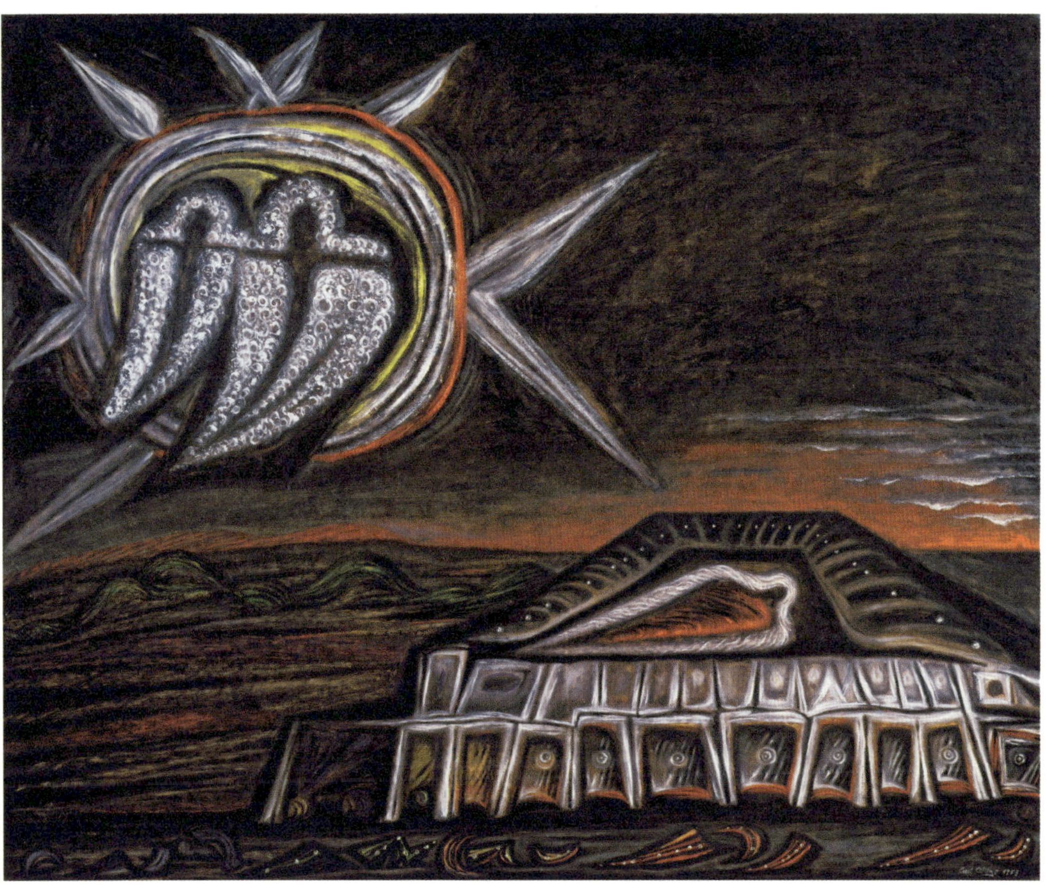

undertones. If two of these landscapes had been shown at the International Exhibition in 1936, Collins might have enjoyed a longer association with the surrealist group. When André Breton realized what had happened and that surrealism had been invaded by despised spiritual imagery, the end was rapid. Breton issued a statement condemning work such as Collins's and ensured that any paintings submitted by him to surrealist exhibitions in the future would be instantly rejected.

After his split from the surrealists, Collins continued to paint his visionary scenes and, when World War II came, with his frail health making him exempt from military duty, he took up teaching at Dartington Hall in Devon.

Cecil Collins, *Hymn*, 1953.

At the height of the Blitz, he held an exhibition in London, and the gallery showing his work was hit by a flying bomb. By a lucky chance, all it did to his paintings was to blow them off the walls so that they landed face-down on the gallery floor. The gallery owner arrived just in time to stop the firemen from flooding the gallery with their hoses – an act that would have destroyed years of Collins's work.

When the war ended, he held another show in London, when his work was attacked for its amateur quality and its 'worn clichés'. A few years later another exhibition, this time in Cambridge, saw him even more savagely attacked. His work was described as 'addled' and 'niggardly'. The critic said that the paintings filled him with revulsion. It is surprising that his pictures should produce such powerful negative reactions. Fortunately for him, there were many others who admired and collected his work, but he always seemed to have been an artist who was both loved and hated in equal amounts. Such is the fate of artists who work outside the mainstream of art, ploughing lonely furrows, driven by personal obsessions and idiosyncrasies.

In 1959 Collins was given a major retrospective of over 200 of his works at the Whitechapel Gallery in London. In the catalogue he struck back at his detractors, saying: 'Pure art is the prettier side of the utterly empty mechanical desert we call modern civilization.' The critics were once again divided, but there was enough praise for Collins to take some comfort from the event. As late as the 1970s, there was an attempt to oust him from his teaching post at the Central School of Art in London. Other staff members disliked his 'spiritual' approach, but he rallied support from students and friends and was reinstated. Right up to the end of his life his work was both coldly rejected and deeply admired.

ITHELL COLQUHOUN

Member of the British Surrealist Group from 1939 to 1940, when she was expelled for not supporting Mesens and because of her interest in the occult

BORN: 9 October 1906 in Shillong, in what was then Eastern Bengal and Assam, British India

PARENTS: Father a civil servant

LIVED: Shillong 1906; Cheltenham 1925; London 1927; Paris 1931; London 1933; Paris 1937; London 1939; Cornwall late 1940s

PARTNER: Married Toni del Renzio 1943–47; divorced

DIED: 11 April 1988 at the Country House Hotel, Lamorna, Cornwall, of heart failure, aged 81

Ithell Colquhoun was one of those artists who had an intense surrealist phase, but whose main focus in life lay elsewhere. She was, first and foremost, an occultist, wrapped up in the gobbledygook of the supernatural. Her interest in witchcraft meant that she was against official religion, and this was something that she shared with the surrealists. She was also obsessed with the mysterious and, again, this was something that appealed to the surrealist mind. The problem for her arose when she realized that the surrealists would treat occultists as just another religious sect and kick them out, along with all other forms of religious practice. This meant that, although she would plunge headlong into the surrealist movement, she would also have to face being ejected from it.

Colquhoun was born in Shillong, in what was then British India, in the middle of the Edwardian period. Her father was a civil servant, and she enjoyed an exotic and uninhibited childhood, full of rich and colourful imagery. Her Scottish family sent her to the exclusive Cheltenham Ladies College in England and then on to the Slade School of Fine Art in London, where, in 1929, one of her paintings was so good that it won a prize and was exhibited at the Royal Academy. It was while she was a student at the Slade that she visited Paris, where she became fascinated by the dark surrealist

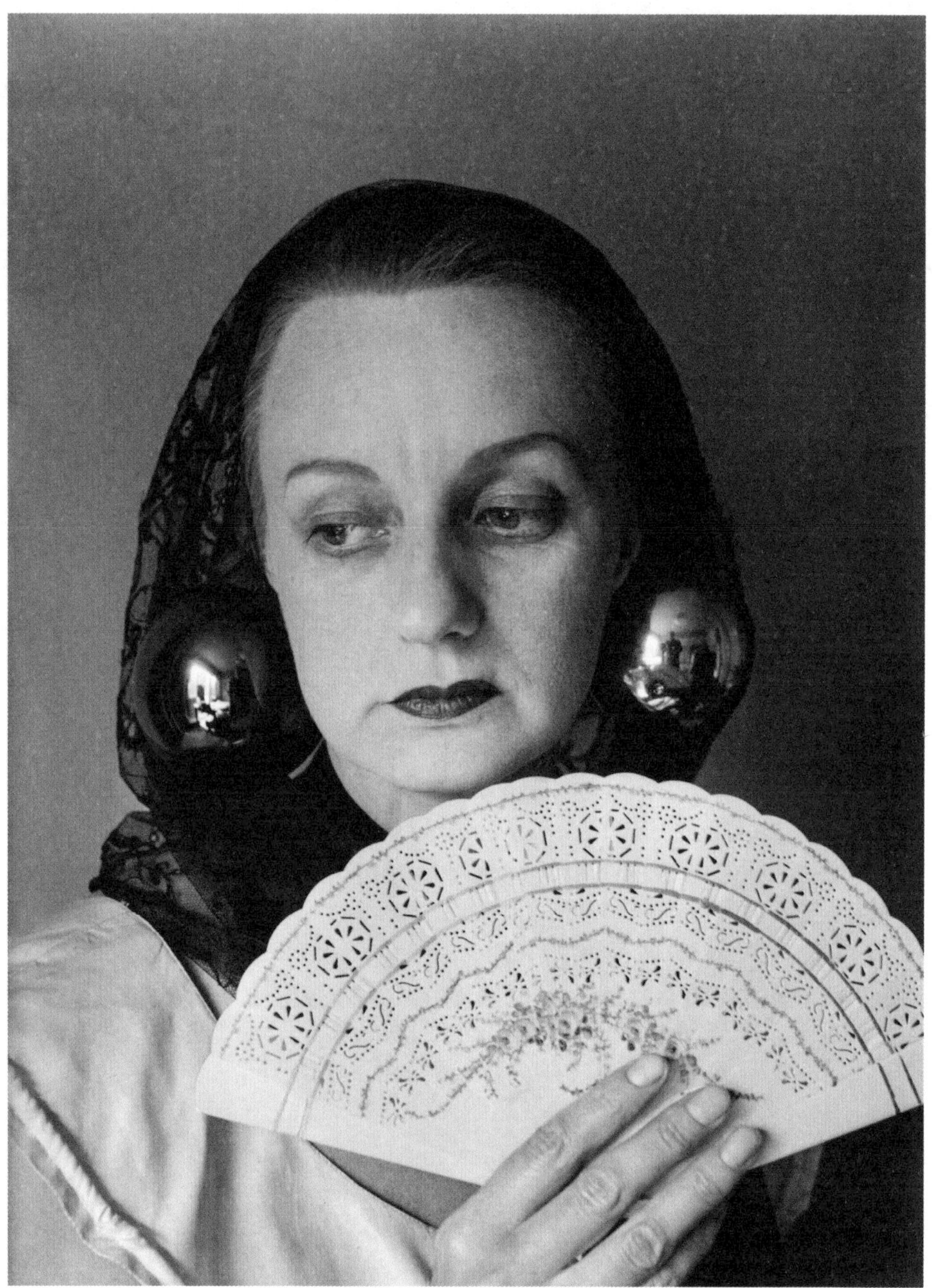

Ithell Colquhoun, photographed by Reg Speller, 1949.

fantasies of Salvador Dalí. In 1931, after graduating from the Slade, she set up a studio in Paris and became more deeply involved with the surrealist circle there. During this period, Colquhoun's imagery revealed a preoccupation with erotic motifs, often involving explorations of a variety of sexual positions. Some of her works depicted symbolic castration and variations in gender roles. Even her botanical subjects carried sexual undertones.

Colquhoun attended the International Surrealist exhibition in London in 1936 but was not included among the exhibitors. It was not until 1939 that she formally joined the British Surrealist Group, then led by the London-based Belgian surrealist Édouard Mesens. Mesens saw himself as the André Breton of England and required his followers to obey the strict rules of Breton's surrealist manifestos, as interpreted by him. When he sensed that the group was becoming rather lax in this respect, he called a meeting in 1940 at which everyone had to swear allegiance to the basic principles of surrealism. This had the effect of splitting the group into two. Those who rejected his demands and left the group included Henry Moore, Paul Nash, Grace Pailthorpe, Reuben Mednikoff, David Gascoyne and Humphrey Jennings – all for different reasons. Ithell Colquhoun wanted to remain in the group but refused to give up her obsession with the occult. Mesens would not accept this and she was expelled. Mesens must have been disappointed by the small size of the group that remained loyal to him.

This expulsion did nothing to dampen Colquhoun's interest in surrealism or her output of surrealist works. It simply meant that she had to do this from outside the now small clique that gathered around their Belgian leader. In 1942, at the height of the war, Colquhoun met a Russian surrealist by the name of Toni del Renzio. He had recently arrived in London and was disappointed to find that, due to the preoccupations of wartime, the surrealist group had lost its impetus. He decided to take over the role of leader, replace Mesens and re-activate the group. As part of his campaign, he published a surrealist magazine called *Arson*. Colquhoun helped to finance this and, when it flopped, she paid off his creditors. He moved into her studio and they became lovers. He also edited a surrealist section of another magazine, where he included a poem 'to darling Ithell' that contained explicit references to 'fresh kisses that fire the night' and 'release the warm thrusts of love'. They became inseparable and on 10 July 1943 they were married.

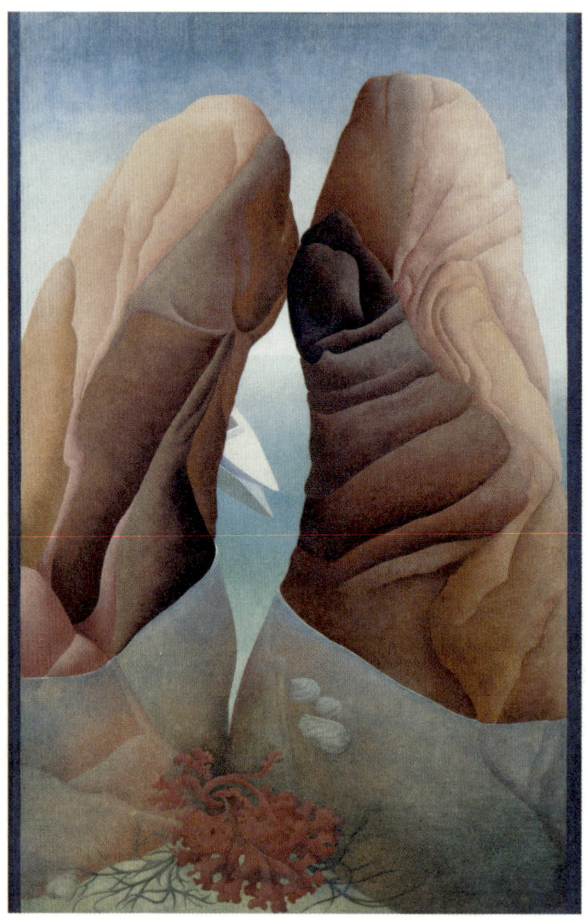

When Mesens got wind of del Renzio's bid to usurp his role, in true André Breton fashion he promptly expelled del Renzio from the group. One of Mesens's followers described del Renzio's published words of love to Ithell as a 'vulgar little poem which bore no conceivable connection to surrealism', adding sneeringly that 'the only link between del Renzio and surrealism was that of a tapeworm in a man's intestine'. Despite these attacks, del Renzio refused to accept his expulsion from the group and, in defiance of Mesens, he and Colquhoun organized a surrealist poetry reading in London at the International Arts Centre. This threw down the gauntlet to Mesens, who

Ithell Colquhoun, *Scylla*, 1938.

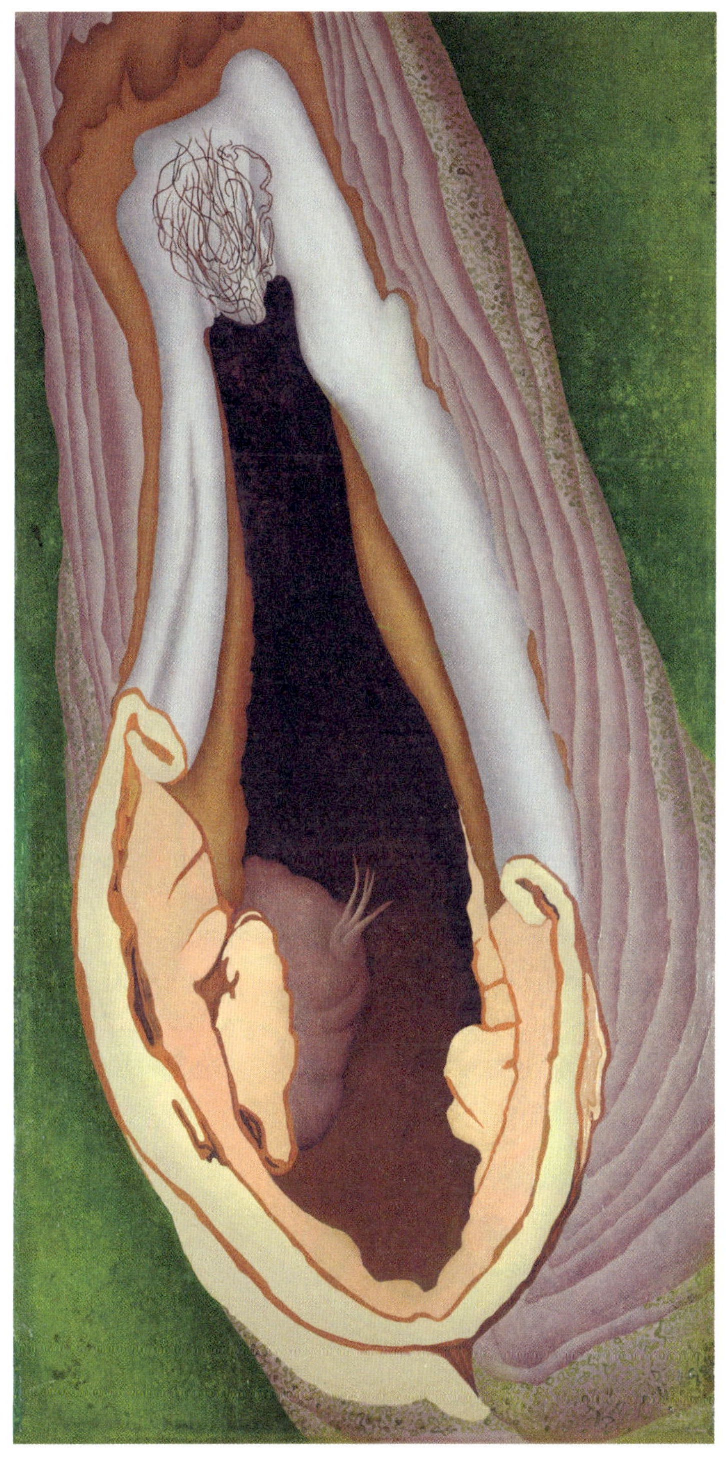

Ithell Colquhoun, *Tree Anatomy*, 1942.

reacted violently. He gathered together a gang of loyal friends and they attended the poetry reading, armed with rotten eggs. They began by demanding that a letter of protest be read out to the audience by Ithell. When this was refused, they started to hurl their rotten eggs at the platform, where Ithell and Toni had to take refuge behind a grand piano. After about half an hour of this bombardment, most of the audience had left and the meeting had to be abandoned.

It has since emerged that there was more to the violence of Mesens's infamous attack on del Renzio and Colquhoun than meets the eye. In addition to the struggle for the leadership role, it seems that Mesens, a well-known sexual predator, had sexual designs on both del Renzio and Colquhoun. When they fell in love and married, he was doubly frustrated, and it is thought to be this that made his protest so extreme – the petulant response of a twice-rejected lover.

After the disastrous poetry evening, del Renzio was defeated and Mesens had regained his crown, but none of this put Colquhoun off producing surrealist paintings, which she continued to do for many years. Her marriage to del Renzio, however, did not last so long. In 1946, because of his infidelities, they separated and were finally divorced in 1947, with much rancour. Shortly after this, devastated by the collapse of her marriage, Ithell moved down to Cornwall, where she would spend the rest of her life and where she became increasingly involved in the arcane world of magic, occult cults and witchcraft.

A final word about Ithell Colquhoun's name. When I talked to her ex-husband, Toni del Renzio, about her, I was surprised to hear him refer to her as 'Eye-thel' rather than 'Ith-hel'. Like most people I have always mispronounced her.

MERLYN EVANS

A peripheral member of the surrealist group in London

BORN: 13 March 1910 in Llandaff, Cardiff

PARENTS: Father an analytical chemist; mother a nurse

LIVED: Cardiff 1910; Rutherglen, near Glasgow 1913; London 1931; Camberwell 1934; South Africa 1938; South African army 1942; London 1946

PARTNERS: Married PHYLLIS SULLIVAN 1933 (ended during World War II) • Married MARJORIE FEW, a pianist, 1950–73

DIED: 31 October 1973 in London, aged 63

THE WELSH ARTIST MERLYN EVANS WAS BORN IN CARDIFF IN 1910, but his family moved to Glasgow when he was only three and he grew up in Scotland. At the age of twenty-one he won a scholarship to the Royal College of Art in London, where he met fellow student Phyllis Sullivan. They were married in 1933, but the marriage was dissolved during World War II.

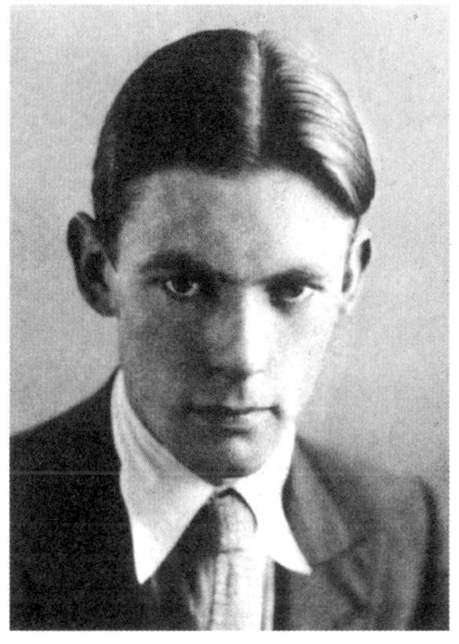

Merlyn Evans, date unknown.

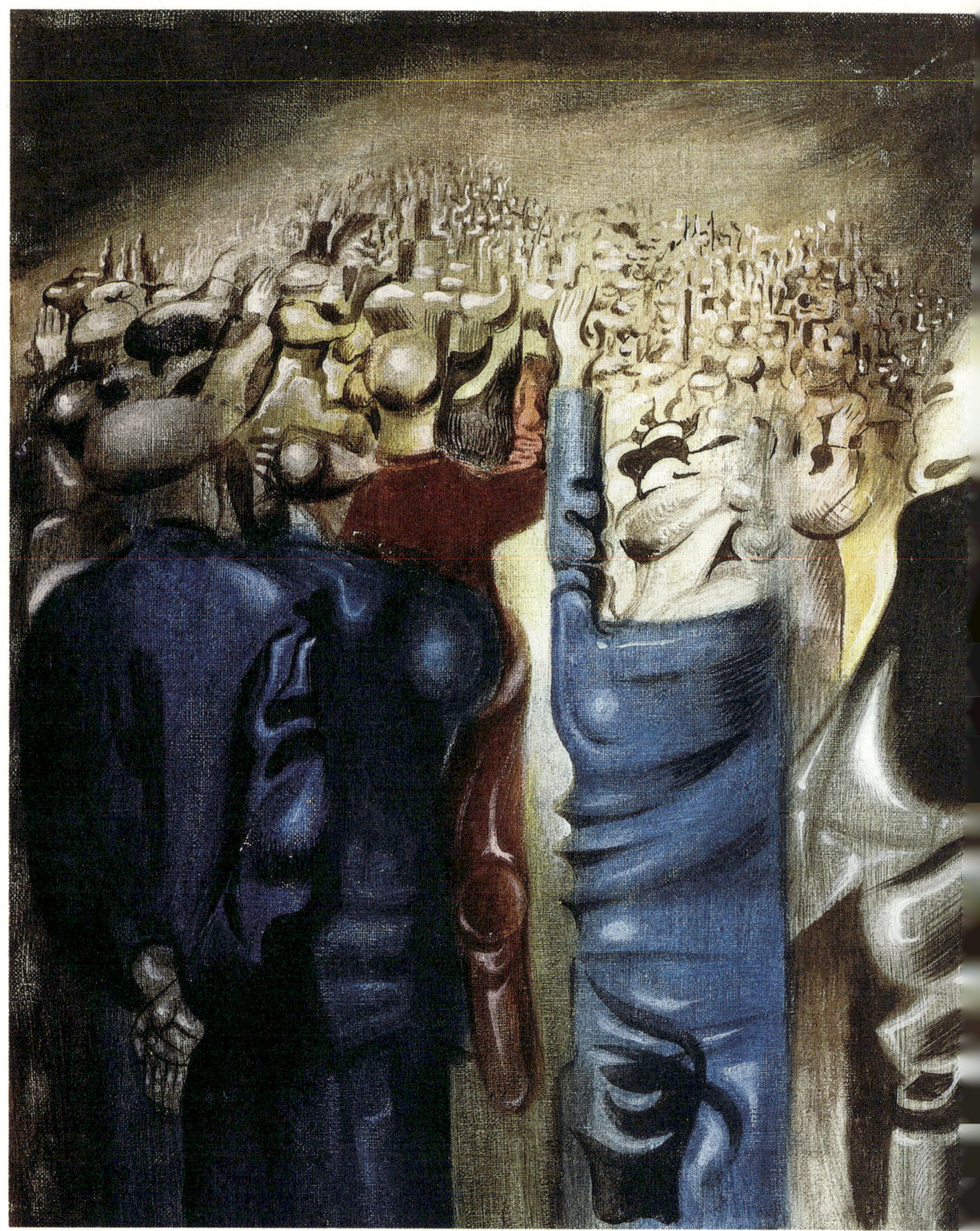

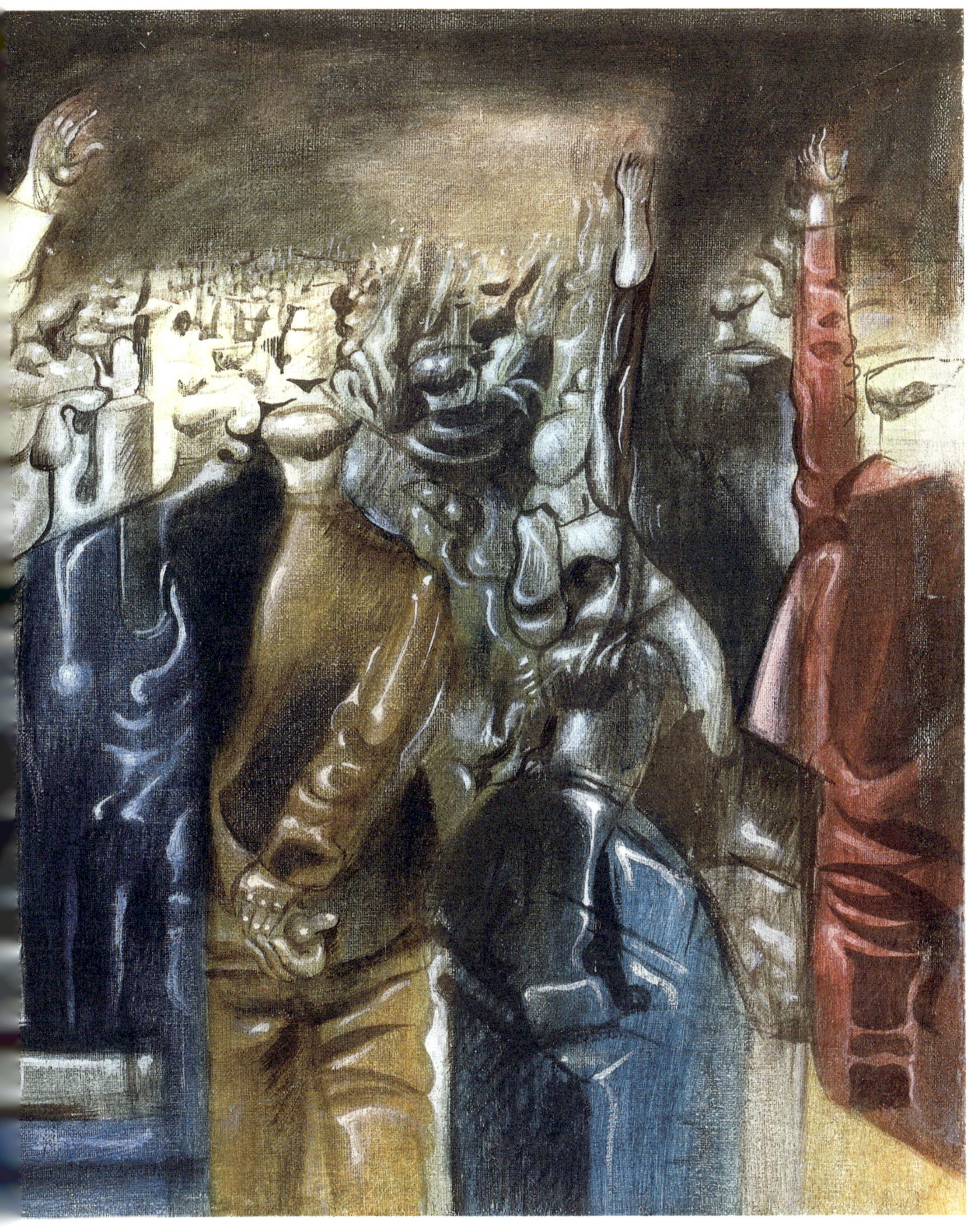

Merlyn Evans, *The Meeting*, 1950.

Cubism and vorticism were the first major influences in Evans's work and, even when he had moved on to surrealist scenes, there was usually a marked angularity to his figures that suggested he had never quite shaken off his first loves. This angularity gave many of his compositions a feeling of aggression, even savagery. When he portrayed a pair of chessplayers, for example, the atmosphere of his painting was more that of a gladiatorial encounter than a cerebral board game. It is said to have been inspired by the relationship between Hitler and Stalin. The title he gave to one of his surrealist works, *Tyrannopolis*, sums up the violence inherent in his compositions. The overall impact of his art is one of stress and tension, conflict and confrontation. Even when his figures lost their sharply pointed angles, they became huddled masses engaged in some sort of protest. If there is a weakness in his work, it is that it lacks a wide range of emotions.

Evans's personality was described as 'many-sided and complex'. He was well read, with a special interest in Freudian psychology. He was perhaps too much of a scholar to be able to release himself from intellectual concerns when he sat in front of a canvas. In his social life he loved nothing quite so much as a good argument and was forever analysing issues involved in psychology, philosophy, politics, optics and the history of art. This made him a good teacher, often witty and irreverent and generous with his time. In his spare moments he wrote a great deal of poetry. He also played the piano and the trumpet, and was a skilled carpenter. These wider concerns can sometimes enrich an artist's visual vocabulary, but there is also a risk that they can clutter the head with complex thoughts that interfere with the rush of pure, intuitive creativity that is needed when engaged in surrealist painting. The artist must learn to free their mind of analytical thought processes while they are at the easel and, if they fail to do this, their work may suffer.

Evans made many visits to Paris in 1934 and 1935, where he met Piet Mondrian, Wassily Kandinsky, Alberto Giacometti, Max Ernst and Stanley William Hayter, learning about the new developments that were taking place there. During this time, he earned a living as a grammar school art teacher. From its inception in 1936, Evans was a member of the surrealist group in England, and six works of his were shown in the International Surrealist Exhibition in London that year. He exhibited with the surrealists again in 1937, but he was becoming increasingly uneasy and pessimistic about the mood of futility that he sensed was developing in the cultural and political

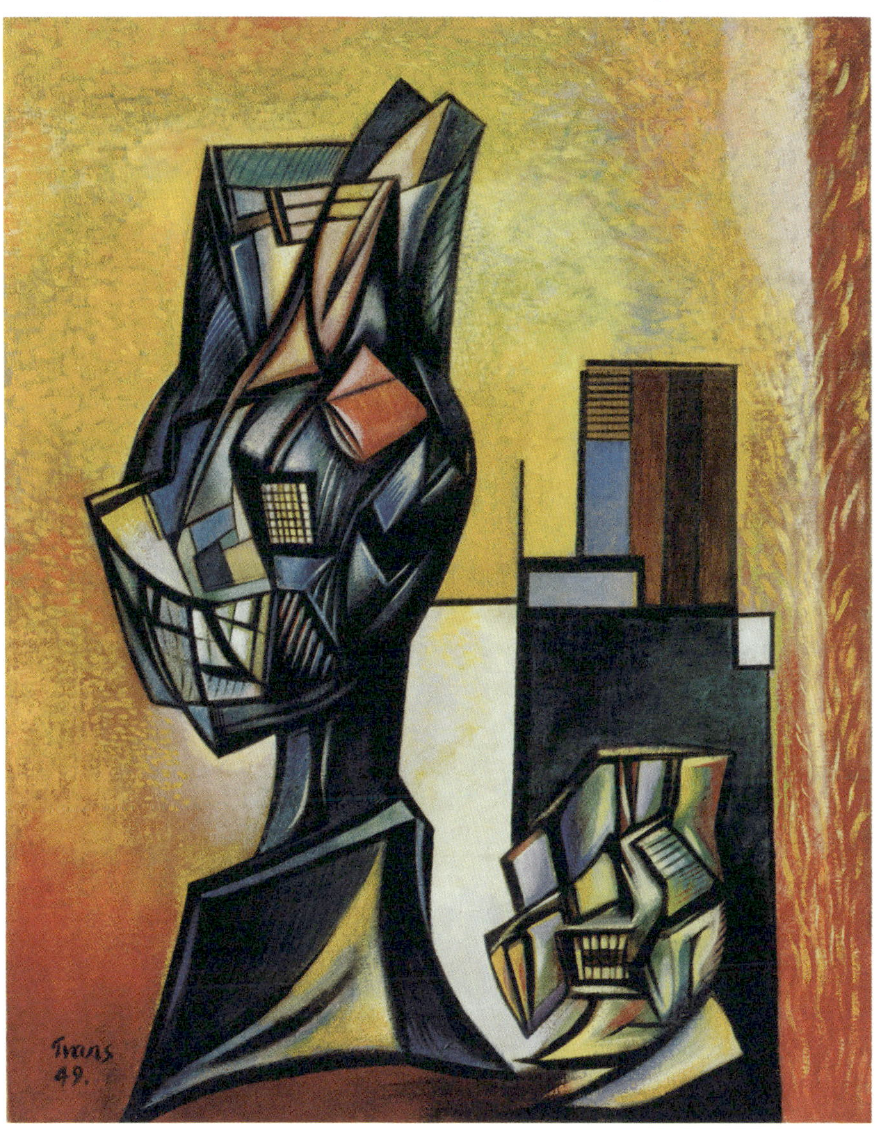

Merlyn Evans, *The Judge and His Clerk*, 1949.

life of Europe at this time. As a result, he left England the following year to take up a teaching post in Natal, South Africa. However, this was disrupted by the outbreak of World War II, and he joined the South African army as an engineer in the Signals Company in 1941. In the Eighth Army he saw service in the North African campaign and then in Italy. He ended up working in War Records in Rome, where he had the chance to meet Giorgio de Chirico. Disillusioned by the horrors of war, in 1944 he was quoted as saying: 'Now we have no trouble in agreeing that humanity is very wicked indeed.'

After the war Evans returned to London and began exhibiting there on a regular basis, although by now he had started to drift away from the surrealist circle. In 1950 he met the pianist Marjorie Few, and she became his second wife. In England during the 1960s, Evans divided his time between London and St Ives, where he spent most of his summers. In 1965 he was appointed to a teaching post at the Royal College of Art. He remained in England for the rest of his life, with only a brief spell in the United States in 1967 when he was an artist-in-residence at the Art Institute of Chicago. While there, he was able to visit New York and make contact with the abstract expressionists, such as Mark Rothko, Barnett Newman and Robert Motherwell. He retained his teaching position at the Royal College until his death in 1973.

SAM HAILE

Joined the British Surrealist Group in 1937

BORN: July 1909 in London, as Thomas Samuel Haile

LIVED: London 1909; New York 1939 (as a pacifist); Ann Arbor 1943; British army 1944; Suffolk 1945; Dartington 1946

PARTNER: Married Marianne de Trey, a potter, 1938 (one child)

DIED: March 1948, Poole, Dorset, killed in a road accident, aged 38

Sam Haile was a promising British surrealist whose life was cut short by a road accident when he was only thirty-eight, and sadly much of the surrealist work that he completed during his short life no longer survives. Many of his earlier surrealist paintings were lost or destroyed when Haile left England for America at the outbreak of war in 1939. Others were destroyed in his fatal car accident, and half of those that did survive were burnt in a fire that broke out at his widow's pottery in 1957. A total of only twelve canvases and fifty or so watercolours, gouaches and drawings remain today out of his entire surrealist output. As a result, he is little known, but he was nevertheless an important and active member of the surrealist movement in London in the 1930s.

Haile was born in London and left school early at the age of fifteen, after which he worked for a shipping firm, attending evening classes at the Clapham Art School. A working-class south Londoner, in 1930 he won a scholarship to the Royal College of Art to study painting, but after a while became more interested in pottery. By 1935 he had a full-time teaching post at the Leicester School of Art, but within a year had returned to London and other teaching posts there.

Haile had his first solo exhibition of pottery in 1937 and it was well received. The following year he married a London-born Swiss art student, Marianne de Trey, who had been studying textiles at the Royal College of Art but who, partly influenced by him, switched to pottery at which she excelled. Sam had a rebellious personality, with strongly held views on many topics, something that appealed to his new wife. She later said of him: 'He was everything I wasn't. He had not been brought up in the same way; he thought all upper-middle-class standards were crazy and was a revolutionary in practically every sense.'

It was in 1938, the year of his marriage, that Haile began exhibiting internationally, in France, Sweden and Canada. He had also, by this time, joined the surrealist group in London and had exhibited at the nerve centre of British surrealism – the London Gallery in Cork Street. His daily routine was described as: 'Night time reserved for the interpretation of dreams and surrealist painting and the days for making and teaching pottery.'

When war broke out in 1939, Haile and de Trey left Europe for America. This was not a case of cowardly flight: it was a positive statement of belief. Haile was an outspoken pacifist and anti-imperialist. He also stated baldly that if the artist 'can keep enough freedom to continue his craft, it matters little to him if it is the people's wish to cut each other's throats'. Underlining his interpretation of the role of the artist in society, he added that, 'Naturally he ignores all calls of duty toward such abstractions as Flag, Fatherland and Freedom, for he has two duties only, or rather two aspects of the same duty which is to art, its two facets being the artistic virtue and the propaganda of the message.' He then explained that by 'propaganda' he meant 'the inevitable propaganda released by the explosion of revealing through the work of art the profound life of the imagination'.

It has to be said that these comments sound much more like the utterances of a rabid surrealist than those of a gently decorative potter. Indeed, Haile also remarked that 'I am convinced that Surrealism is the only proper and valid interpretation of contemporary reality.' He went on, 'This is the big discovery the contemporary artist has made – his contribution towards a more urgent awareness of reality.' He was particularly impressed by the surrealist interest in the *objet trouvé*, or found object, commenting that 'surrealism has demonstrated by means of the object that the aesthetic sensibility exists within the subconsciousness of all, and is not an attribute apart possessed by a favoured few'.

When Haile and de Trey arrived in New York in 1939, he earned a living painting stage sets, decorating porcelain and teaching. He also had several solo exhibitions of his pottery. During these three difficult years he made a number of surrealist gouaches. In 1943 he was inducted into the American

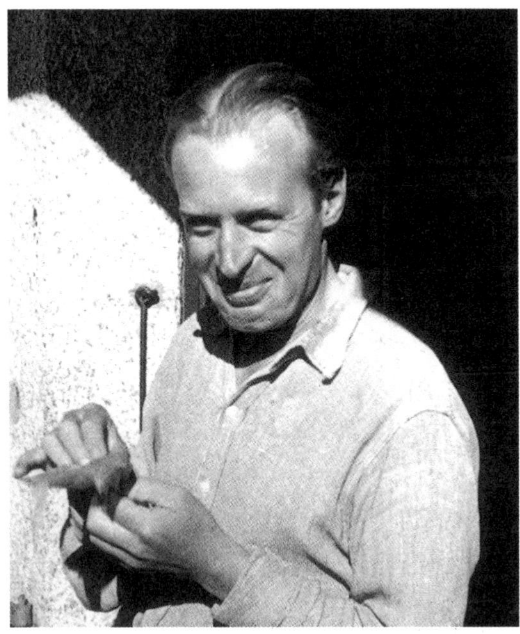

army, but only as a non-combatant, as he stubbornly refused to be made to kill anyone. He found the life of a private in the army extremely boring but did manage to make more drawings in spare moments. Then, in the following year, he was transferred to the British Army and sent back to Britain, where he became an instructor in the Education Corps. In 1945 he was injured in a motorcycle accident and suffered a serious concussion, after which he was released from army service.

Immediately after the war, the couple left London and moved to Suffolk where they set up a pottery. Within two years they had moved again, this time setting up another pottery in the south-west of England, at Dartington in Devon, in a building originally designed for, and recently vacated by, the famous potter Bernard Leach. To earn a living, Sam started working for the Rural Industries Bureau, and this meant a great deal of travelling around southern England. It was on one of these trips, when he and Marianne were just settling into their new life and were on the eve of launching their new pottery, that tragedy struck. Haile was killed in a car accident at Poole in

Sam Haile, 1938.

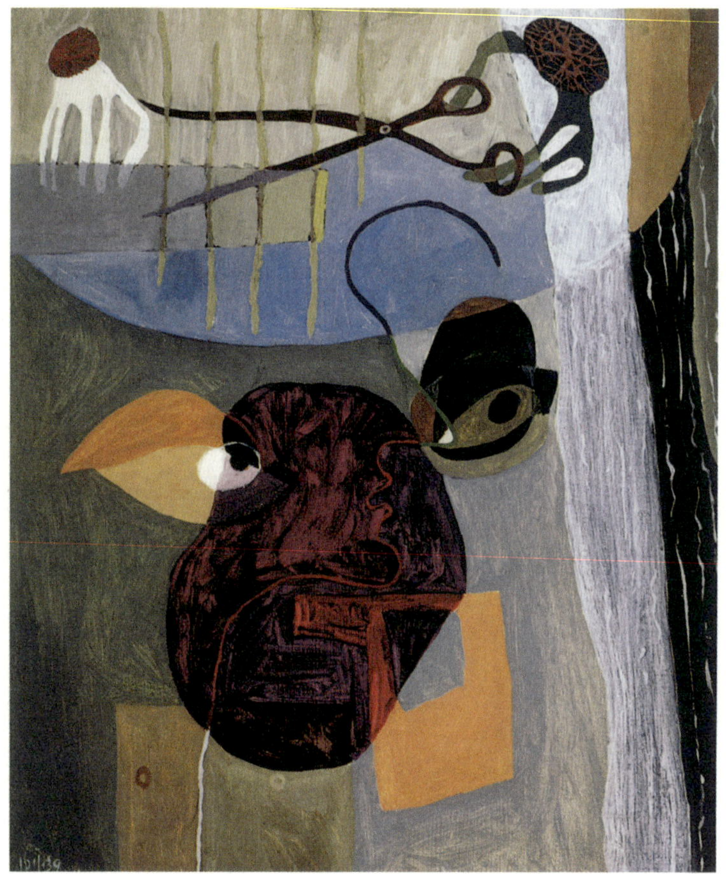

Dorset in 1948. His widow, who was pregnant with their first child, stayed on at the Dartington pottery and ran it successfully for the next thirty-seven years, until she retired in 1985, though she continued to make pottery well into her nineties. Writing about her husband forty years after his death, de Trey described Haile as having an uneven disposition, with periods of elation and periods of depression. She remembered his vitality, his 'huge and ribald sense of humour' and his ability to stimulate almost everyone he met.

After his death, Sam Haile's paintings and drawings appeared in group surrealist shows in England throughout the 1970s and 1980s, including the 1978 'Dada and Surrealism' exhibition at the Hayward Gallery in London.

Sam Haile, *Brain Operation*, 1939.

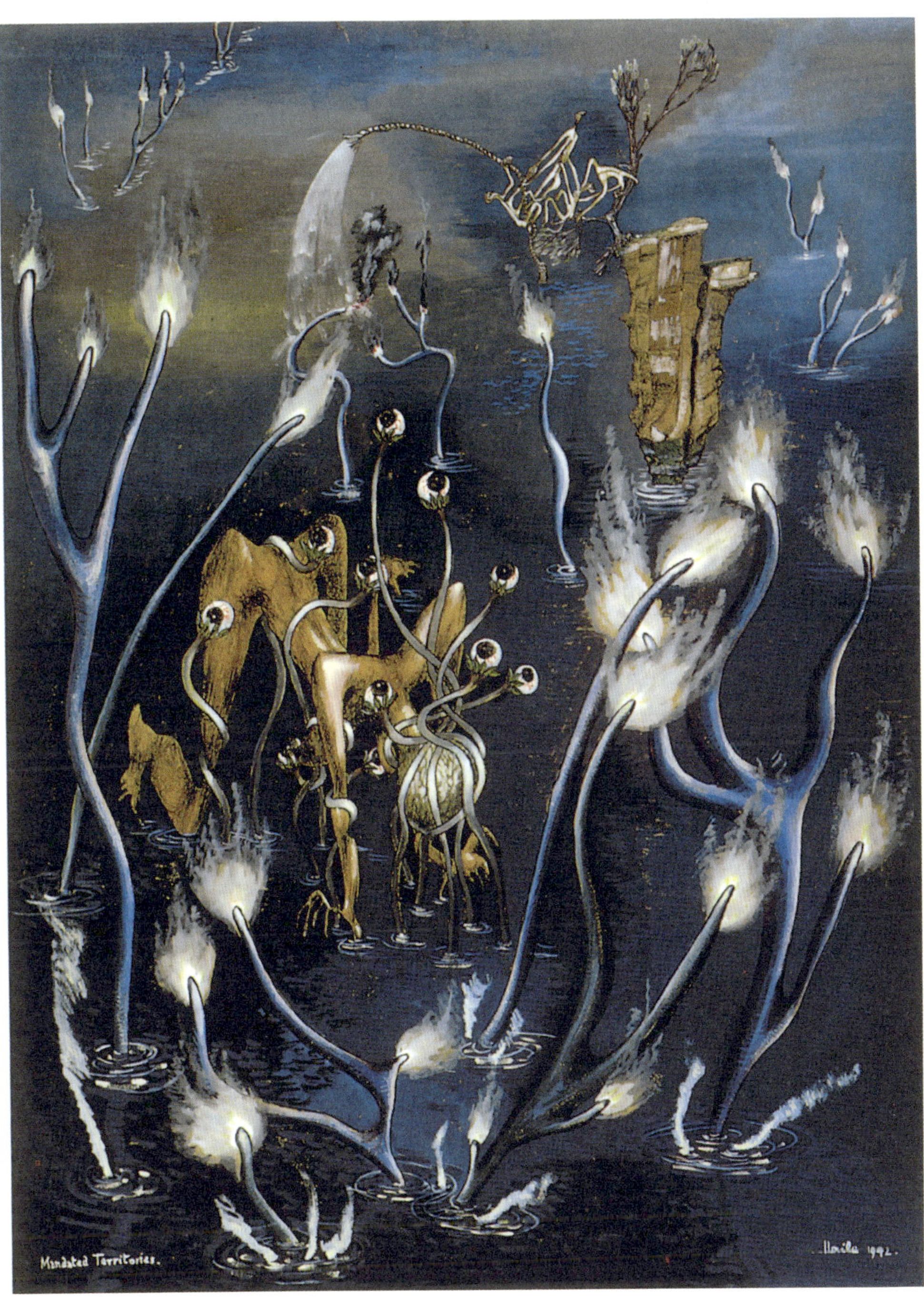

Sam Haile, *Mandate Territories*, 1942.

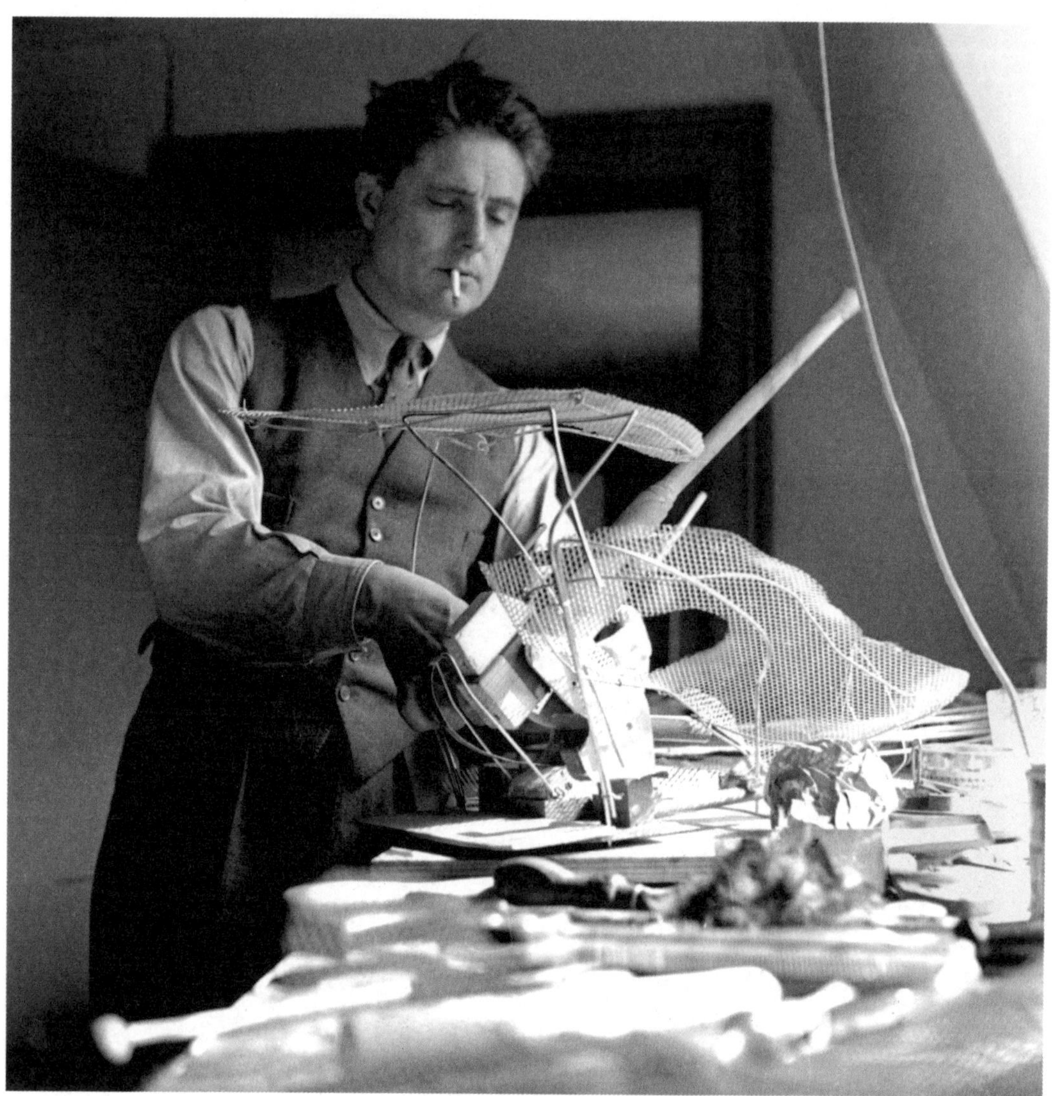

S. W. Hayter, photographed by Lee Miller, 1940.

S. W. HAYTER

Associated with the surrealists in Paris from 1929

BORN: 27 December 1901 in Hackney, London, as Stanley William Hayter

PARENTS: Father a painter

LIVED: London 1901; Abadan, Iran 1922; London 1925; Paris 1926; New York 1939; Paris 1950

PARTNERS: Married Edith Fletcher 1928; dissolved 1929 (one child) • Married Helen Phillips 1940; dissolved 1973 (two children) • Married Desirée Moorhead, an Irish poet, 1974

DIED: 4 May 1988 in Paris, of a heart attack, aged 87

Hayter has been described as the greatest printmaker of the twentieth century. His printmaking studio in Paris, and later in New York, attracted almost all the major avant-garde artists of the day. They went there to cooperate with Hayter on special print productions and also to learn about the latest developments in advanced printmaking that Hayter was pioneering. Pablo Picasso, Wassily Kandinsky, Alberto Giacometti, Joan Miró, Alexander Calder, Marc Chagall, Jackson Pollock and Mark Rothko all worked at printmaking in his studio at one time or another. He hated the term 'teacher', seeing himself more as a facilitator, but the truth was that he had brilliant teaching skills where techniques were concerned.

Stanley William Hayter was born at the start of the twentieth century in London. His father was a painter, but he himself decided to pursue a career in science and obtained a degree in chemistry and geology from King's College, London. It was this scientific training that would stand him in good stead when he moved into the art world, because it provided him with the kind of technical knowledge and the experimental methodology that would help him to pioneer new kinds of printmaking. He was one of the few modern artists who operated in a workplace that was as much a laboratory as it was a studio.

After graduating from college, Hayter left Europe to work for an oil company in Iran for three years. While he was there, he spent all his spare

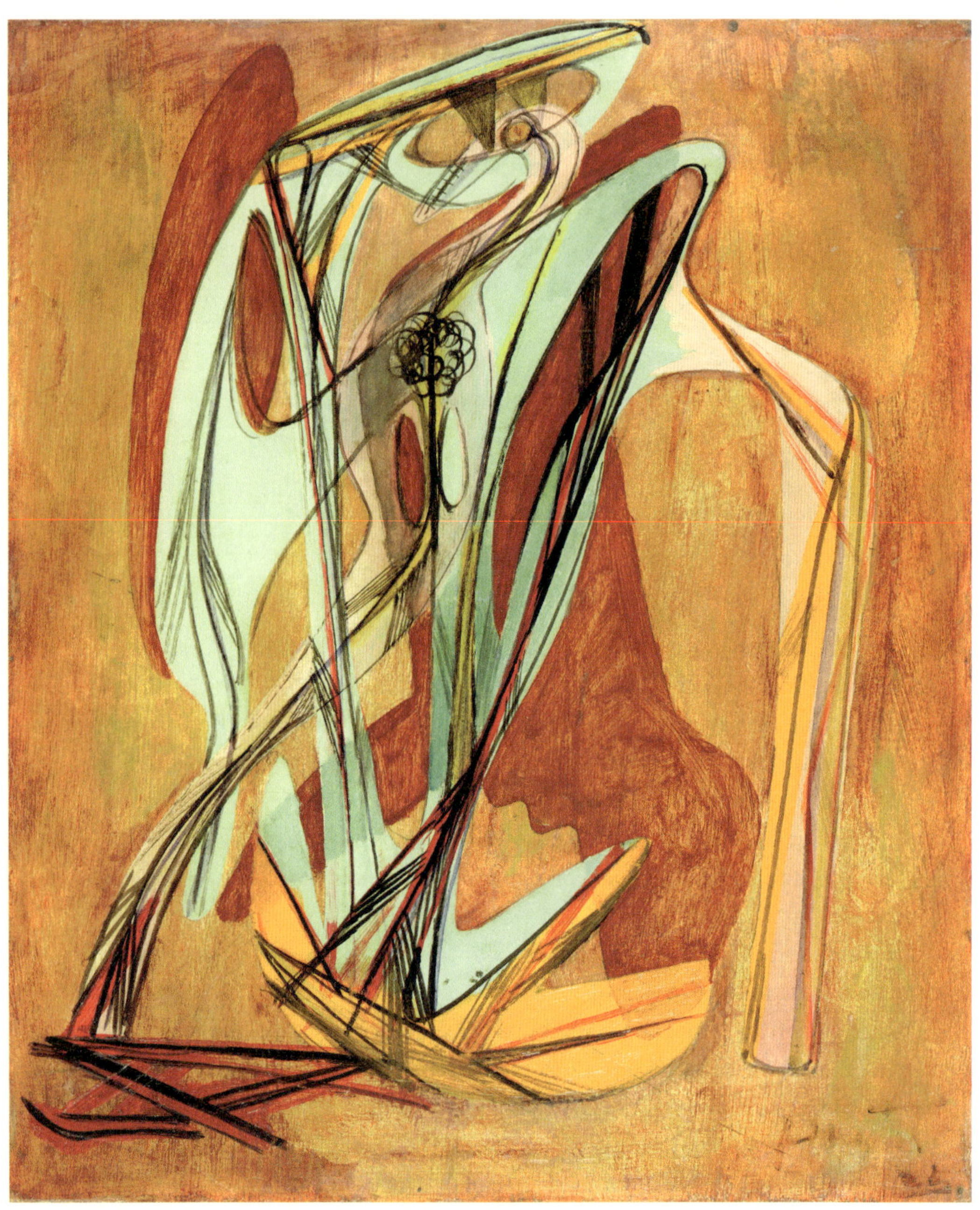

S. W. Hayter, *Composition*, 1935.

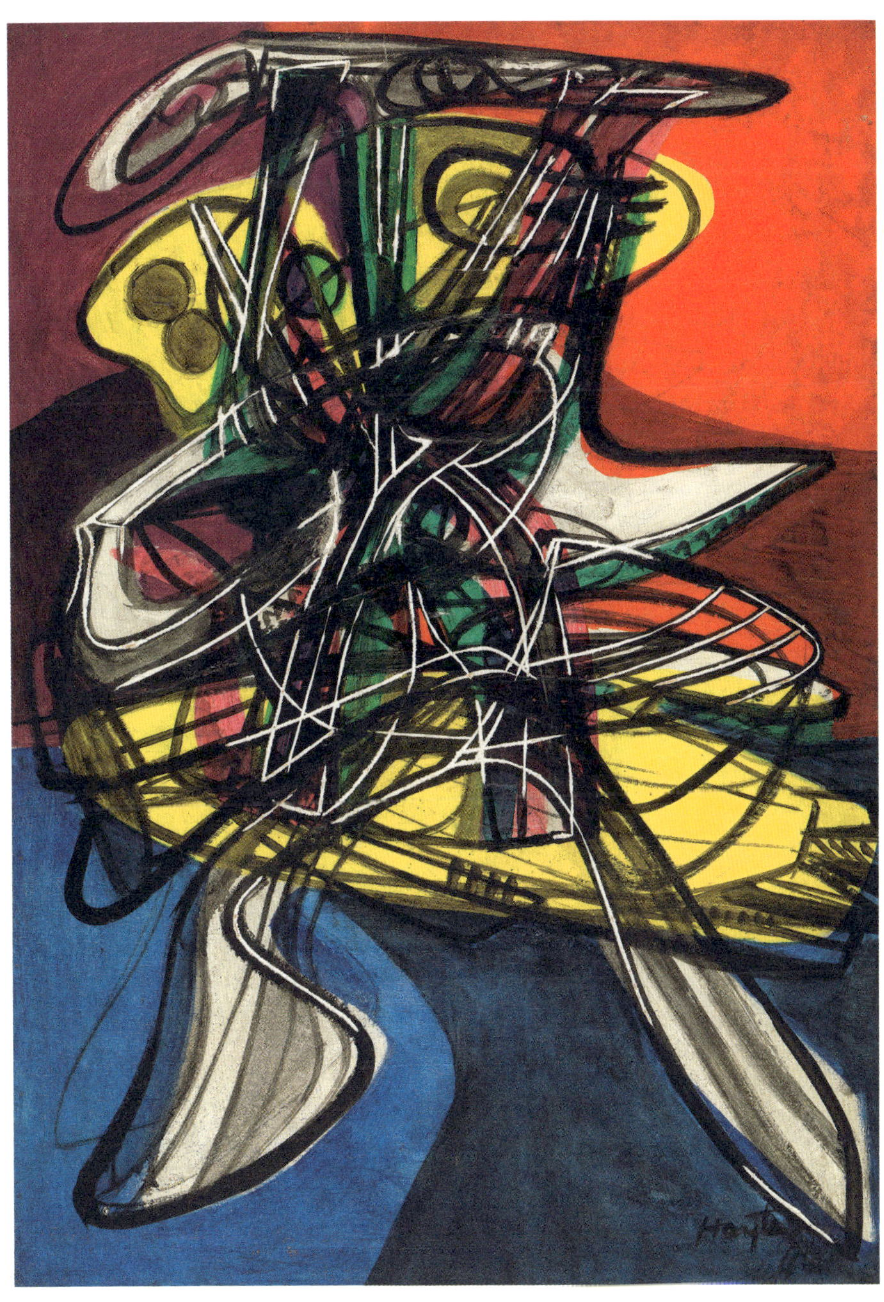

S. W. Hayter, *Child in a Boat* (*Enfant au bateau*), 1946.

time painting and, when he was invalided home after catching malaria, his company gave him an exhibition of his work at their headquarters in London. To his surprise almost everything was sold, and this convinced him that his future lay with art rather than science. In 1926 he decided to move to Paris, the centre of the art world, and soon found himself mixing with artists such as Balthus, André Masson, Calder, Miró and Giacometti. Realizing that printmaking was badly in need of technical development, in 1927 he opened his own workshop, called Atelier 17 – a highly successful enterprise that would run for the next sixty years.

In 1928 Hayter married Edith Fletcher and they had a son, but the marriage was a failure and was dissolved after only one year. He then joined the surrealist circle, and his paintings and prints all began to develop a strong surrealist flavour. During his surrealist phase, he participated in major group shows in London, Paris and New York. He was one of the artists who took Breton's 'psychic automatism' seriously. Nothing was planned beforehand. The lines simply grew and evolved on the paper or canvas, flowing in complex rhythms and patterns that sprang directly from his unconscious. This period would last for about ten years before his compositions started changing to become increasingly abstract.

Following a disagreement with Breton over a political issue, Hayter was expelled from the surrealist group in 1938, never to return. At about this time, he was invited to pay a brief visit to Spain, where the atrocities of the civil war appalled him. Back in Paris in 1939, he took a risk sheltering a number of Spanish war refugees in his studio. This was illegal at the time, and he had to organize transporting gallons of soup to Atelier 17 without arousing suspicions.

The day after World War II broke out in September 1939, Hayter had to abandon Atelier 17 and all its contents and return to London. There, he began war work with Roland Penrose on ways to improve camouflage patterns. When he was declared medically unfit for active duty, he left for New York. Once there, he found himself in the company of a whole group of refugee surrealists from Paris. Despite the fact that André Breton had expelled him from the movement, it was Hayter, along with a few others, who welcomed the great man when he finally arrived at the docks in New York. Having a common enemy mends old wounds.

It was in New York that Hayter met and married an American sculptor called Helen Phillips, with whom he would later have two sons. At the same time, in 1940, he opened a new version of Atelier 17 in the city and was soon attracting young American artists who would later form the abstract expressionist group. In addition to showing them advanced techniques of printmaking, his own work would also exert a strong influence on them. With their cooperation and with mutual influences, Hayter would further abandon the imagery of his surrealist period and plunge deeper and deeper into the meandering visual rhythms of abstraction.

Artists who passed through his Atelier 17 in New York included William Baziotes, Willem de Kooning, Roberto Matta, Robert Motherwell, Rothko and Pollock. It was Pollock who seems to have gained most from the experience, learning from Hayter the value of making unconsciously controlled lines and motifs. 'My notion of a workshop is like a far-out research department,' Hayter said, stressing the importance of ensuring that 'the thinking is done in the medium itself. You find what you want during the operation, by means of the operation.' It was shortly after this period, in 1946, that Hayter invented an important new technique: simultaneous multi-colour printing from a single plate in one passage through the press. It was a technique that would revolutionize colour printing.

As in Paris, Hayter's presence at his atelier made a big impression on everyone who worked there. One observer, Anaïs Nin, commented: 'He always moved about between the students, cyclonic, making Joycean puns, a caricature, a joke. He was always in motion.... His lines were like projectiles thrown in space, sometimes tangled like antennae caught in a windstorm ... to me he was like a wire sculpture, a man of nerves.'

A few years later, in 1950, Hayter returned to France and reopened his Atelier 17 studio in Paris. His fame as a printmaker was now worldwide, and his studio was always busy. By 1957 his experimental mind took him on to new experiments with pattern, and all traces of surrealist influence were now lost. In his new work he was exploring wave motions, flowing currents and rhythmic grids of curving shapes and lines. Young artists flocked to work with him, and he was generous in his advice and guidance.

In personality, he was like the wartime backroom boffin you expect to come across hard at work designing some new bombsight or secret weapon. His floppy, unruly hair, hanging over his forehead, his craggy, deeply lined face with its piercing blue eyes, his gravelly voice and the energetic zeal with which he discussed every small point all made him a commanding figure in the studio, and you could sense the respect that was shown towards him by everyone working at Atelier 17.

Hayter's marriage to Helen Phillips ended in 1973, and the following year he married an Irish poet, Desirée Moorhead, who would stay with him until his sudden death of a heart attack in 1988. Atelier 17, now renamed the 'Atelier Contrepoint', continued with his work after his death and is still active today.

If he had not already been expelled from the surrealist group by André Breton, Hayter would certainly have been removed for the way in which he accepted important honours in the second half of his life. Honours handed out by the establishment were forbidden to hardline surrealists, but he appears to have been happy enough to accept them in recognition of his pioneering work with advanced methods of printmaking. Among his many awards were an OBE, a Légion d'Honneur, a Commandeur des Arts et des Lettres, a CBE and two honorary doctorates.

TRISTRAM HILLIER

Influenced by surrealism in Paris the 1920s and 1930s but not a member of the British group

BORN: 11 April 1905 in Peking (Beijing), China

PARENTS: Father was manager of Hong Kong and Shanghai Bank in Peking

LIVED: Peking, China 1905; Somerset 1914; Cambridge 1922; London 1924; Paris 1927; northern France 1938; London 1940; Somerset 1945

PARTNERS: Irene 'Georgiana' Hodgkins 1931–35; divorced (twin boys) • Leda Hardcastle 1937 (two daughters)

DIED: 18 January 1983 in Bristol, aged 77

To describe Tristram Hillier as a surrealist is to stretch the definition of that word almost to breaking point – almost, but not quite. There was a strong surrealist presence in much of his work, even though he was essentially a landscape painter. This came about in two different ways. When, in his canvases, he moved from the countryside to the city square, he portrayed a sinister empty space devoid of human figures. These works had the same haunting impact as the early paintings of de Chirico. When he stayed on the beaches, strange, twisted objects rose from the sand as though a surrealist sculptor was holding an exhibition there. There were no imaginary, invented beings in his visual world; everything he painted was part of the natural scenery. His talent was for transforming reality into sur-reality simply by the intensity of his paintwork and his carefully chosen viewpoint. The same could be said for the great Belgian surrealist Paul Delvaux.

Hillier's early life was, to say the least, unusual. To be an English child growing up in what was then Peking at the beginning of the twentieth century was strange enough, but then he had to witness his father, who was a diplomat and the manager of an important bank, become suicidal at the age of thirty. The poor man, who had suddenly gone blind, could no longer face living and was only prevented from shooting himself by being converted to the Roman Catholic faith. At an early age, Tristram was shipped back to England with his sickly mother, his brother and his two sisters. Because his mother was so ill, he spent most of his time with the family's Japanese nurse. When he was nine, he was sent away to Downside School in Somerset, where Roman Catholic monks educated him and imposed on him the solemn ritual of the Catholic church. While he was there, he suffered the trauma of learning that his mother had died, his brother had been killed in the war and his two sisters had returned to China. But that was not all. When he was still a teenager, he was told that his father had also died, depriving him of all his close family.

After a brief trip to China in 1922, he returned to England and attended Christ's College in Cambridge, which he described as 'a waste of time'. Then, in 1924, he was apprenticed to a London firm of chartered accountants, but he soon tired of this. It dawned on him that he had the freedom to choose his own future path, and he decided to plunge into the world of art, enrolling at the Slade School of Fine Art in London. There he fell under the influence of the remarkable art teacher Henry Tonks and was able to develop considerable technical skill at painting. In 1926 Hillier began to explore the avant-garde art world of Paris and found himself enjoying the company of the surrealists in their first flush of rebellion. As a reaction against the repressions of his strict Catholic upbringing, he now broke loose and, moving to Paris, pursued a relentlessly hedonistic lifestyle. He spent his days painting or sailing and his nights in the Paris cafés with the surrealists, discussing the controversial art issues of the time 'long into the night'. Max Ernst was one of his closest contacts.

In 1931 Hillier married Irene 'Georgiana' Hodgkins, the daughter of a bookmaker, and they had twin boys together. Sadly, the marriage did not last and, in 1937, he married Leda Hardcastle, the daughter of the man who had invented the torpedo. Together they travelled extensively in Europe, and it was during this time that Hillier met and became a close friend of the British artist Edward Wadsworth. Wadsworth's painting style and his choice of subject matter were to have a major influence on Hillier's work and, in particular, they shared a fascination for the strangeness of objects seen on the seashore or the quayside.

In 1938 Tristram and Leda settled down in northern France, where they were happily enjoying life when war was declared. In 1940 they were forced to flee to England, taking their newborn daughter with them, but little else. Hillier joined the Royal Navy, but after four years suffered a nervous breakdown and was invalided out in 1944. He found it hard to fully recover and could no longer paint.

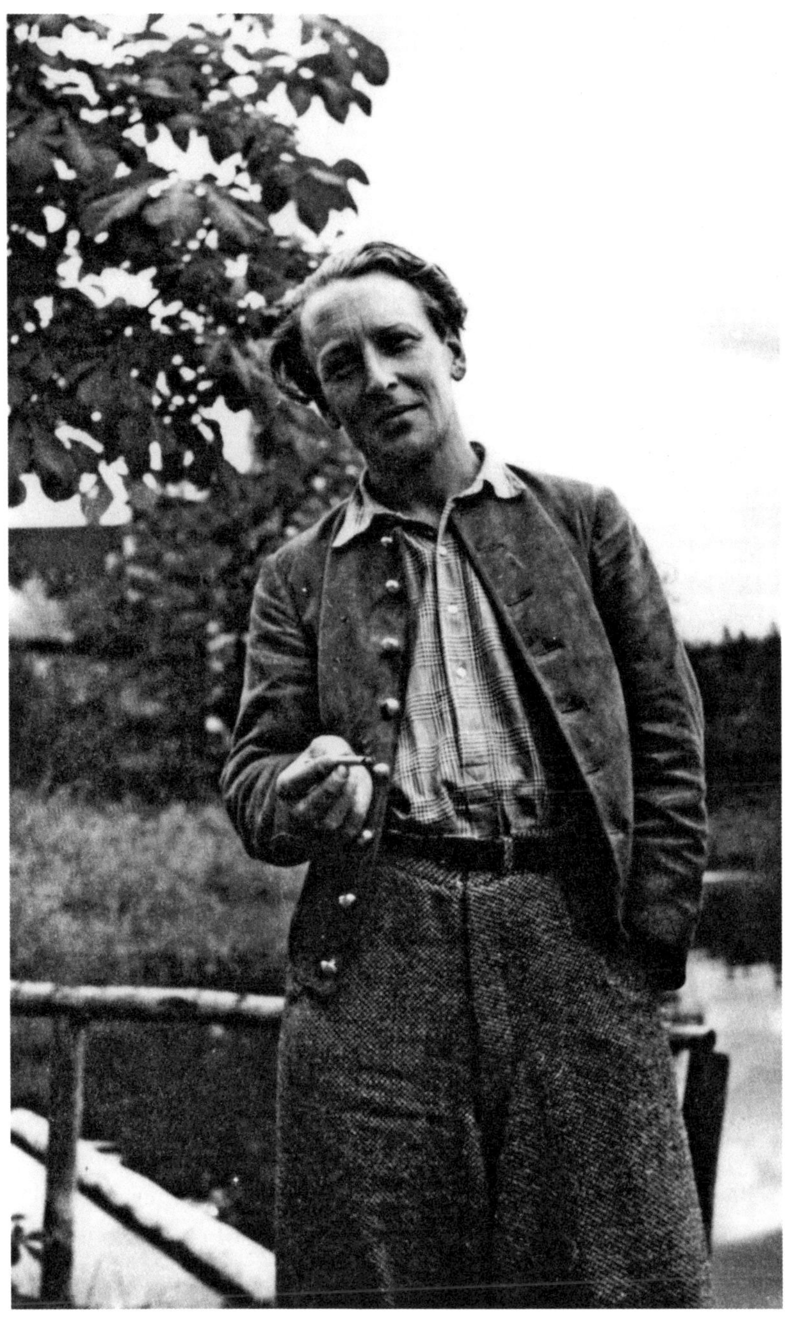

Tristram Hillier, c. 1939.

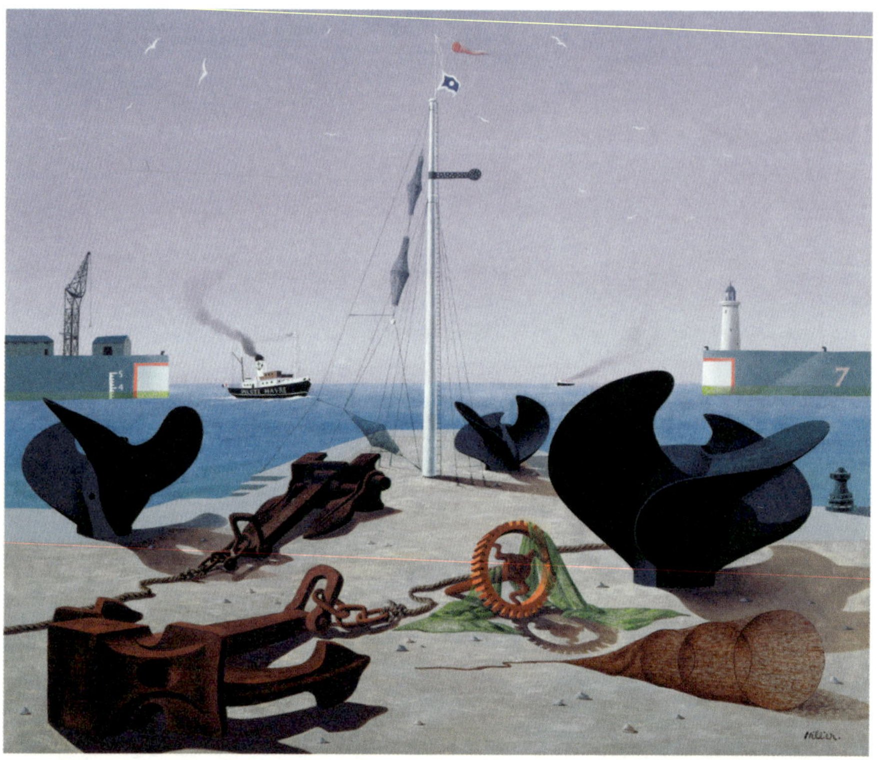

In 1945, when the war ended, he and Leda lived for a while in France and Spain, before finally settling in the small village of East Pennard in rural Somerset. Their now relaxed life in the south of England helped him to recover fully and to return to his art. In 1950 a second daughter was born. At last, Hillier's life became ordered and fulfilling, and he was able to develop a productive painting regime. The wild, surrealist days of his youth in Paris in the late 1920s and early 1930s were now behind him, and he found himself returning to the Roman Catholic faith that he had known as a child. Even so, his hedonism did not entirely desert him, and he spent every summer in the hot sun of either Spain or Portugal, where he would pass the time riding, swimming and drawing in his sketchbook. Then, in the winter months, back in rural Somerset, he would convert his sketches into his meticulous landscape paintings.

Tristram Hillier, *Le Havre de Grace*, 1939.

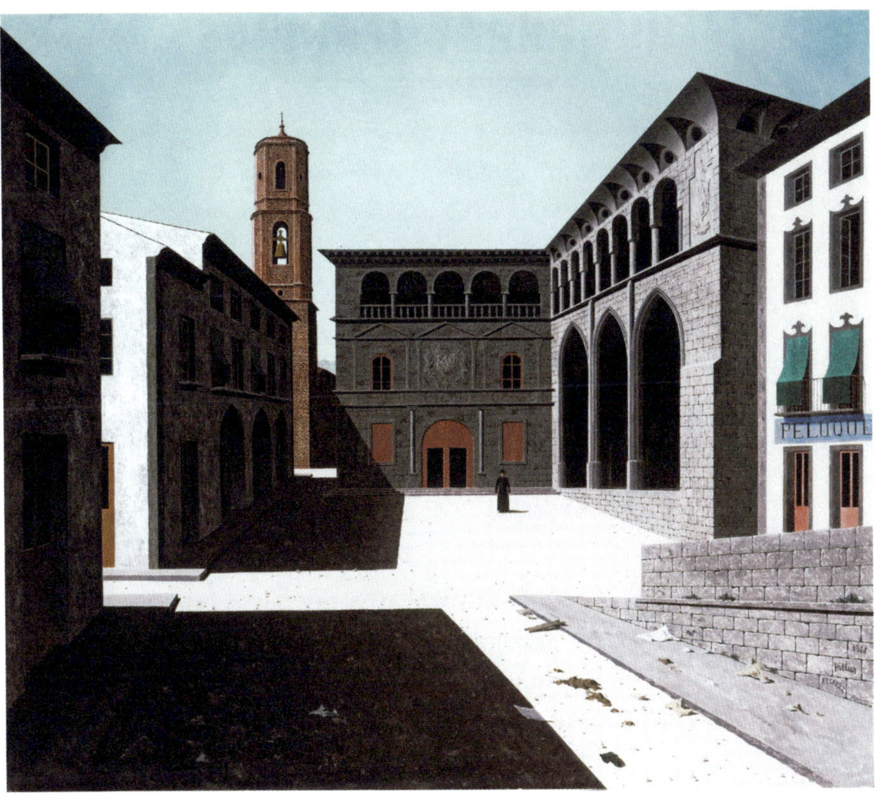

Hillier's work was now gaining him a growing reputation in the art world of London and, in 1967, he was made a member of the Royal Academy, news that his old surrealist companions in Paris would have greeted with horror. Considering the way in which his traumatic childhood had been replaced by a serenely successful later life, one would have expected him to have found peace of mind in his Somerset idyll. However, this was apparently not the case. For some reason he remained a haunted man, and it is said that his paintings became bleaker towards the end of his life because he was now suffering from a 'deep melancholy'. The idea that 'old traumas die hard' seems to be the only explanation.

Tristram Hillier, *Alcañiz*, 1961.

HUMPHREY JENNINGS

Joined the British Surrealist Group in London in 1936; expelled in 1947

BORN: 19 August 1907 in Walberswick, Suffolk

PARENTS: Father an architect; mother a painter

LIVED: Suffolk 1907; Cambridge 1926; London 1934

PARTNERS: Married Cicely Cooper in 1929 (two daughters)
• Emily Coleman 1936 • Peggy Guggenheim 1937

DIED: 24 September 1950, in Poros, Greece, falling from a cliff, aged 43

Humphrey Jennings is best known as a documentary filmmaker, but in private his creative priority was always his painting. The film work was done to make a living, but he never stopped painting and was deeply involved in the great International Surrealist Exhibition in London in 1936.

Jennings was born in a small village on the coast of Suffolk in East Anglia in 1907 and lived there for the first nine years of his life. It was a lonely childhood and, as an adventurous boy, he spent a much of his time exploring the beaches, the sand dunes and the marshes. His parents gave him a great deal of freedom and allowed him to take risks. Even during high seas, with waves crashing on the shore, he was allowed to be out playing, despite the dangers. He was also permitted to smoke, take coffee and drink alcohol from an early age. These childhood freedoms, unusual for the period, made a lasting impression on him, forging an adult personality that felt anything was possible if you put your mind to it. They may also, incidentally, have robbed him of a long life, for it was taking risks on a seashore that ended his life prematurely at the age of forty-three.

When his childhood was coming to an end, a favourite aunt of his was said to have encouraged Humphrey's sexual education by introducing him to a prostitute. This, too, seems to have had a lasting effect on him, giving him an appetite for a large number of sexual adventures later on in his short life. As a young adult he had developed the sort of strong personality that divided opinion. His admirers saw him as energetic, inquisitive, imaginative,

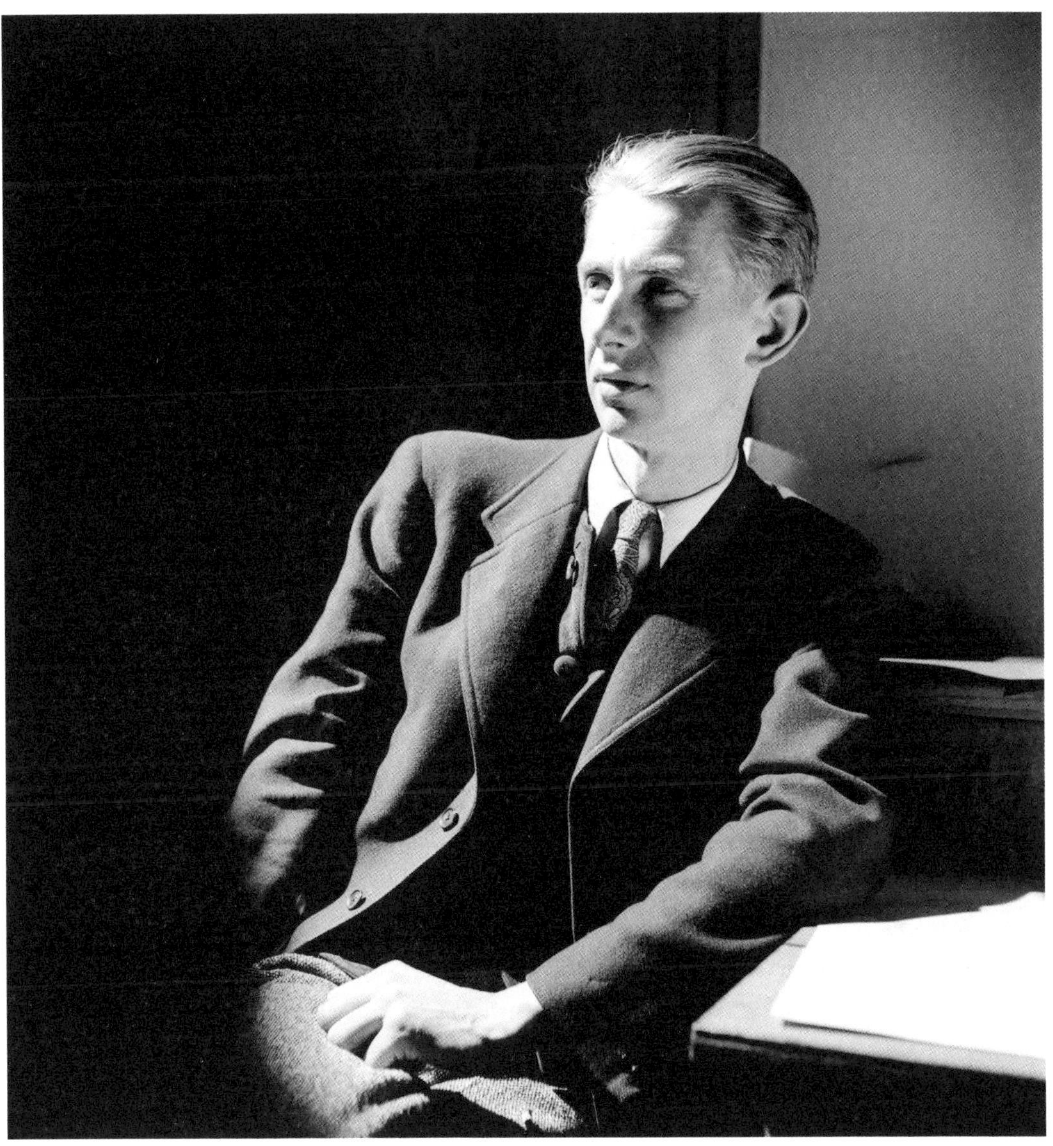

Humphrey Jennings, photographed by Lee Miller, 1943.

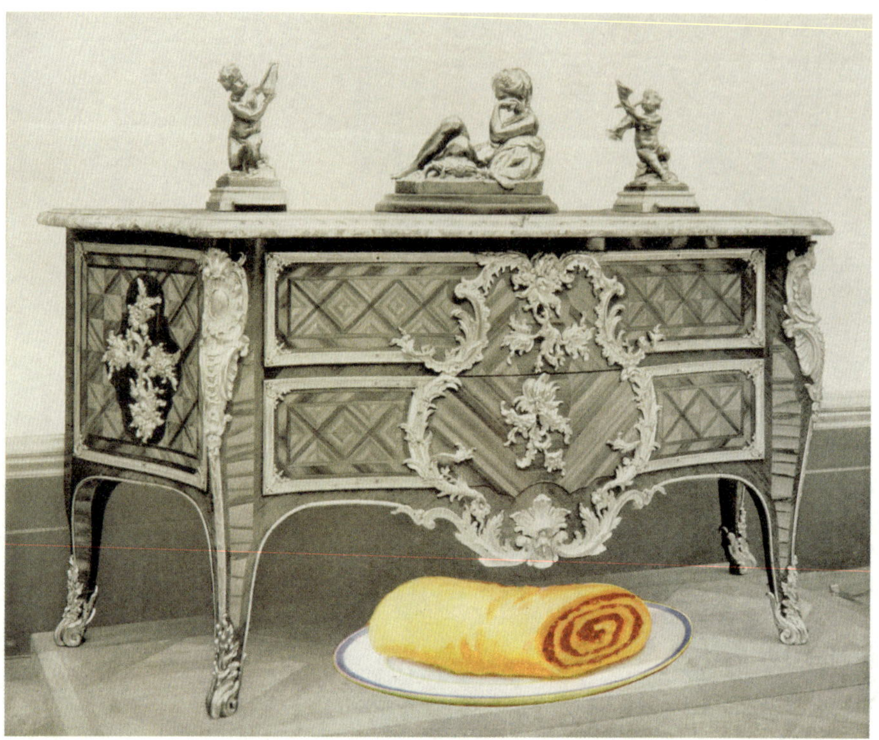

enthusiastic, communicative, lucid, self-confident, independent-minded and full of the joys of life. His critics viewed him as arrogant, bossy, dogmatic, overbearing, excitable, restless, voluble and opinionated. Whichever view you took, you had to admit that the young Jennings was incredibly gifted, and it was no surprise that he graduated with a starred first from Cambridge.

1929, the year of the Wall Street crash and the beginning of the Great Depression, was also the year that saw the first exhibition of paintings by Jennings and his friend Julian Trevelyan. This took place in Cambridge, where Humphrey was now a postgraduate with a scholarship, studying the poetry of Thomas Gray. It was also the year that he became a married man. He was only twenty-two and his bride, Cicely Cooper, was a year younger. It started badly, with both sets of parents refusing to attend the ceremony. Her parents objected because the groom was a penniless young academic, and

Humphrey Jennings, *Commode with Swiss Roll*, 1936.

his parents objected because they considered both bride and groom to be far too immature. As they settled into married life, there were further stresses because Cicely, who came from a wealthy background, now found herself having to scrape by on £2 a week – her new husband's scholarship income. Their flat was so cramped that their marriage bed had to be sawn in half to get it up the stairs.

Despite their poverty, Jennings always managed to find time to paint, not so much to sell his work, but more for his own private satisfaction. Spending time at his painting was a luxury he could not afford, but he did it anyway. His main influences were said to be Klee, Masson, Ernst and Magritte, showing that, at the very start of the surrealist movement, he was already well acquainted with its central figures. In 1930, he and his new wife spent Christmas in Paris, exploring the modern art world there with Julian Trevelyan and staying at his apartment in Montparnasse. The following year Humphrey returned alone to Paris for a month or so, earning some much-needed money working on silk designs. In a letter home, he wrote that he had been to an exhibition by Miró and commented: 'magnificent early work ... thrilling colour'.

The birth of the couple's first daughter in 1933 meant that Jennings had to start thinking seriously about earning a living. He, Cicely and their new baby were living in a freezing basement flat in Cambridge, and his paintings were not creating an income. Something had to be done. In 1934 he moved to London and took a job with the recently formed GPO Film Unit. This would be the start of a long and highly successful career as a documentary filmmaker. Indeed, it was so successful that it overshadowed his work as a painter.

This did not mean that he abandoned painting, but simply that it became pushed into the background. Then, in 1936, something happened that brought it into the foreground, if only briefly. Roland Penrose had just returned to London from Paris, where he had been living for some time, determined to introduce surrealism to the British public. He needed support in his project, an d the person who offered this support was Jennings, a figure who impressed Penrose more than anyone else in the London art world at the time. Together they set up a London Surrealist Group and gathered a team around them who would help to organize a major exhibition. Many years later, Penrose recalled that: 'Humphrey was an exception among that group because he had something which was very fascinating – he had a life about him – a sparkle about him. A wit. A violence – which was a bit un-English. In fact it seemed to me very much to link up with ... my friends among the surrealists in Paris.'

Jennings was increasingly busy in his private moments, making surrealist collages, objects and photographs, in addition to his paintings. Six of his works were included in the International Surrealist Exhibition that opened at the New Burlington Galleries in London in June 1936. Paul Éluard bought one of them, and Jennings himself bought a work by Magritte.

Jennings's involvement with the surrealist group brought him into contact with some exciting young women and, a few months after the exhibition had closed, he began his first extramarital affair, with an American called Emily Coleman who had written a novel about her time in an asylum. It was reported that she was so in love with him that, in a moment of elated abandon, she threw her hat over Waterloo Bridge. Before long, however, she had moved on, but before doing so she introduced Jennings to her friend the eccentric American heiress Peggy Guggenheim, who was in London in 1937 trying to decide whether she should open a modern art gallery there. Jennings was excited by the idea and encouraged her, promising to help in any way he could. They soon became lovers, which was not surprising since Peggy had entered a contest with her sister Hazel to see who would be the first to sleep with 1,000 men. She called Jennings, who was thirty at the time – nine years her junior – 'a sort of genius who looks like Donald Duck', adding that 'his art is divine'.

When Peggy left London on a trip to see her sick mother in Paris, Jennings, in the role of toy-boy, followed her there and introduced her to André Breton and Yves Tanguy. He managed to persuade Tanguy to have a solo exhibition in London if Peggy opened her gallery there. Peggy, for her part, introduced Jennings to Marcel Duchamp. Peggy was supposed to be staying with her ailing mother, but instead she and Jennings holed up together in a small hotel on the Left Bank. However, although she found him intellectually appealing, full of exciting ideas and enthusiasms, she was less impressed by his performance in bed and, when he returned for a second weekend, she refused to leave her mother's side. She ended the affair as diplomatically as she could, telling him that it was her fault, but he was distraught. She commented: 'We were standing on one of the bridges of the

Seine, and I remember how Humphrey wept. I think he had hopes of some kind of a wonderful life with me, surrounded by luxury, gaiety and surrealism.' She replaced him in her bed with a young Irish writer called Samuel Beckett. When the Guggenheim Jeune gallery finally opened its doors in London's Cork Street in 1938, Tanguy did, indeed, come over and exhibit his work there. He also, in the process, became Peggy's next lover.

In the years that followed, Jennings embarked on many more brief affairs but never abandoned his long-suffering wife. She knew what was happening but was prepared, miserably, to put up with it. She loved him until the day he died and was heard to emit a terrible scream when a telephone call told her that he had been killed.

During the war years the surrealist group in London was, inevitably, broken up and became inactive. Jennings was now more and more involved with his documentary filmmaking, and this continued after the war ended.

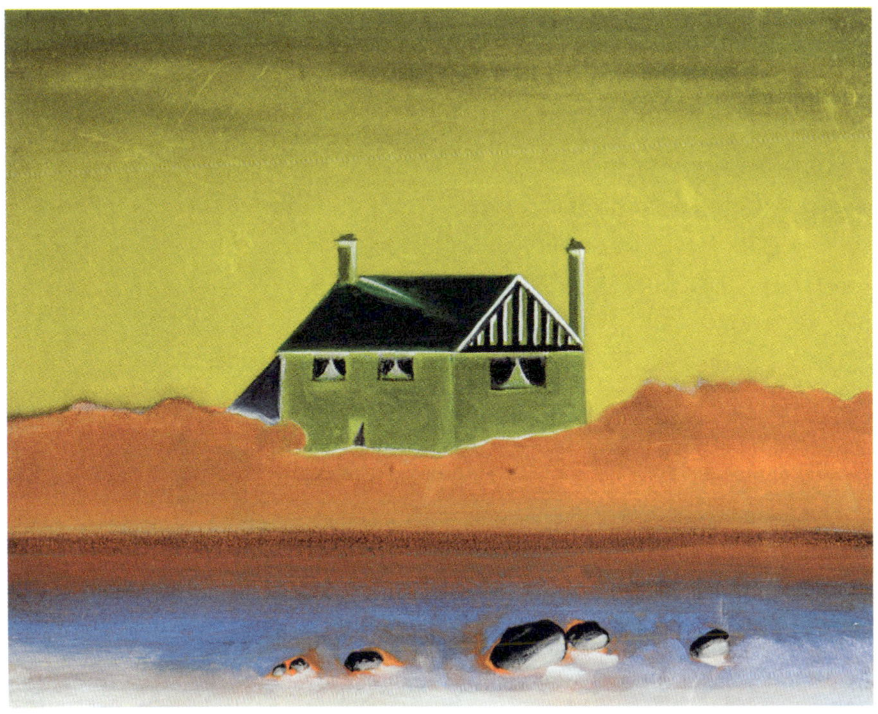

Humphrey Jennings, *Concealed House by the Water*, 1938.

He did still produce surrealist paintings in private, but did not become involved in post-war surrealist activities in the way that he had done with such enthusiasm in the 1930s. In the summer of 1950 Jennings set off with a film crew to travel across Europe to Greece. It was there that he was going to make a film called *The Good Life*, on the subject of health. After several days filming, he and his continuity girl travelled to the island of Poros to scout for new locations, with Jennings making sketches for good camera positions. At one point they decided to climb to the top of a cliff to get a good view from the summit. It seemed a simple enough climb, but when they were about twenty-five feet up, Jennings grasped hold of a rock to pull himself up and it gave way. He fell onto the beach below. Had it been a sandy beach, it would have been a soft landing and done little harm. Sadly, however, it was a rocky shore, and he crashed onto his head and was knocked unconscious. He was rushed to the naval hospital on the island, but never regained consciousness and died two hours later despite all attempts to revive him. Four days later he was buried in the Protestant Cemetery in Athens. The epitaph on his tombstone quoted Shelley and read: 'Death is the veil which those who live call life; they sleep and it is lifted.' Poignantly, it was a line from a book that he had in his pocket when he fell.

When his widow went to the bank to take out some rent money in the week after his death, she discovered that their joint account held the sum of precisely £1. It was the exact same sum that they had had in their account on the day they were married. Humphrey Jennings's wild enthusiasm for life meant that he had always lived on the edge, as well as dying on it. His daughter Marie-Louise summed up her father in the following words:

> Tall, skinny, bony-faced with short blond hair and blue eyes, he was in some ways a lonely man.... Being good at writing, painting, acting, languages and sports did not make him popular. He could speak French like a Frenchman, and read and spoke Latin and Greek at school. Everyone who knew him commented on his energy, his incessant talking and discussing, his sometimes over-enthusiastic pursuit of ideas and his inability to curb his workaholic tendencies.

CONROY MADDOX

Active member of the British Surrealist Group from 1938

BORN: 27 December 1912 in Ledbury, Herefordshire

PARENTS: Father a seed merchant and publican

LIVED: Ledbury 1912; Chipping Norton 1929; Birmingham 1933; London 1955

PARTNERS: Married Nan Burton 1948–55 (two children)

• Pauline Drayson 1960s and 1970s • Deborah (Des) Mogg 1979

DIED: 14 January 2005 in London, aged 93

In its early days, when surrealism was an active movement, there was a special category of surrealist – the group leader. In Paris, of course, it was André Breton. His counterpart in London was Édouard Mesens; and in England's 'Second City' – Birmingham – it was Conroy Maddox. I was lucky enough to join Conroy's group in 1948 and later wrote about it:

> As soon as I arrived in Birmingham in 1948 I set about exploring the local art scene and found a thriving surrealist group centred on the home of the painter Conroy Maddox. Perhaps painter is the wrong word for him – he was a theorist, an activist, a pamphleteer, and a writer, as well as an artist – in fact, the total surrealist.

Maddox was as much concerned with surrealist ideas as with the production of art objects. Frequently it was enough simply to have an idea, without bothering to carry it out. For example, one winter evening Conroy suddenly announced to the assorted group of students, painters and poets who, time and again, were drawn to his Birmingham home, that he would like to buy a piece of land and have a house built on it. It would be an ordinary-looking house, made of bricks. Ordinary except for one detail: it would be completely solid. Solid right through. No rooms – all bricks. And when it was finished, he would simply leave it there. There would be no announcements, no fanfare. It would quietly make its own statement.

His solid brick house was only one of a flood of surrealist images that flowed incessantly from his fertile, eccentric brain. Some, like the house, remained no more than ideas. Others, like his savage typewriter, with inverted, sharp nails where the keys should have been, and a streak of blood on the paper coming out of the roller, were actually realized; still others were rendered as collages or paintings. Paint as paint, however, was of little interest to him. Although he was a meticulous craftsman, it was the symbol, the concept, that was all important. If an idea could be expressed better with glued photographs than with oil paint, so be it. For Conroy, the message was the message, and to hell with the medium. Such was the intensity of his ambiguously erotic, obscurely sinister visions that they had the power to convert even the most commonplace magazine cut-outs into vivid works of art.

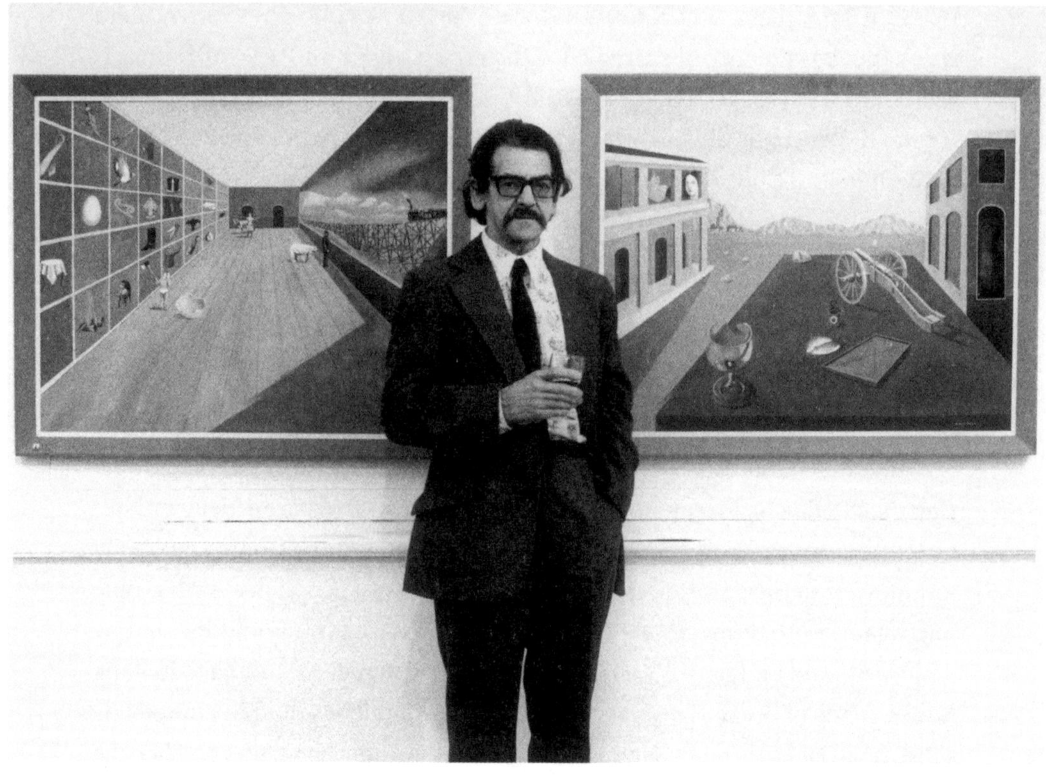

Conroy Maddox, date unknown.

Conroy Maddox was born in the market town of Ledbury, about forty miles south of Birmingham, in 1912, the son of a seed merchant. His father was wounded in World War I, and Conroy's earliest memory was of visiting him in hospital. As with many surrealists, this experience started him off on a lifelong hatred of the establishment. In 1933 the family moved to Birmingham, where his father was employed in the wine trade. He himself began earning a living as a solicitor's clerk. By 1935 he was working as a commercial designer but, in this year, he discovered surrealism in the city library and was fascinated by the possibilities that it offered.

1936 was a key year in his development because it was then that the major International Surrealist Exhibition was held in London. It made the headlines, and the young, twenty-four-year-old Maddox travelled to the capital to attend the extraordinary opening ceremony. It made such a powerful impression on him that, sixty-five years later, during an interview, he recalled every detail, especially the lecture given by Salvador Dalí, wearing a deep-sea diver's suit, carrying a billiard cue and holding two Russian wolfhounds on leads: 'He nearly died. They screwed the headpiece up and it was very hot in those suits. And they couldn't find the spanner. He was twisted up with a couple of Russian wolfhounds on a lead, and they got twisted around his leg, so he clomped along – and of course the audience thought it was marvellous. He was sitting there trying to recover and Mesens introduced me to him.' Conroy would later write a book about Dalí.

After this colourful encounter with the surrealists, Conroy knew that he had to go to Paris to learn more about the movement and made two lengthy visits there in 1937 and 1938, meeting, among others, Marcel Duchamp and Man Ray. On his final visit, in 1939, he decided it was time to leave when he saw workmen putting sandbags around public monuments. He sailed on the last but one ship to leave France before World War II broke out.

Back in England, Maddox had become part of the London Surrealist Group, attending their meetings and exhibiting with them. Even during the war, when he was working for a firm making parts for warplanes, he managed to keep in touch with the other surrealists in London. At one point, some of his rather sinister collages were seized by the police in a raid on the house of a friend of his. Bizarrely, they suspected that these were somehow a means of sending coded messages to the enemy. The irony was that, at this particular point, Maddox himself was now engaged in secret war work, drawing blueprints for aircraft parts.

It was during the war years that he met a lively, strong-minded young woman by the name of Nan Burton. Although she was married, they began a lengthy affair and had two children together. Eventually, in 1947, she obtained a divorce, and she and Conroy were married early in 1948. This was the year when I first met him, and I was impressed by the fact that Nan was more than a match for his waspish tongue and his black humour. Their relationship was an entertainment in itself. When she was suffering from jaundice, he wrote to me, unsympathetically, that there were evenings when he didn't switch the light on but 'just bathed in a marvellous yellow glow'. He never minced his words. His comments about other modern artists were nearly always scathing, unless they happened to be card-carrying surrealists. Even the work of close friends was criticized if they strayed from the surrealist path – 'not too unsuccessful' was the best he could offer them.

His own work consisted of three distinct types. There were his collages in the classic surrealist tradition established by Max Ernst; his small, colourful gouaches of biomorphic beings parading in a simple landscape; and his major works, all of which were in oil on canvas. In these less colourful oils he portrayed meticulous, dreamlike scenes that were stylistically somewhere between Giorgio de Chirico and René Magritte, but with his own special flavour. If anyone asked him to explain one of his paintings, he was stubbornly uncooperative: 'You can't explain an image like this and you shouldn't. A surrealist does not know what he is doing. Dalí didn't know what he was doing. I don't know what I'm doing. Something happens and it develops, but you don't analyse it. By doing that you destroy a surrealist image.'

One of his passions was attacking religion. A later painting of his that is hardly ever shown, called *Short-cut to Calgary* (1990), depicts Christ with his cross getting a ride to his crucifixion in a vintage motor car. He also dressed a friend up as a nun and then proceeded to have himself photographed assaulting her, after which she did her best to crucify him by nailing his hands to a wall. He is on record as describing religion as 'a brutal insignia of a slow moral decomposition'.

When his Birmingham group had finally dispersed, Maddox moved to London in 1955. His marriage to Nan collapsed, although she continued to visit his exhibitions. When I expressed surprise at seeing her there, she smiled and replied, 'Just checking the sales.' He would later enjoy two more

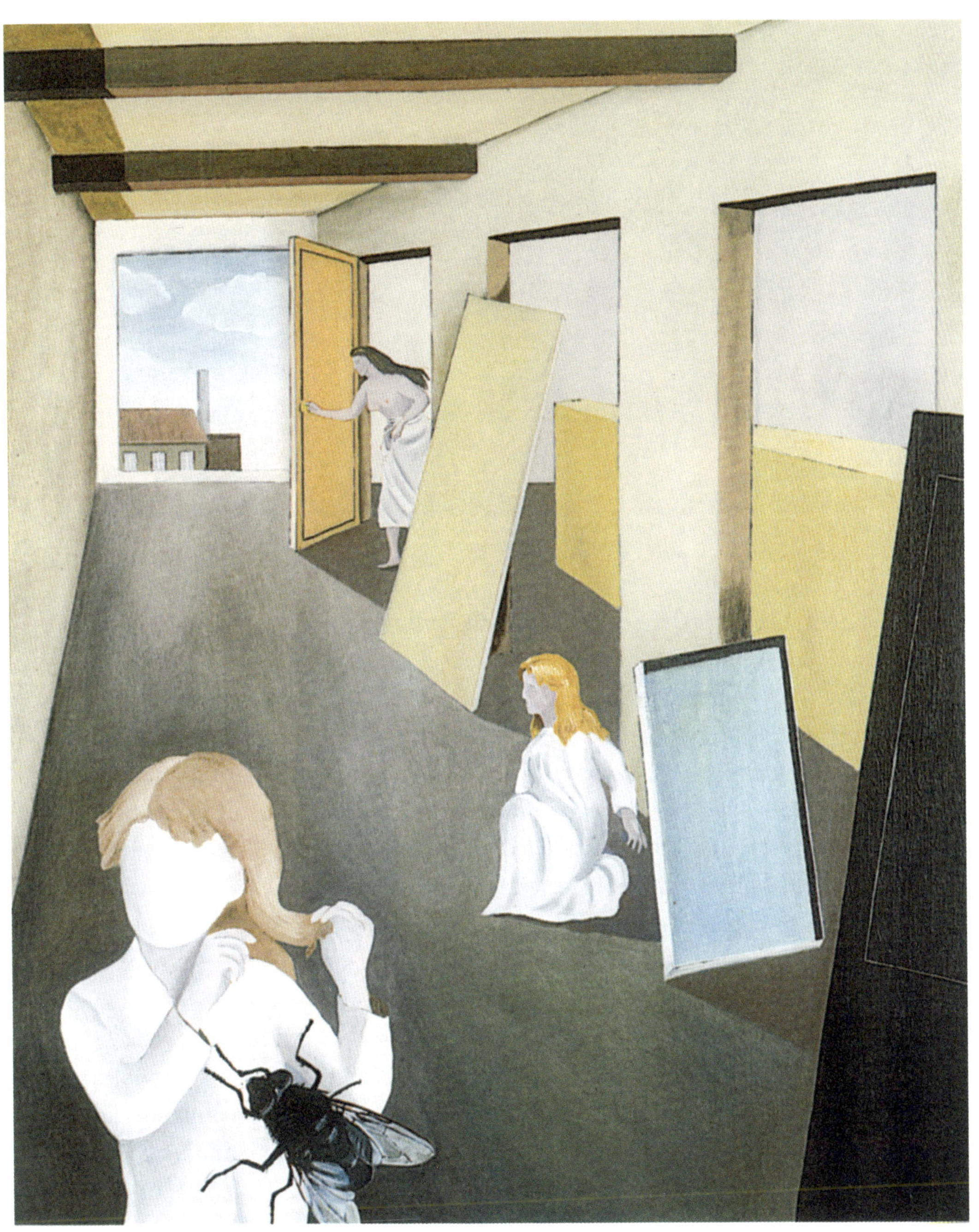

Conroy Maddox, *The Stillness of the Day*, signed 1943 but may be later.

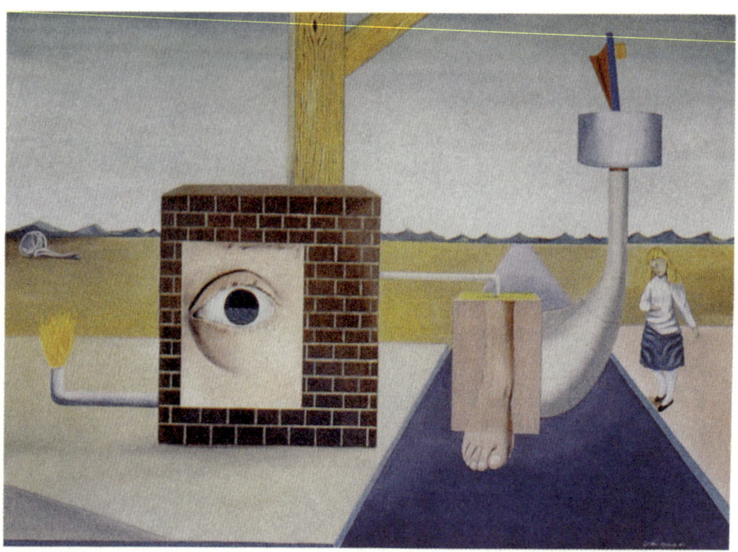

long-term relationships – the first with Pauline Drayson in the 1960s and 1970s, and the second, from 1979, with Des Mogg, who was fifty years his junior – but he never remarried.

During his first years in London, Conroy had to earn his living as an advertising designer, but as the years passed surrealist paintings enjoyed better sales, especially in the case of someone who had originally been active in the 1930s. By the time he reached old age, he was at last able to survive financially from his art alone. He did hit one snag, however, owing to his disdain for what he called 'the art merchants'. Angry that his earlier paintings were selling better than his (more accomplished) later ones, he decided to make a stand against the commercialism of the art world. He went round his studio changing the dates on his canvases, making them thirty or forty years older than they really were. If people were stupid enough to pay for the date of a painting rather than for the work itself, more fool them. Unfortunately, he came unstuck when he put an early date on a collage that contained part of a photograph from a magazine that had been published later. The game was up, and the galleries were furious with him.

Conroy Maddox, *Morning Encounter*, 1944.

One of the attitudes that made Conroy cross was the idea that surrealism had passed into history in the 1950s and was now a dead movement, confined to a time slot in the history of art. For Maddox, surrealism was an act of rebellion that, once initiated, would live forever in one form or another. He said: 'The work of surrealism can never be conclusive. It is more of an exploration ... and a struggle.... I will remain on my quest for surrealism until my last breath.' In 1987 he wrote to me, saying: 'Surrealism is dead, long live Surrealism.' Nobody in Britain did more than Conroy Maddox to keep its spirit alive into the twenty-first century.

A final word concerning a criticism of Conroy Maddox's painting that I have heard repeated on a number of occasions. It is said that he was a derivative artist, lacking in originality. This is only true of some of his work and, even there, I am sure that he would have argued that André Breton would have put no store by originality or individuality, seeing surrealist statements as a shared, common ground in the assault on the respectable and the traditional.

F. E. MCWILLIAM

Exhibited with the British surrealists from 1937

BORN: 30 April 1909 in Banbridge, County Down, Northern Ireland, as Frederick Edward McWilliam

PARENTS: Father a local doctor

LIVED: Banbridge 1909; Belfast 1926; London 1928; India (in RAF) 1944; London 1946

PARTNER: Married Beth Crowther, a painter, 1932 (until her death in 1988) (two children)

DIED: 3 May 1992 in London, of cancer, aged 82

The Irish sculptor F. E. McWilliam, known to his friends simply as 'Mac', belongs to that class of artist who produced important surrealist work but rejected any kind of group activity. Mac was a quirky loner who had no time at all for fancy theories or organized movements. He admired the surrealists for wanting to break down the traditional conventions of the art world and for letting the imagination run freely; but he would have shaken his head in disbelief if he had ever found himself at the centre of a querulous theoretical or philosophical debate by the surrealist group under the headmastership of André Breton. He was not even at ease at a gallery exhibition. I have watched him sidle in, his thin frame cutting gently through the throng of a private view, quietly study the works on display and then vanish. Yet, despite this, his best works make bold visual statements with a confident air that transforms them into surrealist icons.

McWilliam was born in Banbridge, a small town in Northern Ireland where, as a child, he became fascinated by the local craftsmen who made barrels, furniture, rope, harnesses and saddles. He would wander around their workshops, watching them transform raw materials into finished products. The son of the local doctor, he had an idyllic childhood in the period just before World War I, the only dark cloud being the sectarian disputes between Catholics and Protestants. It was this needless violence that gave McWilliam his lifelong hatred of group allegiance of any kind, even if it

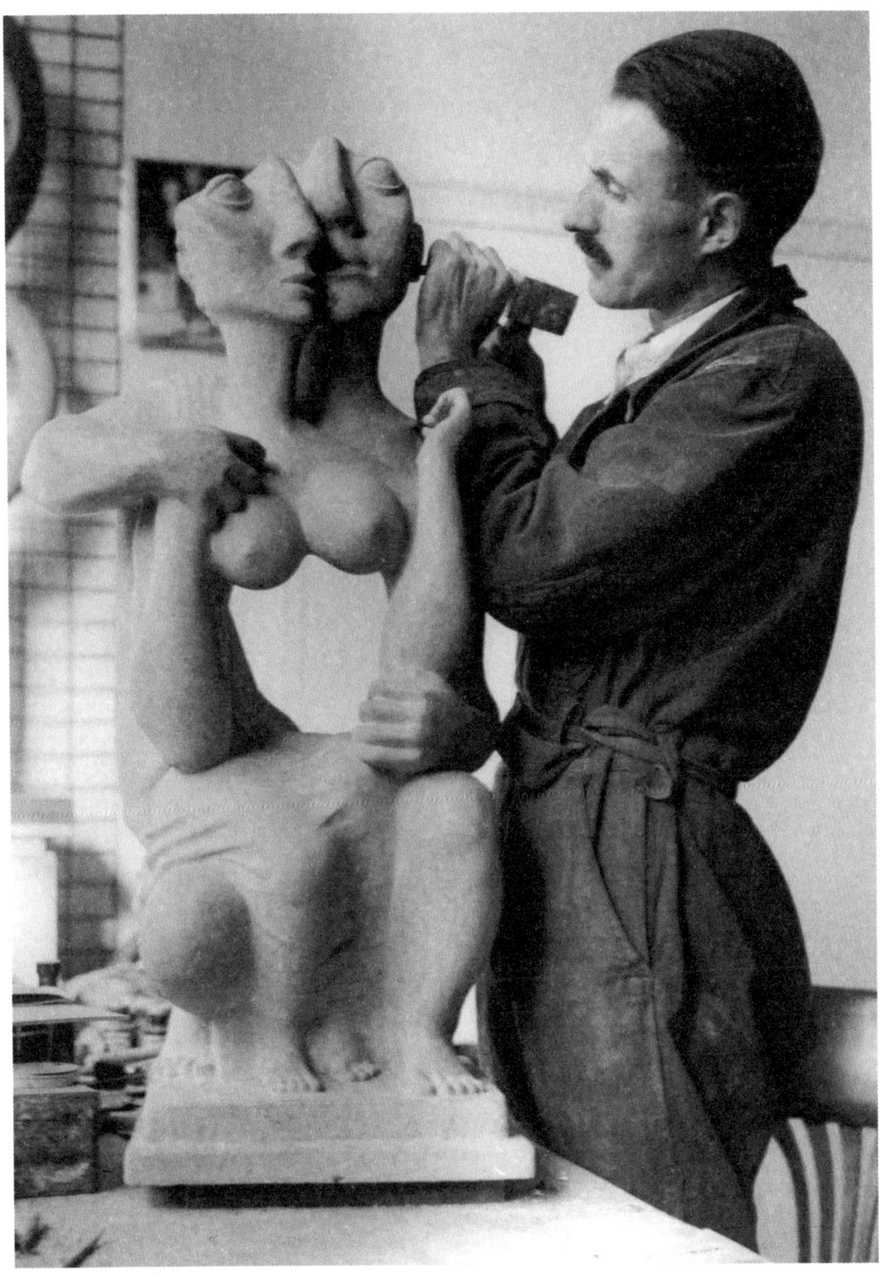

F. E. McWilliam, 1948.

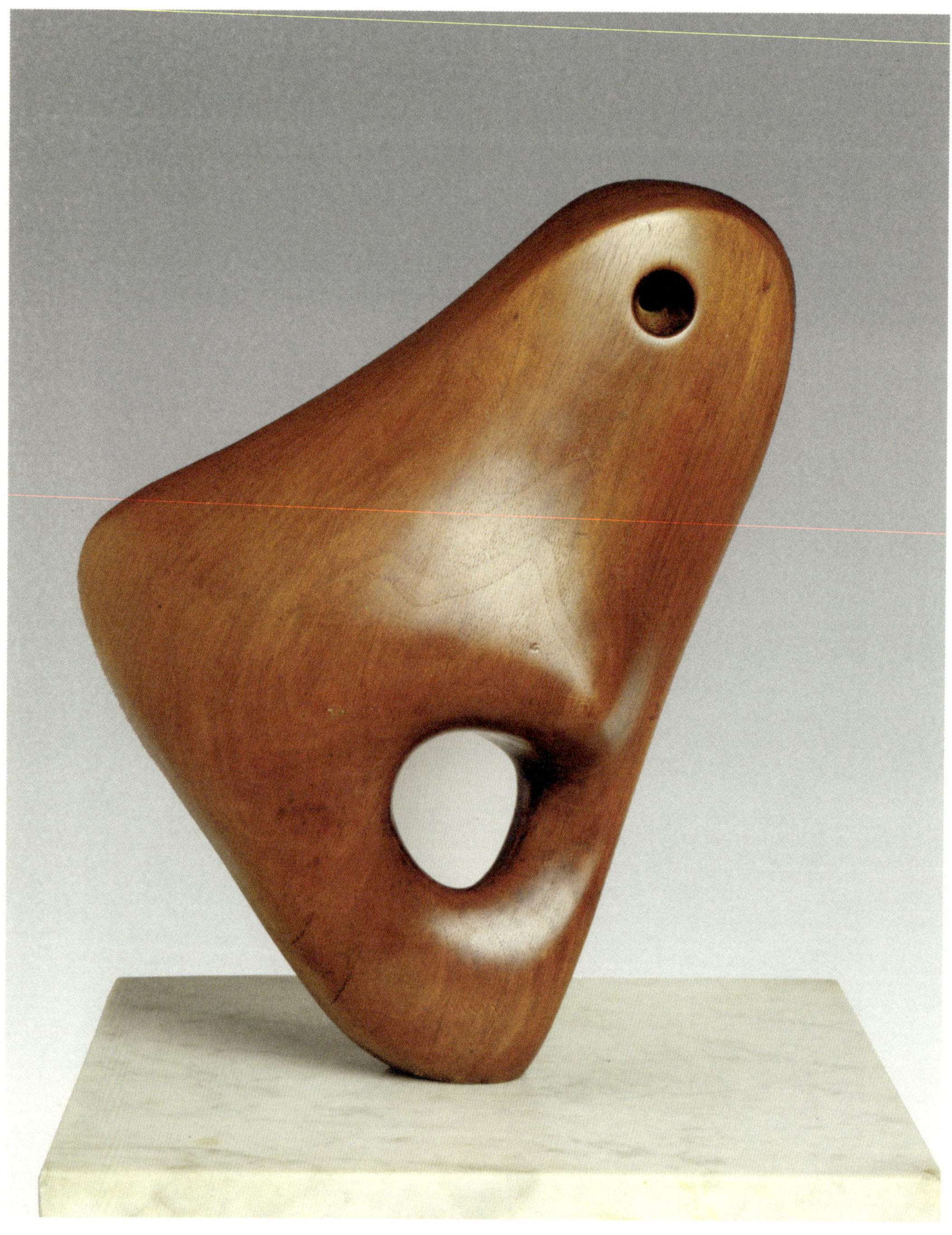

F. E. McWilliam, *Carving*, 1936.

was as harmless as an art movement. For the rest of his life, he would remain a devoted non-joiner, his own man, working outside all the usual cliques and coteries.

Even when he developed a style of his own, he would soon move on to something else. It was as though he was such an extreme form of loner that he didn't want to belong even to his own one-man group. Once he had explored a particular style of work, he felt restricted by it and refused to go on making more examples, even if they were successful. Instead, he had to switch to something else, something different, that gave him a new challenge. He is on record as saying, 'I have never set any store by consistency – life is too short for restrictive practices.' This meant that, during his working life, he tackled a whole series of different types of sculpture, giving him a wide scope but also destroying something that is valued by art collectors: the immediate recognizability of a particular artist. It was this creative restlessness that meant that he never reached the level of fame enjoyed by sculptors such as Henry Moore or Barbara Hepworth, despite the fact that some of his works were just as memorable. Roland Penrose summed it up well when he said that 'McWilliam is an inventor of styles'.

After studying at the Belfast College of Art, McWilliam left Ireland and, still a teenager, moved to London in 1928. There, he attended the Slade School of Fine Art, where he met Henry Moore, who would become a lifelong friend, and Beth Crowther, who would become his wife in 1932 and who would remain with him until her death in 1988. It was during his time at the Slade School that he developed a special interest in sculpture rather than painting. A success at the Slade, he won a scholarship that enabled him to visit Paris in 1931, at the height of the surrealist explosion. He was deeply impressed by what he encountered there and was especially delighted to be able to buy and read a copy of James Joyce's *Ulysses*, a book that was still banned in England.

Back home a year or so later, and newly married, he moved out of London and, in isolation from the art world, began to make sculptures in carved wood. In 1936 he visited the International Surrealist Exhibition in London and was fascinated by what he saw there. Perhaps he felt he should have been part of it himself and regretted his isolation outside the capital, because shortly afterwards he and Beth moved to Hampstead to join their friends Henry Moore, Roland Penrose, Paul Nash, Ben Nicholson, Barbara Hepworth and Herbert Read, in what was rapidly becoming an exciting enclave of modern artists.

In 1937 McWilliam began exhibiting in earnest with the surrealists, saying, 'I chose the surrealist camp because of its more liberal, non-doctrinaire attitude, but it would be true to say that I remained more a fellow traveller than a zealot.' He continued to show with them until World War II broke out, when he joined the Royal Air Force. Towards the end of the war, he was serving in India, a posting that enabled him to study the sculptural forms on the Hindu temples.

After the war he returned to London and taught sculpture at the Chelsea School of Art for a while, before being put in charge of sculpture teaching at the Slade, a post he would retain for twenty-one years. During this time, he was able to exhibit his own work extensively and was flattered when he was made an associate of the Royal Academy in 1959. He soon regretted this, however, and resigned a few years later following a disagreement with the selection committee. He had briefly forgotten his golden rule of non-joining and was happy when, in 1963, he found himself once again unattached to any official art faction. And that was how he remained until his death thirty years later.

When I first met him, in the later 1980s, he was excited by an accident that had occurred during a terrible storm that had just swept the country. An ancient mulberry tree had been uprooted in his garden, and its trunk was twisted into all kinds of exciting knobs and lumps. He cut it up into pieces and then started to convert the pieces into tortured sculptural shapes. When he had finished, he held a one-man mulberry show in London that was unlike anything he had done before. Once again, in his restless way, he had moved on and become yet another sculptor. Some critics thought that he had done too little to the mulberry logs – had not tamed them enough – and that they still looked too much like pieces of sawn-off tree-trunk. They had a point, but the knobbly, warty, lumpy pieces of polished wood were still wonderful to contemplate, and Mac had obviously been seduced by the natural qualities of the wood.

Although F. E. McWilliam was never a full-blown member of the surrealist group, it is nevertheless true to say that his very best work was done when he was in one of his surrealist phases. His life's work can be divided up into distinct periods, each quite different from the others, thanks to his

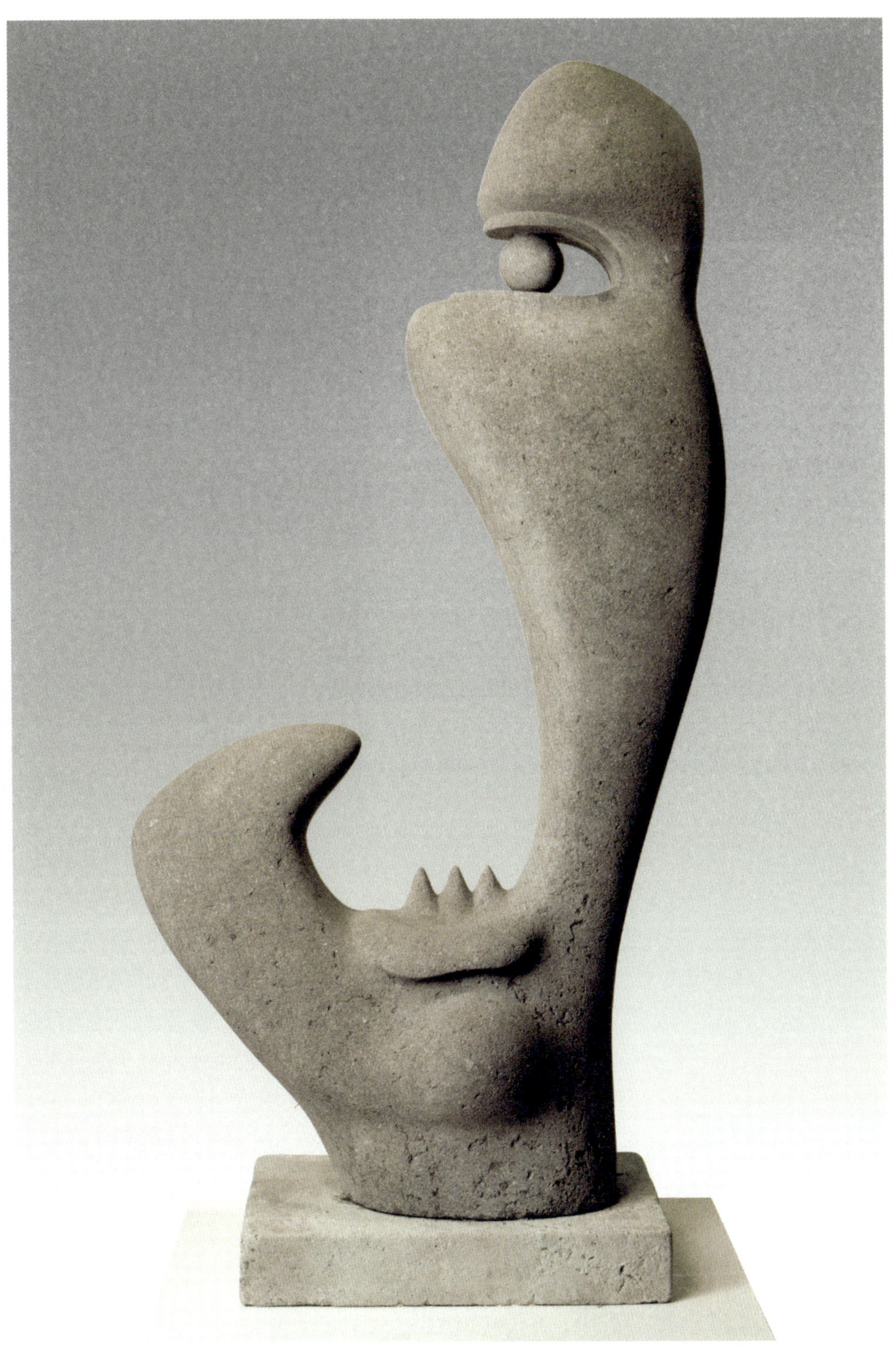

F. E. McWilliam, *Spanish Head*, 1939.

restless curiosity. There were seven main ones: his brilliant wood carvings of the mid-1930s; his powerful stone carvings of the late 1930s and the late 1940s; his rough-surface Giacometti-influenced bronze figures of the 1950s; his sharply pointed compositions of the early 1960s; his faintly obscene, joyously playful 'bean' figures of the mid-1960s, based on the buttock-like shape of the coco-de-mer nut from the Seychelles; his disembodied, elongated bronze legs of the late 1970s and early 1980s; and, finally, his mulberry tree-trunk wood carvings of the late 1980s.

Some works of art, when you put them in your home, eventually become boring and you cease to notice them. You know them so well that they cease to surprise you. However, I have lived for half a century in a house that contains two of McWilliam's sculptures, and they still capture my attention whenever I walk into a room and catch sight of them. Their verve, their surrealist inventiveness and their visual ambiguity never cease to amaze me.

In 2008 Mac's hometown of Banbridge in Northern Ireland honoured him by opening a McWilliam Gallery and Studio, complete with a sculpture garden, a reconstruction of his workshop, a permanent display of his work and a large exhibition space. It attracted 43,000 visitors in its first year alone.

REUBEN MEDNIKOFF

Member of the British Surrealist Group from 1936; expelled by Mesens in 1940

BORN: 2 June 1906 in London

PARENTS: Russian Jewish immigrants

LIVED: London 1906; New York 1940; Vancouver 1941; London 1946; Dorking, Surrey 1950; Battle, East Sussex 1953; Crowborough, Sussex 1958; Ninfield, East Sussex 1962

PARTNER: Married MARIE DE SOUSA 1932–35; dissolved

• GRACE PAILTHORPE 1935 (until her death in 1971)

DIED: 3 May 1972 in Hastings, Sussex, aged 65

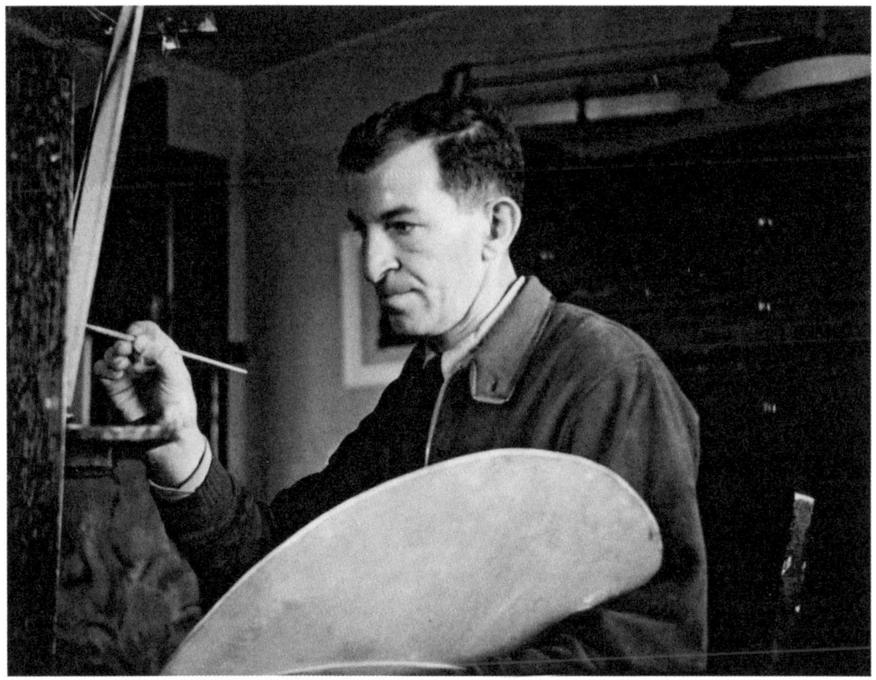

Reuben Mednikoff, 1938.

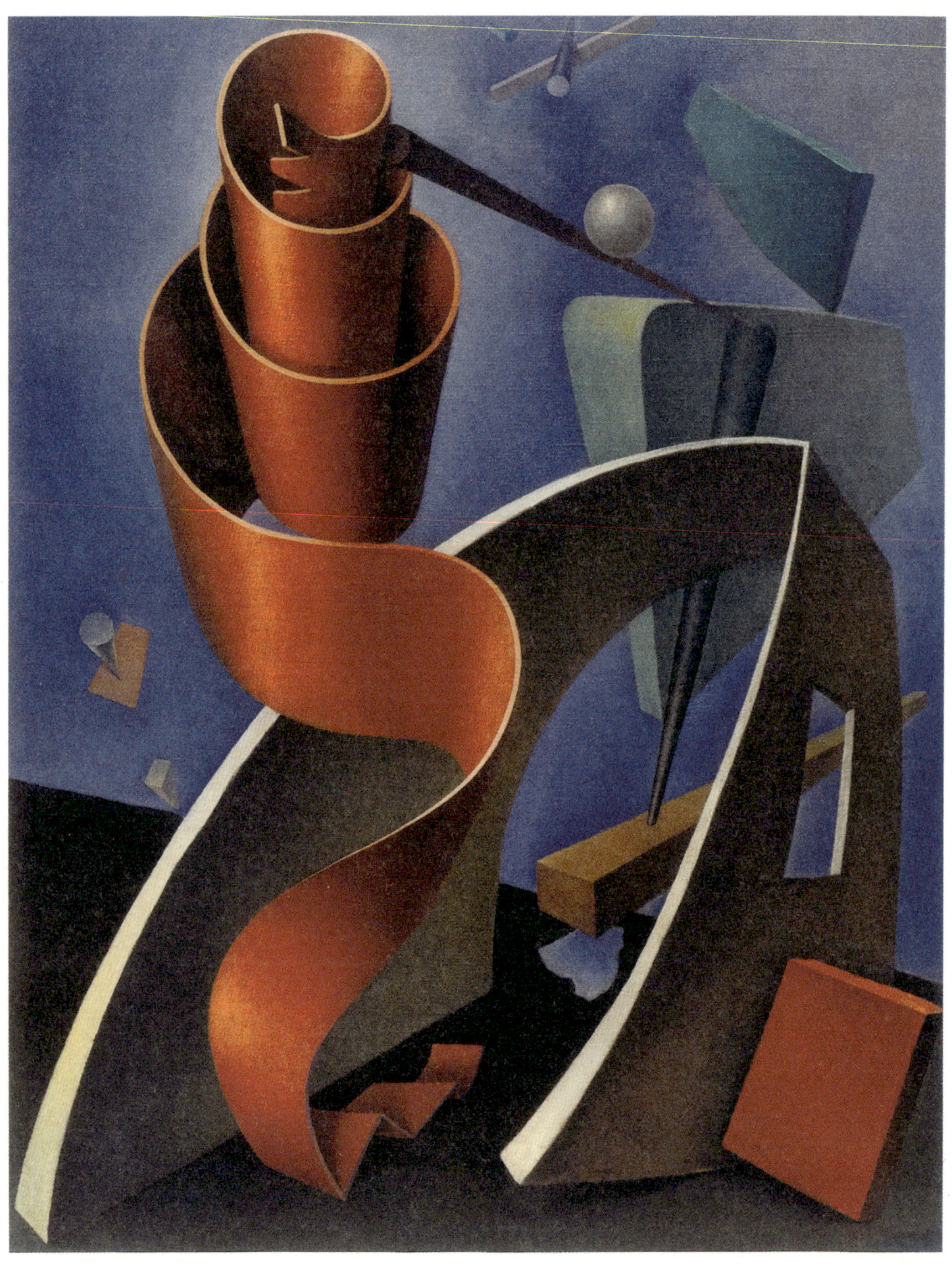

Reuben Mednikoff, *The Anatomy of Space (21 January)*, 1936.

THE SON OF RUSSIAN JEWISH IMMIGRANTS, Reuben Mednikoff's surrealist paintings were skilfully made and contained powerful, sometimes startling imagery. But he is best known for the strange partnership that he formed with the forceful psychoanalyst, surgeon and artist Grace Pailthorpe, a partnership that lasted from 1935, when they met at a satanic party, until her death in 1971. She was twenty-three years older than him, and the other British surrealists who knew them repeatedly commented on what a very odd couple they were.

Mednikoff had studied art at St Martin's School in London, which he attended from 1920 until 1923. Then, from 1923 until 1935, he was earning a living in advertising. It was during this time that he met his first wife, Marie de Sousa. The marriage only lasted three years and was dissolved in 1935. It was then that his meeting with the extraordinary Dr Pailthorpe would change his life forever. It is not known why they were both attending a sinister, satanic gathering, but what is clear is that they were soon ignoring proceedings and were huddled together in a corner, excitedly comparing their views about

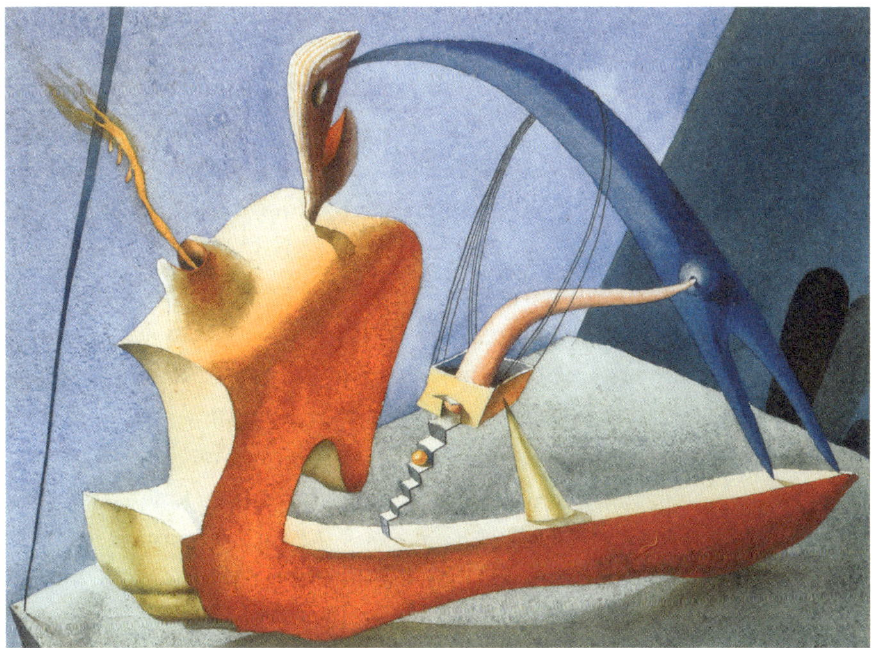

Reuben Mednikoff, *The Stairway to Paradise (20 March - 1)*, 1936.

art and therapy. Within days, they were already a devoted couple – mentally if not physically – who had decided that, since surrealism was based on allowing the unconscious mind to take over the creative process, while conscious control, reasoning and analysis were all prohibited, it must therefore have great therapeutic value. It followed that, by carefully studying the surrealist imagery that was being created by this means, it could be used to understand the mental problems and obsessions of the painters. In this way, they believed it would be possible to short-circuit what they referred to as Freud's interminable couch treatment.

To experiment with this idea, they started painting surrealist works, Reuben skilfully, Grace rather less so, and then proceeded to clinically analyse what they both had done. Their work was shown in the great International Surrealist Exhibition of 1936 in London and received special praise from André Breton. They became members of the British Surrealist Group, and all was going well until they started insisting on the therapeutic value of surrealism. This caused dismay and even ridicule among the other surrealists, with matters coming to a head at a meeting in London in 1940. Reuben and Grace felt superior to the rest of the group, because of their crusade to improve mental health, and were shocked and angered when they found themselves being formally expelled. They were so angry, in fact, that they did not simply leave the group: they left the country and moved to America. With a common enemy, their relationship was becoming closer and closer and, in 1942, Reuben began to refer to himself as Richard or Ricki. A few years later, Grace took the extraordinary step of adopting him as her son, and he then changed his name to Richard Pailthorpe.

The pair continued their art therapy work in the United States and Canada for several years but eventually, in 1946, they returned to England and Grace took up a post as a consultant psychiatrist at a London clinic, with Reuben enrolled as her assistant. In 1950, their next step was to set up their own School of Art Therapy at Dorking in Surrey, the first of its kind.

In 1955 it is recorded that Reuben opened the Little Georgian Antique Shop in Battle, Sussex, taking a break from the intense world of psychotherapy for a while. After this, with their role in British surrealism far behind them, they sank into obscurity but they never left one another. When Grace died of cancer in 1971, Reuben, despite being so many years her junior, would soon follow her, dying only ten months later.

OSCAR MELLOR

Member of the Birmingham Surrealist Group in the 1940s

BORN: 7 June 1921 in Manchester

LIVED: Manchester 1921; Birmingham 1939; Oxford 1948; Exeter 1969

PARTNERS: Married Iris Poulton 1948–67; divorced (two children)

• Married Yvonne Taylor 1969–78; divorced

• Married Maureen Sandford 1983–98; divorced

DIED: 24 October 2005 in Exmouth, Devon, aged 84

In the late 1940s, Oscar Mellor and I, armed with André Breton's phone number, visited Paris to seek out any surrealists we could find there. World War II had scattered most of them from their original haunts, and we found their favourite street cafés ominously empty. Oscar had a special interest in the French surrealist Frédéric Delenglade, who told us that he was working on a project to build a full-scale Egyptian pyramid underground in Wales. At the famous Minotaure bookshop Oscar was able to purchase one of the Marquis de Sade's books that was banned in Britain. Fearful that it would be confiscated by British customs, he carefully took it to pieces and posted it to himself, page by page, in a long series of letters.

Mellor was born and educated in Manchester, where his father had his own business in the cotton industry. Oscar's earliest painting dates from 1936, when he was still a teenager, and it already revealed strong surrealist influences. At the end of the 1930s, the family business was hit by a slump in the cotton industry, and the Mellors moved to Birmingham in 1939, where Oscar's father found employment in a firm making shrouds. During World War II Mellor served in the Royal Air Force. He volunteered in 1940 and was accepted in 1942, training at various locations in England and Canada. Demobbed in 1946, he joined the surrealist circle that had gathered around Conroy Maddox in Birmingham and, by the late 1940s, was fully engaged in Surrealist activities. His paintings were skilfully executed in meticulous detail, with human figures – often nude women – engaged in dreamlike rituals.

Mellor was one of the founder members of the Birmingham Artists Committee in 1947, an avant-garde organization set up in opposition to the conservative Royal Birmingham Society of Artists. He exhibited in their annual group shows between 1947 and 1951, alongside the other Birmingham surrealists.

In 1948 Mellor married Iris Poulton, and they moved from Birmingham to Oxford, where he studied at the Ruskin School of Art from 1948 to 1951. He and Iris then established the Fantasy Press while living in Swinford, just outside Oxford, publishing surrealist poetry and other documents, carrying

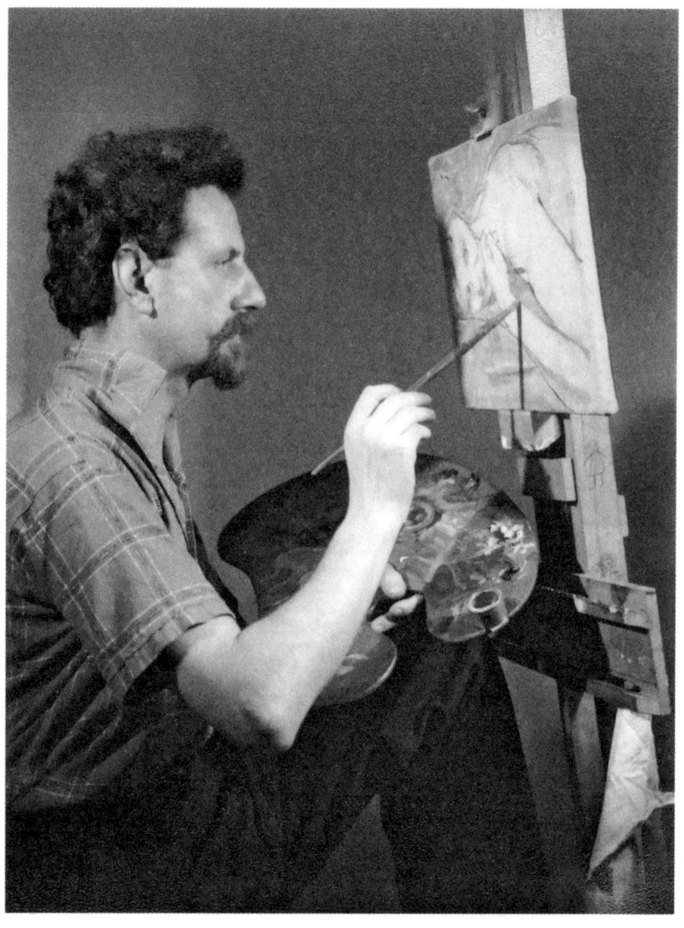

Oscar Mellor, early 1950s.

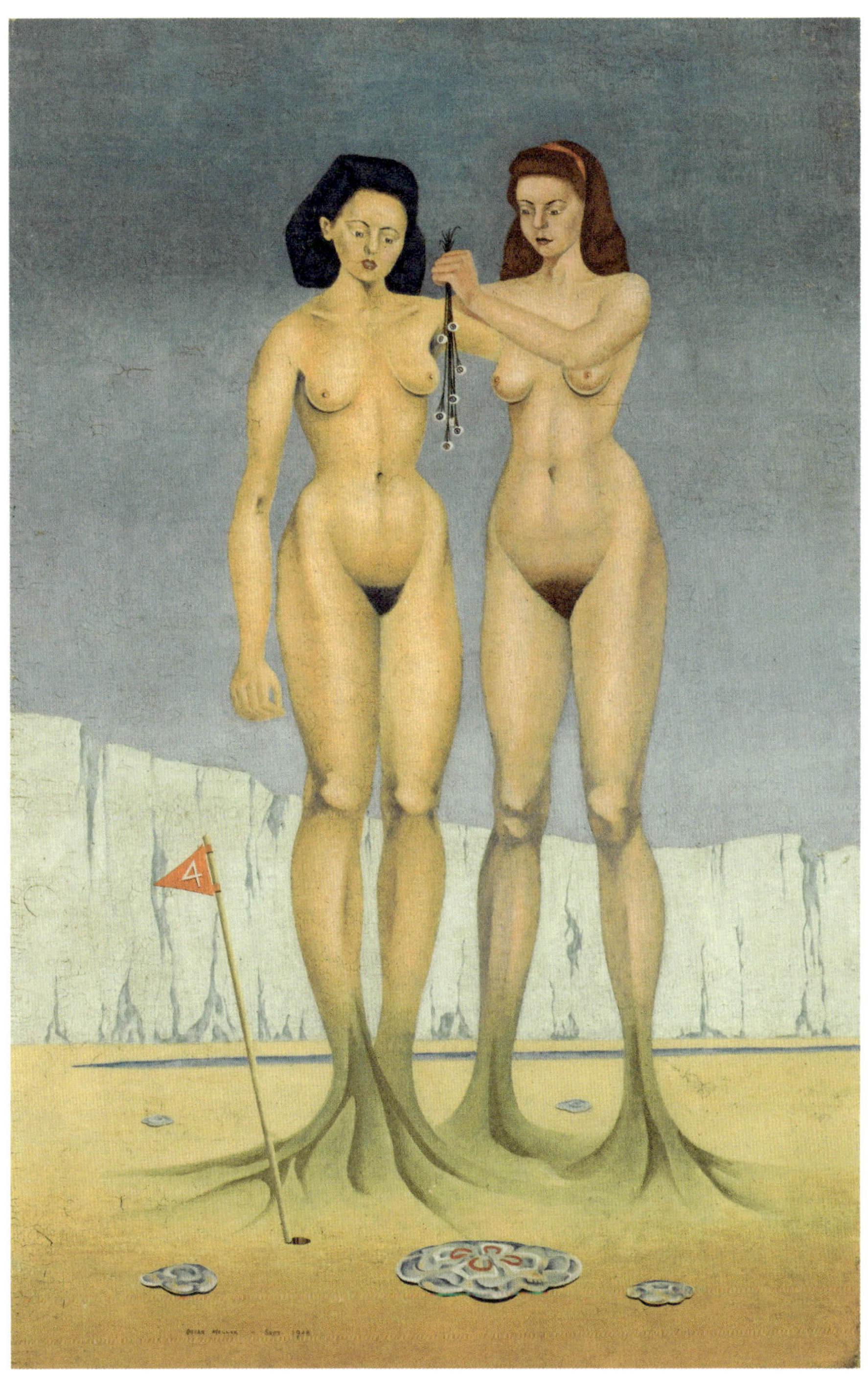

Oscar Mellor, *A Small Bunch of Eyes*, 1948.

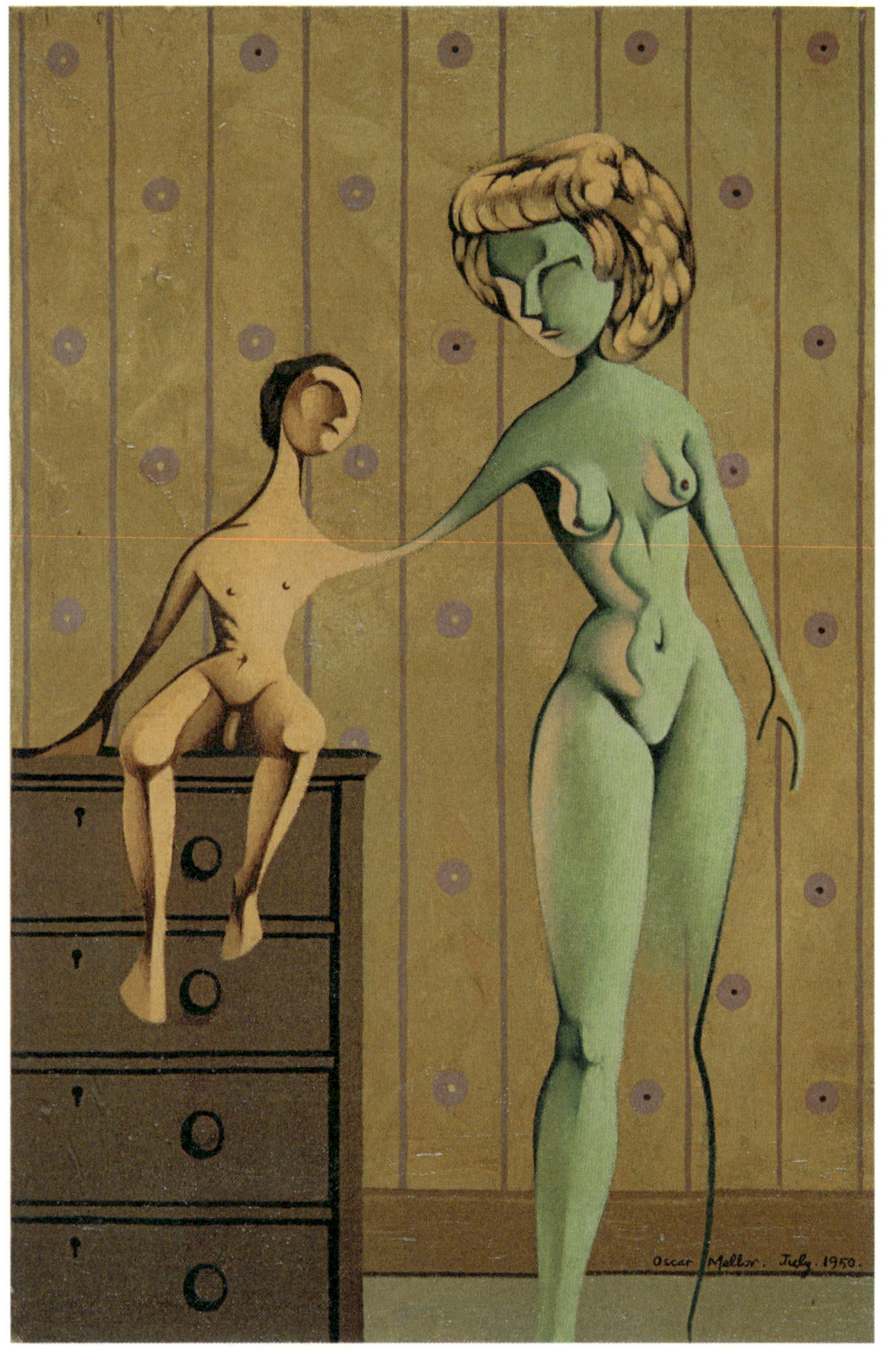

Oscar Mellor, *The Green Child*, 1950.

out all the printing and binding work themselves. Oscar's paintings during the 1950s included a strange series of portraits of women with large, winged insects. His landscapes were often bleak, and the mood of his pictures at this time was usually both haunted and haunting. He also earned a living as a professional photographer and, in 1966, he was elected an associate of the Royal Photographic Society.

He and Iris were divorced in 1967, and in 1969 he moved from Oxford to Exeter in Devon, where he became senior lecturer in photography at the Exeter College of Art. He married Yvonne Taylor, whom he had met when she had been a student at St Anne's College in Oxford in the 1960s.

During the 1960s Mellor began to focus more and more on the female form in his paintings. In the early 1970s he was led astray from pure surrealism by his association with the Nicholas Treadwell Gallery in London. Treadwell was obsessed with erotic images and encouraged his stable of artists to make their paintings more and more sexually explicit until, in some cases, the work was starting to approach what can only be called soft porn. Mellor was swept along by this trend, and it distracted him from his serious work. For a short period, until 1975, he continued to supply erotic paintings to the Treadwell Gallery for its group shows. In 1971, a critic in *Art and Artist* magazine said of one Treadwell's exhibitions: 'The place blisters with work of searing eroticism, high camp, coarse belly laughs and hideous vulgarity.' Mellor was not one of the worst offenders, but it was a relief to his friends when he eventually broke free from Treadwell's influence and, later in his life, returned to mainstream surrealist works once again.

Oscar and Yvonne were divorced in 1978 and, in the 1980s, following his retirement from college teaching, he was able to devote much more time to his canvases. He pulled together, again in meticulous detail, all the various elements and symbols that had fascinated him over the years. Strange light bulbs, candles, lions, lamps, mirrors, lobsters, waterfalls, butterflies, brides and bulls milled around in dreamlike scenes, rendered with the academic precision of traditional art.

Mellor married for a third time in 1983, to Maureen Sanford, but they were divorced in 1998. In 1996, at the age of seventy-five, he suffered a serious stroke that ended his painting career and, after a long illness, he died in 2005.

JOHN MELVILLE

Joined the British Surrealist Group in 1938

BORN: 25 August 1902 in London

LIVED: London 1902; Birmingham 1913

PARTNER: Married Lily Beatrice (Betty) Samuel 1929 (one child)

DIED: 8 December 1986 in Birmingham, aged 84

John Melville is one of the forgotten surrealists of British Art. Although he did produce some important surrealist paintings in the 1930s, for him it was only a passing phase, and his other work falls well outside the genre. Also, he did not live in London, where most of the British surrealists were gathered, and he was not represented at the major International Surrealist Exhibition there in 1936. This had the effect of sidelining him. Melville was born in London, but when he was still a teenage boy his family moved to Birmingham, where he spent the rest of his life. He was largely self-taught, although he did attend some classes at the Birmingham College of Art. His brother Robert shared his feelings about modern art and would later become an important author and critic, specializing in surrealist work.

At the height of his surrealist phase, in 1938, six of Melville's paintings were banned by local government councillors from inclusion in an exhibition in Birmingham, because they were said to be 'detrimental to public sensibilities'. This was a polite way of saying that they were considered obscene. Melville tried to defend himself in the local press, but to no avail. His most famous work, *The Museum of Natural History of the Child* (1937, Leeds City Art Gallery), described as one of the key paintings of British surrealism, labels him clearly as one of the paradoxical surrealists, featuring a realistic portrayal of a bizarre event in which a child, bent forward, is seen carrying a heavy wooden chair upside-down on her back. She is approaching an outsized apple, sliced in half, out of whose core a phallic, blue caterpillar is emerging and aiming itself at her body. In the background, a crossed-legged female figure suggestively shows off her naked thighs and a glimpse of her

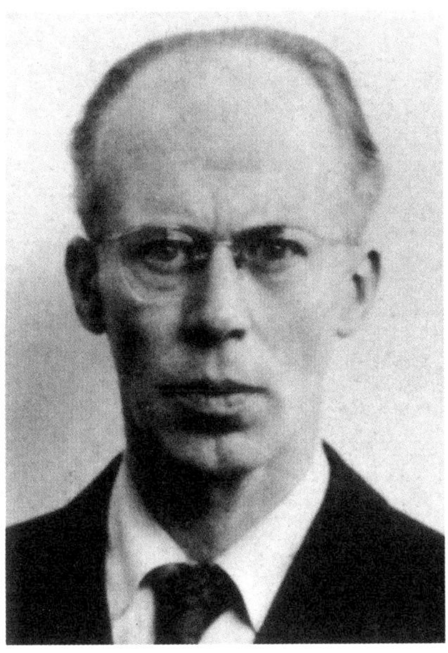

pubic hair, while insects and bits of floating vegetation drift out through a window. The atmosphere of this haunting scene is oppressive and strangely sinister, despite its attractive colours. It shows that Melville had grasped one of the central ideas of surrealism – the disturbing power of an irrational arrangement of familiar figures and objects, presented in a contrastingly realistic, conventional style.

During his surrealist period, Melville seems to have become something of a purist, intolerant of those who did not become totally immersed in the principles of surrealism. It has often been said that he and his brother, along with another Birmingham surrealist, Conroy Maddox, refused to exhibit at the International Surrealist Exhibition in London in 1936 because too many non-surrealists had been included in the show by its organizers, Roland Penrose and Herbert Read. They were accused of dragging in people who did not belong there, simply to boost the number of British artists who were included. This criticism was certainly justified, but was it the real reason for Melville not participating?

John Melville, date unknown.

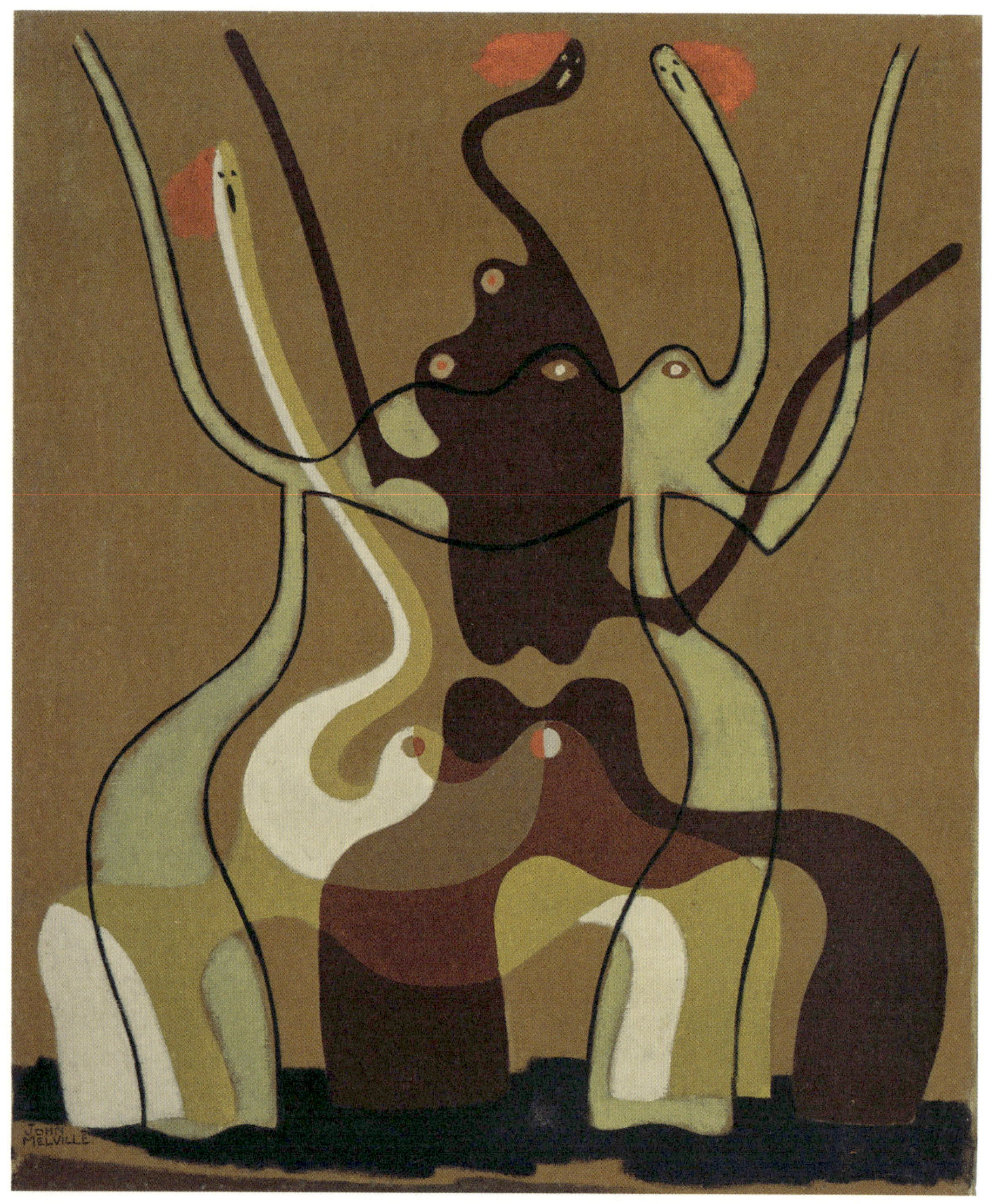

John Melville, *Dancers No. 3*, c. 1934.

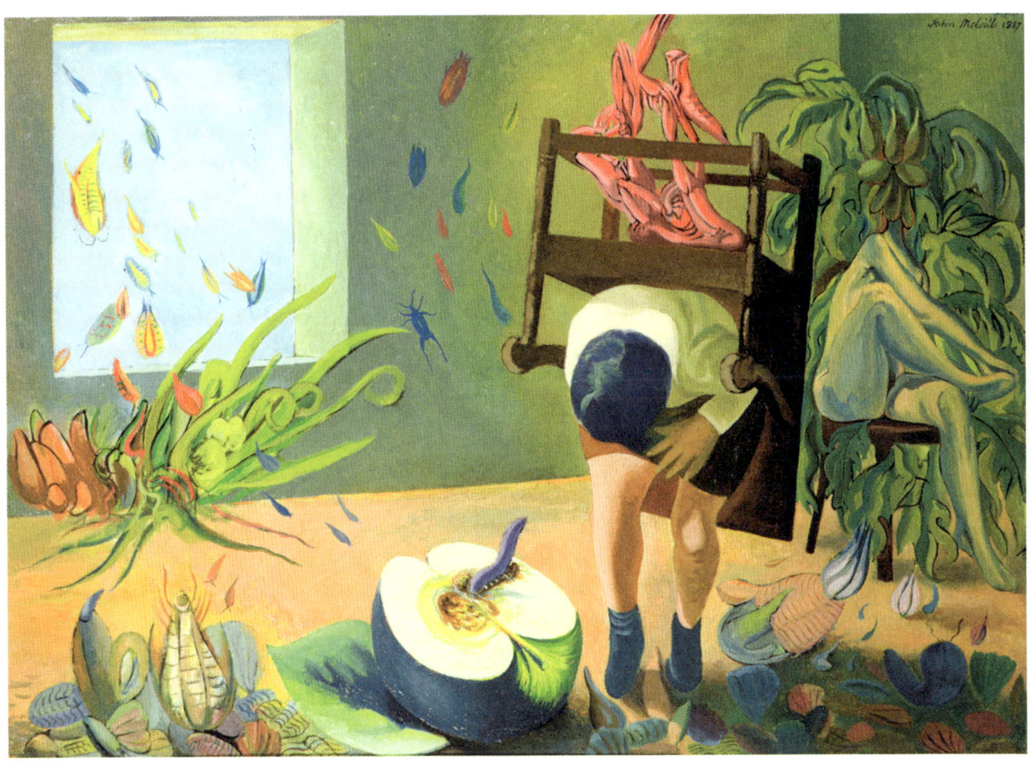

The story goes that the Melvilles and Maddox made a formal protest at the opening of the show. Travelling to London from Birmingham, they went to the gallery and pinned up a notice stating that, in their opinion, most of the English exhibitors were not true surrealists and that this was why the Birmingham surrealists were refusing to exhibit. If they did carry out this protest, then either nobody bothered to read their notice, or those that did simply ignored it, because there was no reference to it in any of the reports of the show. When David Gascoyne, who had initiated the exhibition, was asked why Melville and Maddox had not been included, he replied, rather sheepishly, 'We didn't know about them.' In other words, they could not have refused to exhibit, because they were not asked in the first place. The inference is that they were so piqued at not being asked to join in that they pretended they had rejected their invitations.

John Melville, *Natural History Museum of the Child*, 1937.

Whatever the truth, the fact remains that the Birmingham enclave were out of the limelight in 1936, so it is not surprising to find that, in 1938, Melville joined the London group of surrealists as a way of becoming better known and being part of the central action of the group. Unfortunately, his campaign was disrupted by the outbreak of war in 1939; after the war, his art was neglected for many years, and the important surrealist paintings he had done in the 1930s were overlooked. He himself had seemingly had enough of the surrealist crusade by that time and had moved on to other types of work.

In the 1950s Melville taught art at Birmingham University in the extra-mural department. His reputation was eventually revived when, fifty years after the 1936 exhibition, that seminal event was commemorated in a number of anniversary shows in various parts of England. This time he was included among the exhibitors, and his work was, at last, singled out for the praise it deserved.

HENRY MOORE

Member of the British Surrealist Group in 1930s; expelled by Mesens in 1948

BORN: 30 July 1898 in Castleford, West Yorkshire

PARENTS: Father of Irish origin, under-manager of the Wheldale colliery

LIVED: Castleford 1898; Army in World War I; Leeds 1919; London 1921; Hampstead 1929; Perry Green, near Much Hadham, Hertfordshire 1940

PARTNER: Married Irina Radetsky, an art student at the Royal College, in 1929 (one child)

DIED: 31 August 1986 at Perry Green, Hertfordshire, aged 88

With Henry Moore, the great mystery is how on earth he became associated with the surrealists, for his personality and his lifestyle were as far as it is possible to get from the spirit of surrealism. When you sat chatting with him you felt that you were in the presence of a down-to-earth, work-toughened Yorkshire farmer rather than a major avant-garde artist and arguably the greatest sculptor of his generation. He was never keen to talk about his work and appeared to have no interest in what other modern sculptors were doing. The only time I ever annoyed him was when I suggested that it might be worth making a visit to see the huge new sculpture garden of a Scandinavian artist who was making the news in the 1960s. To my surprise, Henry dismissed the man's work as appalling rubbish and a waste of space. This seemed so uncharacteristic of him because, on all other topics, he was the epitome of modest, friendly enthusiasm. I soon learned that there were two Henry Moores – the reserved, easy-going, eager-to-learn companion and the passionately driven sculptor who took no prisoners.

Knowing that I was a zoologist, Henry wanted to spend all our time together discussing animals. He would, for example, want to analyse in great detail the differences in the silhouette and skin texture of the Indian and the African elephant. It was clear to me that he was seeing these giants as pieces of moving sculpture. In particular, he loved the shape of their skulls. It so happened that a mutual friend of ours, the zoologist Julian Huxley, had an African elephant's skull at the bottom of his garden, and when Henry, the affably polite visitor, caught sight of it he was immediately transformed into that other Henry – the ruthless sculptor. 'It is magnificent, I must have it,' he gasped. Julian and his wife were taken aback. You don't walk into a friend's house and demand that they hand over one of their prized personal possessions. They told him firmly that he could not have it – 'if only because birds are nesting in its eye-sockets'. Henry's response was to say that he would wait until the nestlings had fledged. The Huxleys, trapped by having used an excuse, instead of saying simply that they didn't want to part with their splendid skull, had no choice. When the birds left the eye sockets, the couple dutifully telephoned Henry with the news. Julian told me that, within hours, a large van had arrived and the skull was gone. Henry was thrilled and used it as the basis for several important sculptures and a number of drawings.

So that was Henry Moore – tough when it mattered and tender when it didn't. And the only thing that really mattered to him and filled most of his waking hours was the creation of sculpture. How did this lifelong obsession begin?

Moore was born in a Yorkshire mining town, the sixth of the seven children of a tough coal miner. The family lived in a house that was so small that the children always had to sleep three or four to a bed. But when people referred to his hard childhood, Moore insisted that it was happy, not hard. Where he lived, everyone had the same sort of lifestyle, so he had no concept of a soft childhood with which to compare his own. It was the norm; it was what you expected of life. But he was lucky because his father, a typical Victorian head-of-the-house whose word was law, respected learning and wanted his children to be well educated.

Moore was also encouraged to go out into the local countryside at the weekends, where he became fascinated by the forms of the branches and roots of trees and by piles of rocks he came across in the woodlands. One rock pile in particular looked like a sphinx worn smooth by time, and in later life he remembered it. He also visited the local church, where he saw his first sculpture and was especially impressed by the recumbent figure of a woman whose face had been simplified without robbing it of its beauty or its serenity – something that could be said of the faces of many of his own stylized, figurative sculptures.

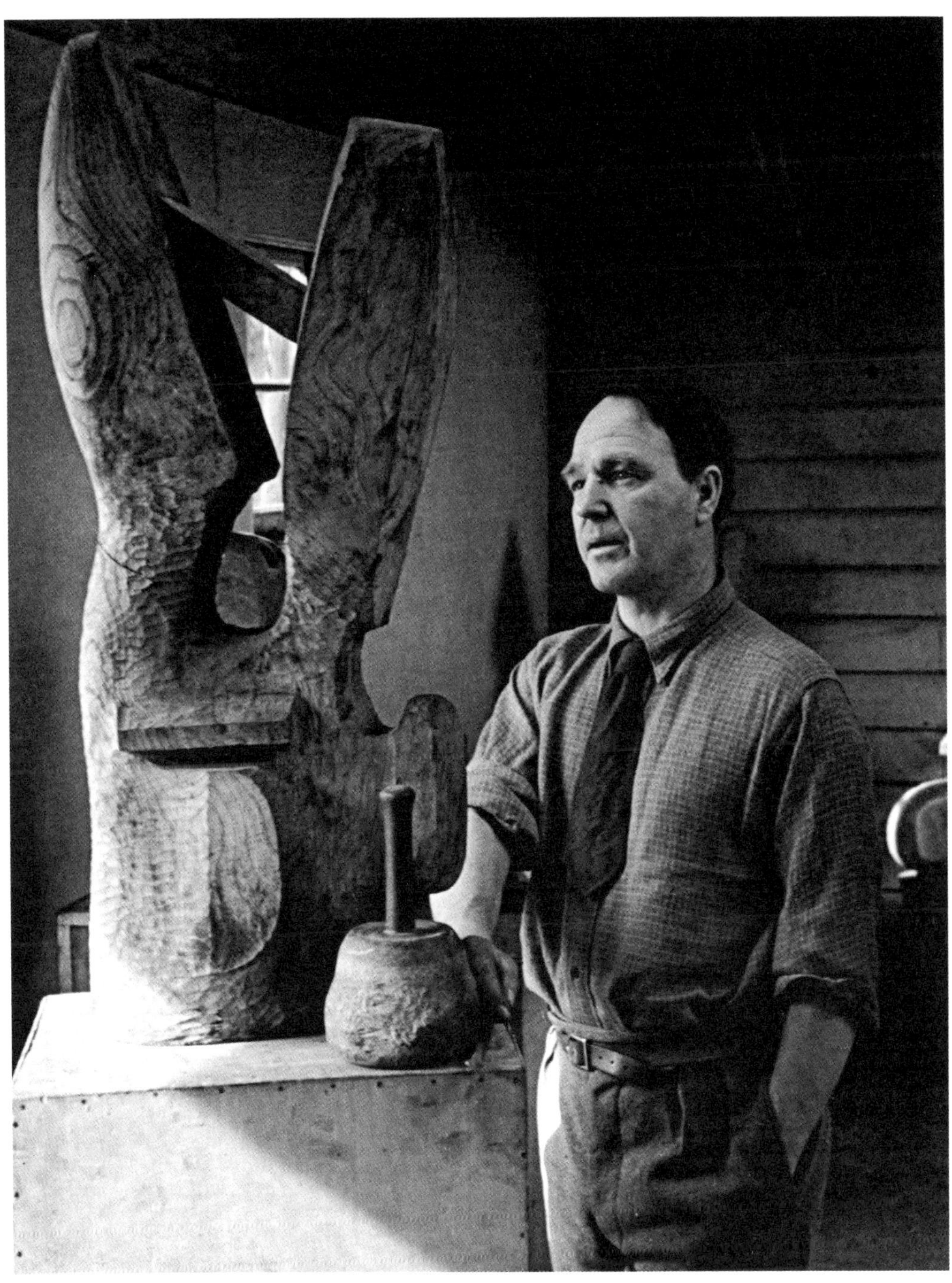

Henry Moore, 1945.

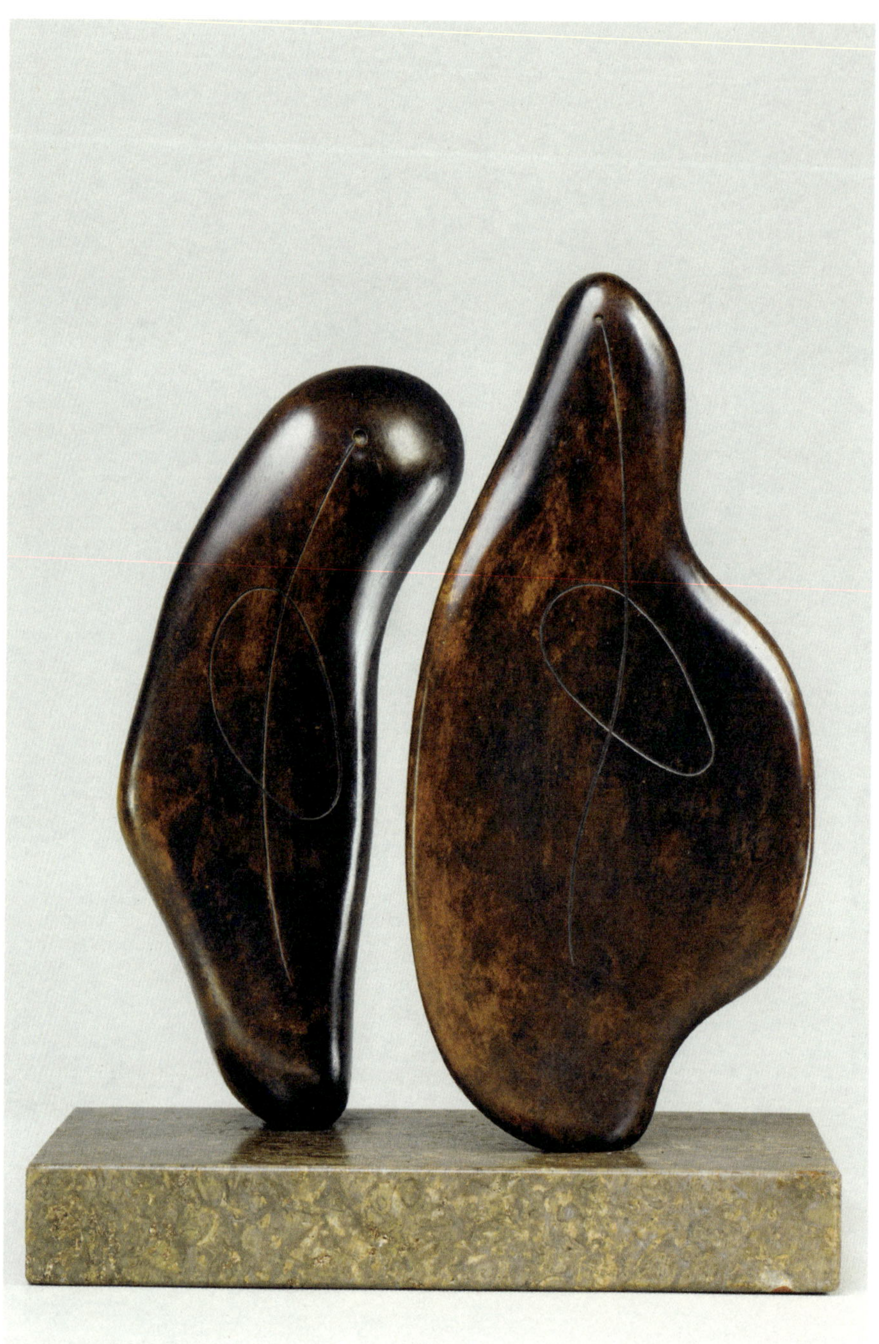

Henry Moore, *Two Forms*, 1934, cast 1967.

When he was eleven, following a Sunday school lesson in which he was introduced to the work of Michelangelo, he decided that he wanted to be a sculptor. His father was against this because he considered sculpting to be manual labour – something he wanted his children to rise above. Henry eventually became a schoolteacher, but this career was interrupted by World War I, in which he served and was lucky to survive. After one battle, only 42 of the 400 men in his group remained alive. After the war, Moore was given a grant that enabled him to attend Leeds School of Art and to pursue his sculptural work in earnest. While there, he fell for a young student called Barbara Hepworth and managed to convince her to switch from drawing to sculpting – thereby setting in motion a lifelong rivalry. Moore eventually moved to London and the Royal College of Art. There he lived in Chelsea in a room that was only eight feet by nine, but he loved it because he didn't have to share it. In his spare time, he haunted the British Museum and the Natural History Museum, but avoided the Tate Gallery because, strangely, he wasn't interested in contemporary art.

I once asked him if he enjoyed his art classes or found them too rigid. He told me that he hated still-life classes and would sneak off if he had the chance. One day, he said, when he was avoiding the boring still-life compositions with their meaningless subject matter, he idly opened some old drawers in the corner of one of the art rooms. Inside he found some dusty animal bones that had long ago been used for drawing lessons. He was fascinated by their shapes and began sketching them. After telling me this he paused for a moment and then said, in a soft voice, 'I think they have stood me in good stead, don't you?' Of course I agreed, because it was these biomorphic shapes that would become the very basis of all his later work, in which he saw beneath the surface of human and animal forms to get at their structural essence.

It was later, when he was teaching at the Royal College of Art, that Henry met a young art student, the Russian-Polish Irina Radetsky, who became his wife and lifelong partner. (When René Magritte visited the Moores in London in 1937, Irina made a deep impression on him, and he wrote to a friend, describing her as 'a young Russian wife with a SUPERBLY shapely body, like a sturdy wasp'.) After a period in Hampstead in the 1930s, the Moores moved out of London and bought a farmhouse at Much Hadham in Hertfordshire that would remain their home for the rest of their lives. They lived a simple, almost Victorian existence, with Henry going 'down the mine' into his sculpture workshop each day, where he would hammer away at a stone surface for hour after hour, just as his father had once hammered at the coalface. When I was once foolish enough to say to him that it must be very hard work, he gave me the look of someone who was tired of having to answer this question and said, 'No, no, it's just a matter of knowing how to let the mallet hit the chisel.' And that was the end of the discussion.

Family life changed little over the years for Moore. When he and Irina were young, they had little money and lived frugally. When, in later life and following global success with his work, he was immensely rich, they still lived frugally and saved their money. Moore was his own man and would have little to do with the establishment in London. Offered a knighthood, he refused, saying that he couldn't bear the thought of being greeted in his workshop with 'Good morning Sir Henry'. And he refused all attempts to get him to exhibit at the Royal Academy. It was as if his experiences on the battlefields of World War I had turned him against anything to do with official society.

Here, perhaps, we can see the seeds of his involvement with the surrealists. The surrealist movement had been spawned by a hatred of the pointless slaughter of World War I. When Moore first visited Paris in the early 1930s, a time when the surrealist movement there was at its height, he met André Breton and learned about sculptors such as Jean Arp, Constantin Brancusi and Alberto Giacometti. He disliked some aspects of the movement – its tendency towards what he considered pornography and some of its wilder excesses – but he admired the openness of its ideas and the encouragement of unconscious experimentation. The way in which he was starting to play with the human form and metamorphose it in various ways in his sculptures fitted well with the surrealist approach. Above all, he embraced it because 'it was an antidote to absolute pure abstraction'. His lifelong obsession with biological forms meant that he was always the enemy of hard-edge abstraction, with its geometric refinements, and the growth of the surrealist movement provided a welcome ally.

One art critic referred to Moore's involvement with the surrealist movement as a 'brief flirtation', but it was much more than that. It lasted for about eight years, from 1936 to 1944. It became serious in 1936 when a neighbour of his in Hampstead, Roland Penrose, recently returned from Paris, decided to organize a major International Surrealist Exhibition in London that year.

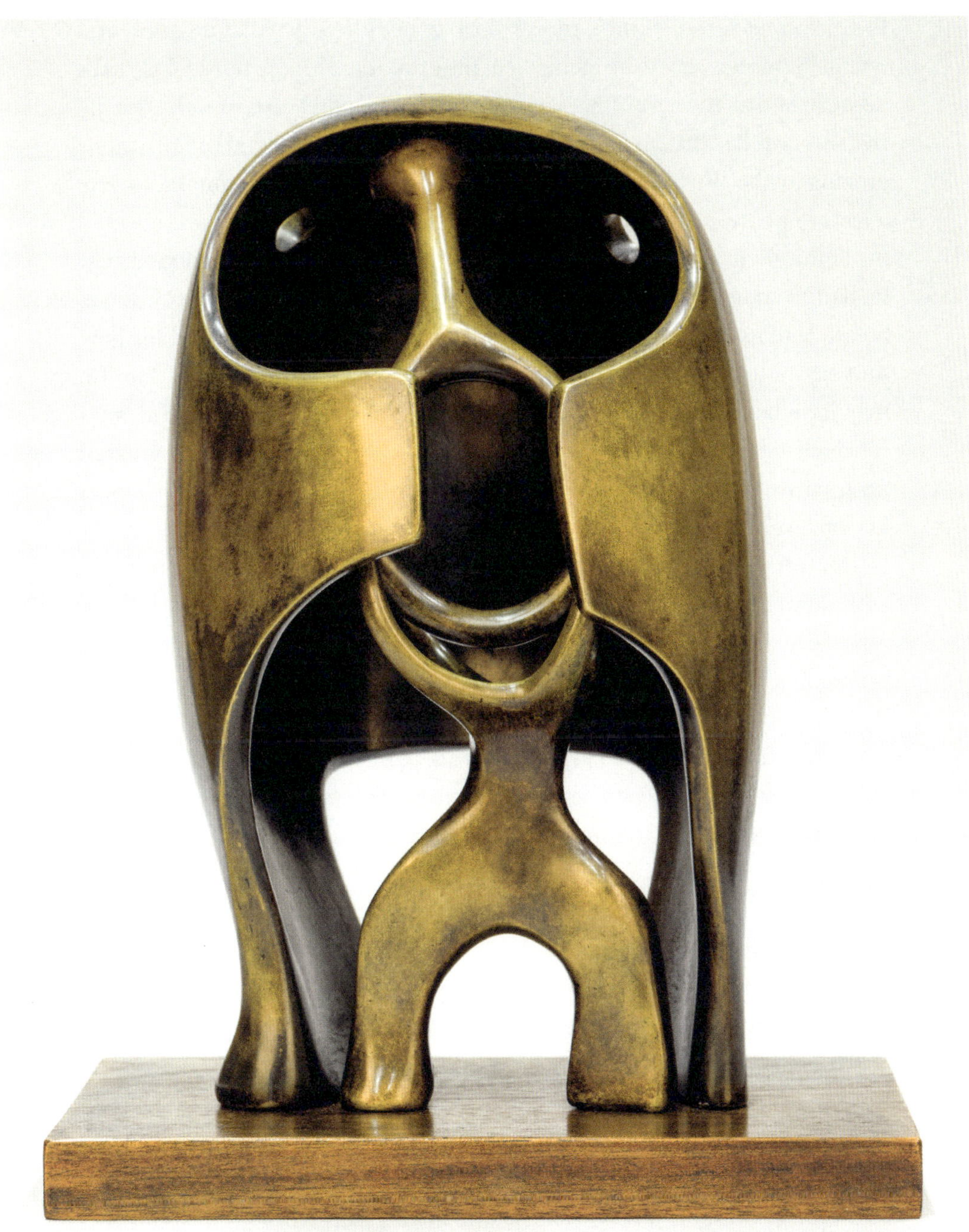

Henry Moore, *The Helmet*, 1939–40.

Penrose considered Moore's recent work to be fully surrealist in spirit, and four of his pieces were to be included in the exhibition. Moore himself, perhaps because he was the sort of person you knew you could trust, was elected the treasurer of the 'British Organizing Committee'. He attended the notorious evening at the Burlington Galleries when Salvador Dalí attempted to give a lecture wearing a diving suit. Moore's comment on the occasion reflected his ambivalent attitude towards the surrealist group. He complained that he had to wait for twenty-five minutes, sitting in front of an empty stage, before Dalí made his entrance. The precision with which he timed his long wait says a lot about the sensibly controlled way he organized his life. He may have been an out-and-out surrealist in the strangely wonderful ways in which he manipulated the human form in his sculptures and created imaginative biomorphic shapes, but in the way he lived his daily life he was far too level-headed for the totally committed surrealists.

Matters came to a head in 1944 when he accepted a commission to make a Madonna and Child for a church in Northampton. There was nothing especially religious about the actual sculpture: it showed what could be any proud, healthy peasant woman with a sturdy baby boy sitting on her lap. But when it was placed in a church it became a religious icon, and this broke one of the cardinal rules of surrealism, leading to Moore's eventual expulsion from the movement. A few years later, in a formal declaration signed by nearly all the British surrealists, Moore was attacked for 'making sacred ornaments'. Surprisingly, his friend Roland Penrose was one of the fourteen signatories. I asked Moore if he had been upset at being expelled. He smiled and said, 'Not a bit. If they didn't want me, that was fine by me.'

He had taken what he wanted from the movement and enjoyed the release it had given him. Some of his best pieces from the 1930s are great examples of surrealist sculpture. Thanks to his involvement with the surrealists, he had been freed from conscious control to create excitingly novel forms, still with a basis in biology but with a much more extreme metamorphosis than could be found in his earlier or, for that matter, his later work. He was not a complete, out-and-out surrealist, but he did pass through a significant surrealist phase.

Earlier, I said that the only thing that really mattered to Henry Moore was the creation of sculpture. I have recently discovered that this was not strictly true. To be more precise, it was only true for fifty of the fifty-two weeks of the year. For a two-week period each summer, even sculpture had to take a back seat. The two weeks in question were the Wimbledon fortnight, for it turns out that Henry was passionate about tennis. He would draw a line right through the two weeks in his diary when the tennis finals were taking place and would sit glued to his television screen, not missing a single moment. There is something charmingly out of character about this minor passion of his. It also explains the fact that he was upset when Eileen Agar beat him one day in a friendly tennis match.

PAUL NASH

Active in the British surrealist movement for a few years in the 1930s

BORN: 11 May 1889 in Kensington, London

PARENTS: Father a barrister; mother mentally unstable

LIVED: London 1889; Western Front in World War I 1917; Dymchurch, Kent 1921; Rye 1925; Swanage 1934; London 1936; Oxford 1939

PARTNERS: Married MARGARET ODEH, suffrage campaigner, 1914–46 • EILEEN AGAR, 1935–44

DIED: 11 July 1946 at Boscombe, Dorset, of a heart attack, aged 57

PAUL NASH IS SOMETHING OF A CONTRADICTION. He was a leading light in the British surrealist movement in 1936 and was an active member of the committee organizing the important International Surrealist Exhibition in London that year. Despite this, it has to be said that, at heart, he was a pastoral landscape artist with a love of the pale, washed-out colours typical of the politely restrained English art establishment. He seems somehow out of place in the rebellious world of the true surrealists, but his canvases of the 1930s demand that he should be considered in their company.

Nash was born in London, the son of a barrister, but when he was thirteen the family moved out of the city and Paul was able to grow up in the countryside, becoming absorbed in the English rural scene. His mother died young in an asylum when he was only twenty-one. Family tradition decreed that he should start training for the navy, but he conveniently failed his entrance exams and switched instead to a career as an artist, studying at the Slade School of Fine Art in London. His year was a remarkable one, his fellow students including Edward Wadsworth, Ben Nicholson and Stanley Spencer. Poor at figure drawing, Nash focused his attention on unusual landscapes, especially those that included some sort of ancient features such as megaliths or earthworks.

He was twenty-five when war broke out in 1914 and he joined the army, where he was given the rather strange duty of guarding the Tower of London.

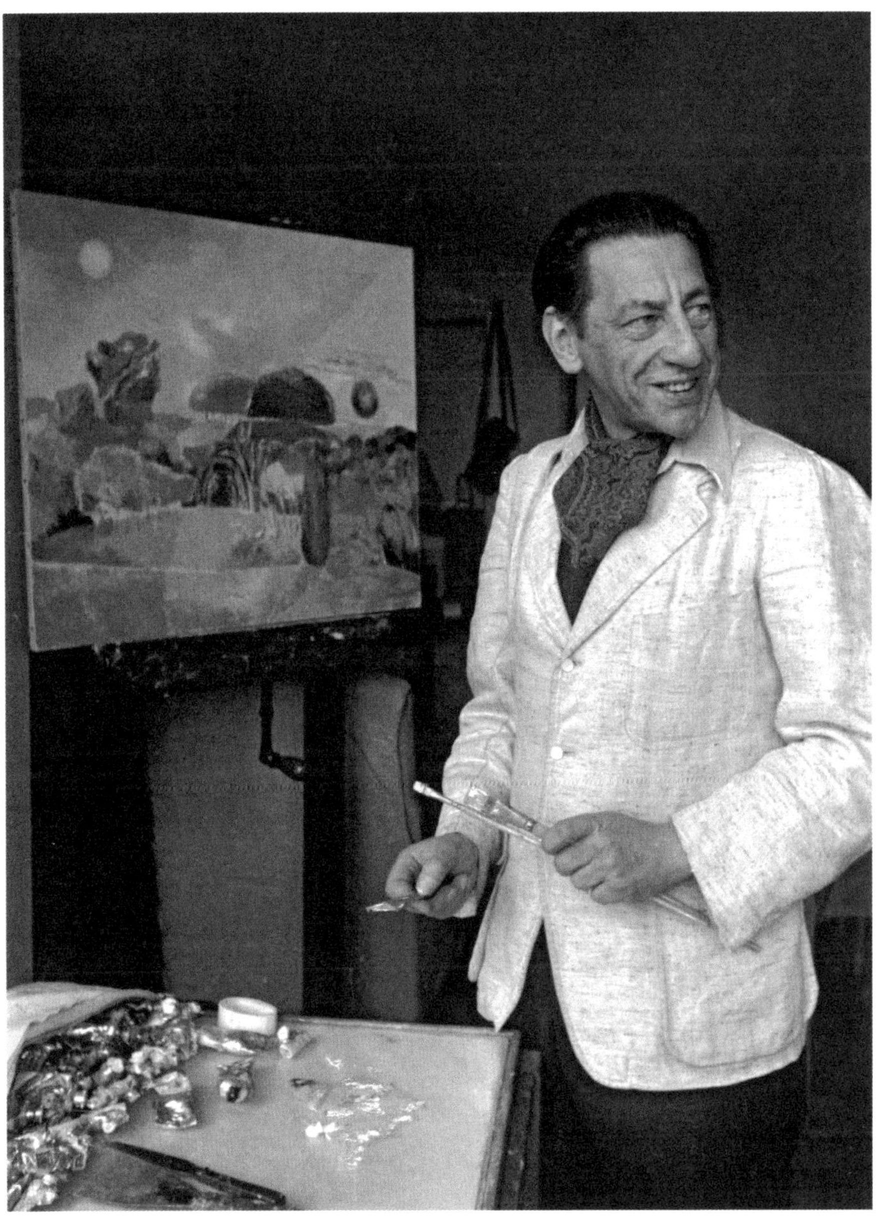

Paul Nash, 1944.

Before the end of that year, he had married Margaret Odeh, an Oxford-educated suffragette. In 1917 he was sent to the Western Front, where he started making sketches of the scenes he encountered there. He was lucky to survive, escaping almost certain death because he injured himself falling into a trench and was invalided home. No sooner had he left than nearly his entire unit was killed in fierce fighting.

Back in London Nash worked up his front-line sketches and, when they were exhibited, was advised to apply to become an official war artist, which he did. He returned to France in that role and began the gruesome task of portraying the horrors of trench warfare. He wrote home: 'It is unspeakable, godless, hopeless. I am no longer an artist interested and curious, I am a messenger who will bring back word from the men who are fighting to those who want the war to go on for ever. Feeble, inarticulate, will be my message, but it will have a bitter truth, and may it burn their lousy souls.' It was this same disgust at the appalling slaughter that had been initiated by the European establishment that would be the trigger for the dadaist and, later, the surrealist art movements. So it may be that it was there, on the front line, that Nash found the source for his sympathy with the surrealists in the inter-war period of the 1930s.

After the war, his paintings of the devastated landscape of the trenches made him nationally famous. On this tide of success, he appeared to have survived the horrors he had witnessed, but in 1921 he suffered a delayed reaction, experiencing a nervous breakdown that was described as 'suppressed war strain'. When he recovered, he went on to become a successful landscape artist throughout the 1920s until, in 1928, he made a deliberate change, moving towards surrealism. It was in that year that he visited an exhibition of the early work of Giorgio de Chirico in London, and the Italian's haunted compositions may well have been the trigger that encouraged him to change the nature of his own landscapes. In the years that followed he became obsessed with prehistoric standing stones and other ancient monuments. The giant megaliths of Avebury in Wiltshire particularly fascinated him and featured in some of his paintings.

He began to collect surrealist objects – strangely shaped flints and flotsam from the seashore on the south coast of England. It was there, at Swanage in 1935, that he met the surrealist artist Eileen Agar and fell in love with her. They began a lengthy affair that caused trouble for both of their marriages.

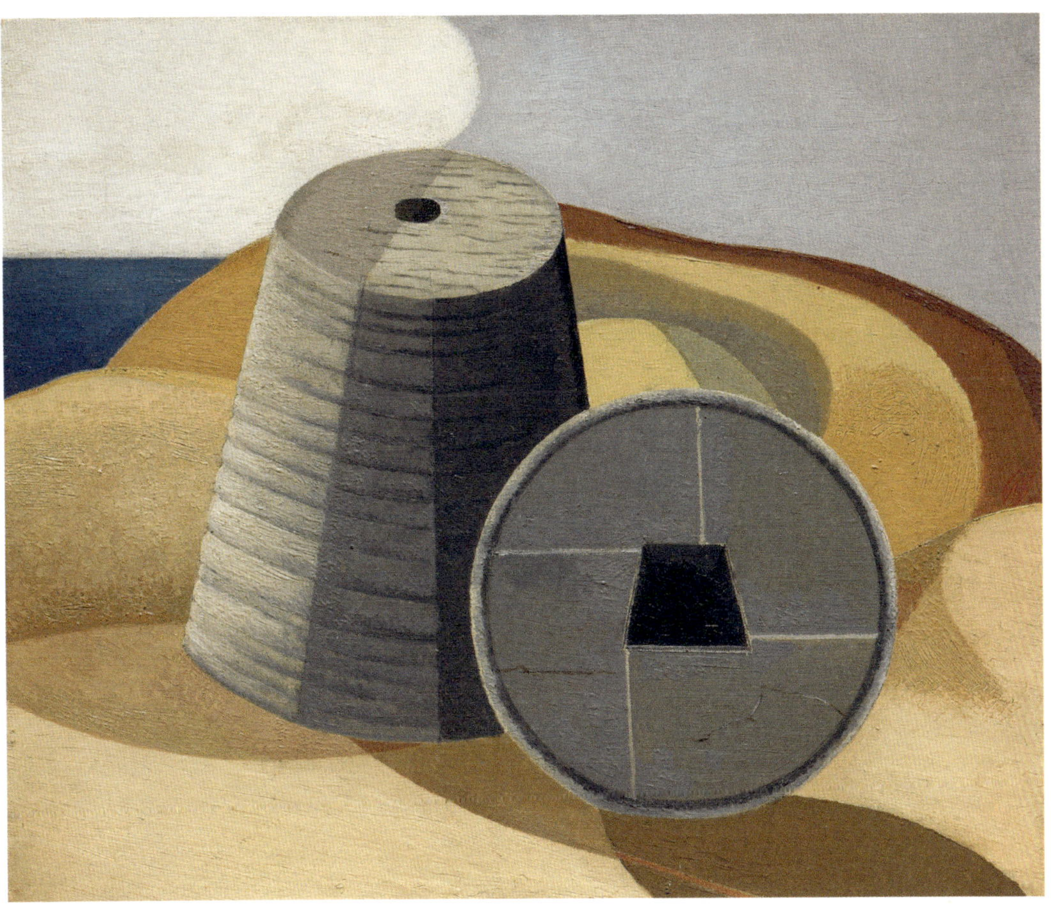

Their official partners knew about it, and there was so much pain involved that, the following year, Agar decided to end their relationship. Nash wrote to her: 'This year we have had together has given me something I don't feel I shall have again while I live ... it fed me and gave me new energy and poignant joy.'

For Nash, this intense romantic experience must have been something of a shock to the system. It was not like him to let himself go in this way. In his more usual state of mind, he was described as being 'aloof and living in a private world'. Those who knew him well commented that he was highly

Paul Nash, *Mineral Objects*, 1935.

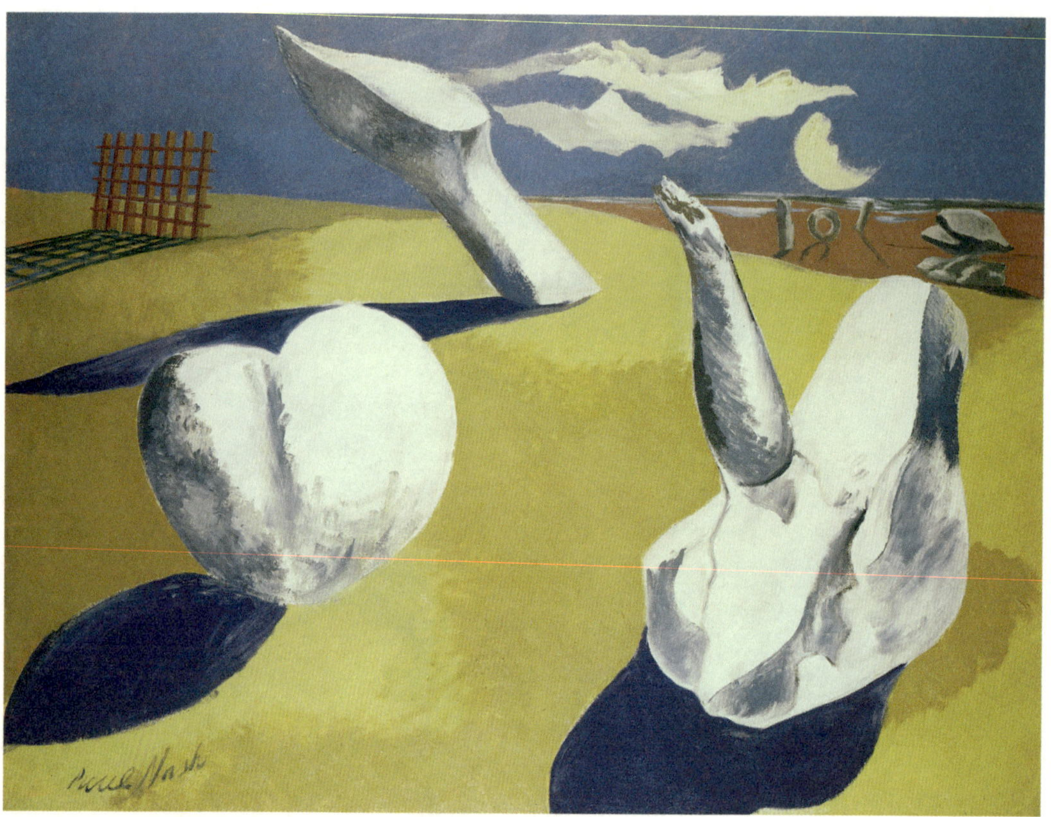

self-disciplined and that, although emotional, he managed to keep his emotions controlled by his intellect. A close friend of his said that he 'took everything seriously, most of all himself'. His wife, when asked to describe his personality, remarked that he had a 'very intellectual make-up'. It is hard to see such a man in the role of a besotted lover, desperate to keep his affair with Agar going after she had called a halt to it. But clearly Agar had cut through his armour and had found an inner version of Nash that was busy breaking all his usual rules for himself. He managed to win the struggle to keep the affair going, and they continued to meet secretly for another eight years.

In 1936 Nash and Margaret moved to Hampstead in north London, and it was there that he finally became fully engaged in the world of the surrealists.

Paul Nash, *Nocturnal Landscape*, 1938.

His new neighbour, Roland Penrose, was busy organizing the big International Surrealist Exhibition, and Nash joined the committee and helped with the selection of the artists to be included. Unsurprisingly, one of the artists chosen was Eileen Agar, who said she was startled to find herself becoming an official surrealist overnight. Nash's own work was included in the exhibition: four oils, five collages and three surrealist objects. It was praised by such major figures as André Breton, Max Ernst and René Magritte. Magritte called him 'The Master of the Object' which, coming from him, was praise indeed.

It is probably no accident that the surrealist phase in Nash's art coincided with his intense affair with Agar. At other times in his life, his usual painting methods were too self-conscious, too planned and organized to lend themselves to the free-flowing, unconscious stream of images required by surrealist doctrine. Agar cut him loose from his usual restraints and released the poetic side of his personality. This is borne out by a comment made by Nash himself in 1942 when discussing his relationship with the surrealist movement. He claimed 'I do not pretend to be a member of the surrealist party. I did not find surrealism, surrealism found me ... its expression and my expression came together at one point only – what I know as Poetry.'

In other words, the aloof intellectual Englishman took from surrealism the poetic freedom it offered to his visual imagery but rejected all the rest of its philosophical theories and its political dictates. He was not alone in this. Several of the other British surrealists made much the same point, if in different terms. They all relished what Nash called the 'inspiration and refreshment of mind' offered by surrealism, but they did not wish to be part of any hardline collective.

After the end of World War II, Nash was beginning to lose a long battle with asthma, and his poor health gave increasing cause for concern. In 1946 he was on holiday on the south coast when he suffered a heart attack and died at the young age of fifty-seven.

GORDON ONSLOW FORD

Joined surrealist group in Paris in 1938

BORN: 26 December 1912 in Wendover

PARENTS: Father and mother both artists

LIVED: Wendover 1912; Dartmouth and Navy 1926; Paris 1937; New York 1939; Erongarícuaro, a Purépecha village, Mexico 1941; San Francisco 1947; Inverness, California 1957

PARTNER: Married JACQUELINE JOHNSON, American writer, 1941

DIED: 9 November 2003 in Inverness, California, aged 90

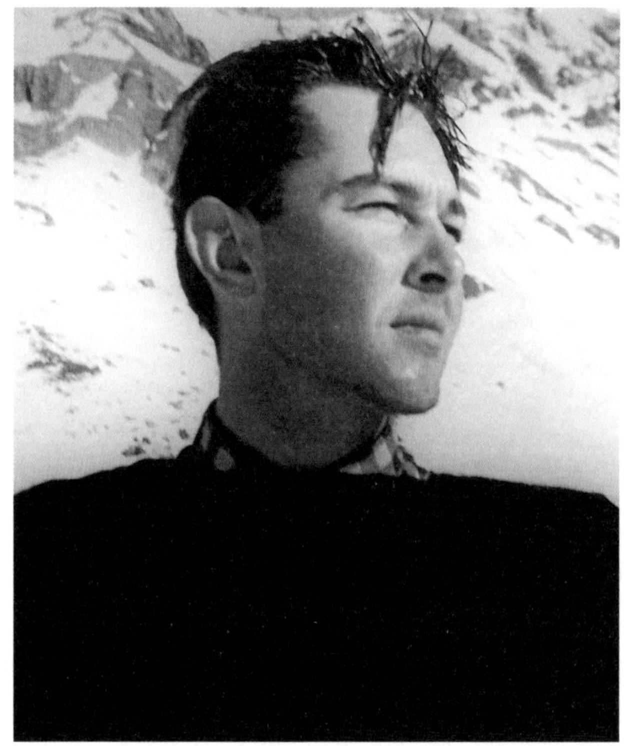

Gordon Onslow Ford, Switzerland, c. 1938.

Gordon Onslow Ford was born into a family of artists in southern England shortly before World War I. His grandfather Edward was a well-known Victorian sculptor, but it was his uncle Rudolph whom he remembered with a particular fondness, because he would take the small boy out into the country on the back of his bicycle when he went on sketching trips. Even as an old man, Onslow Ford could still recall details of those idyllic trips, such as the way his uncle would clean his paintbrushes on the stumps of trees.

As a result of this family atmosphere, Onslow Ford knew from a very early age that he wanted to be an artist. Reminiscing, he said that the great advantage of being a painter was that you didn't have to know anything. He made the perceptive comment that if you were stuffed with too much knowledge it could interfere with the directness of your visually creative actions. Painting, he argued, should be done 'on the spur of the moment'. He began painting landscapes at the age of eleven and then, when he was fourteen, his father died and he was packed off to the Royal Naval College at Dartmouth. The visual impact of the ocean had a deep effect on him but, after some years as a naval officer, he decided to pursue his first love of painting and in 1937 resigned his commission and moved to Paris.

He had chosen Paris because it was the centre of the modern art movement at the time and was permissive and tolerant of the behaviour of artists. England, by contrast, he said, was stuffy, conventional and preoccupied with matters of good taste. He made friends with the Chilean surrealist Roberto Matta and they spent a whole summer discussing surrealism and where it was going. They were almost exactly the same age, Matta having been born only six weeks before Onslow Ford. They were comparative newcomers on the scene, more than a decade younger than the central figures in the surrealist movement. Together they began attending the gatherings at the Deux Magots café. André Breton and his inner circle of about ten surrealists sat at a central table and around them, at other tables, there was a gathering of minor surrealists and followers. At the time, Matta was working as an architect in the offices of Le Corbusier in Paris but was making surrealist drawings in his spare time. Onslow Ford was so fascinated by these drawings that he persuaded Matta to give up architecture and switch to surrealist painting full time.

Eventually, Breton started to take notice of Onslow Ford and visited his studio. In 1938 he invited the young Englishman to become an official member of his surrealist group. Through Breton's introduction, Onslow Ford was then able to make contact with all the important surrealist artists, including Tanguy, Ernst, Victor Brauner, Miró and Masson. Breton admired what Onslow Ford was doing. In 1939 he said of his work that he 'describes a kind of world in which the last clear angles of cubism are fragmented'. Two years later he added that Onslow Ford had 'the eye of a man sure of conquering whatever still offers resistance'.

Just before World War II broke out, Onslow Ford rented a chateau in eastern France, near the Swiss border, and entertained his friends there in the last summer before hostilities began. Breton and his wife, Tanguy and Kay Sage, Matta and Esteban Francés were all guests there, painting and discussing the future of surrealism. A few months later, that future became a group exile in America as they all fled the Nazi invasion. In New York, some of them, like Breton himself, suffered from language problems, but English-speaking Onslow Ford found himself suddenly at a social advantage, and his status in the group began to rise. He was invited to give a series of lectures about surrealism and he also organized exhibitions. Young American artists who listened to him included Jackson Pollock, Mark Rothko and Robert Motherwell, who would later go on to found the American school of abstract expressionism – a noisy offspring of surrealism – in the 1950s. It should be recorded that, like Max Ernst, Onslow Ford was dripping paint onto canvas long before Pollock made a career out of this action.

It was at one of his lectures that Onslow Ford met an American writer called Jacqueline Johnson. They were married in 1941 and, dissatisfied with the commercialism of New York, moved to Mexico, settling in a remote village on the shores of Lake Pátzcuaro. There they mad e a close study of the indigenous beliefs and rituals and were visited by many of their surrealist friends, including Wolfgang Paalen (who was also a near neighbour), Matta, Remedios Varo and Esteban Francés. It was also there that Onslow Ford decided to end his official relationship with the surrealists, so he wrote a letter to Breton in 1943, formally resigning. He recounted how 'I told him that I had deep respect but I was no longer a revolutionary and I didn't have time to occupy myself with the politics of the movement. I was interested in investigating the unconscious and that was a full-time occupation.'

After six years in Mexico, Gordon and Jacqueline moved to California in 1947 and Onslow Ford became an American citizen. They settled in the

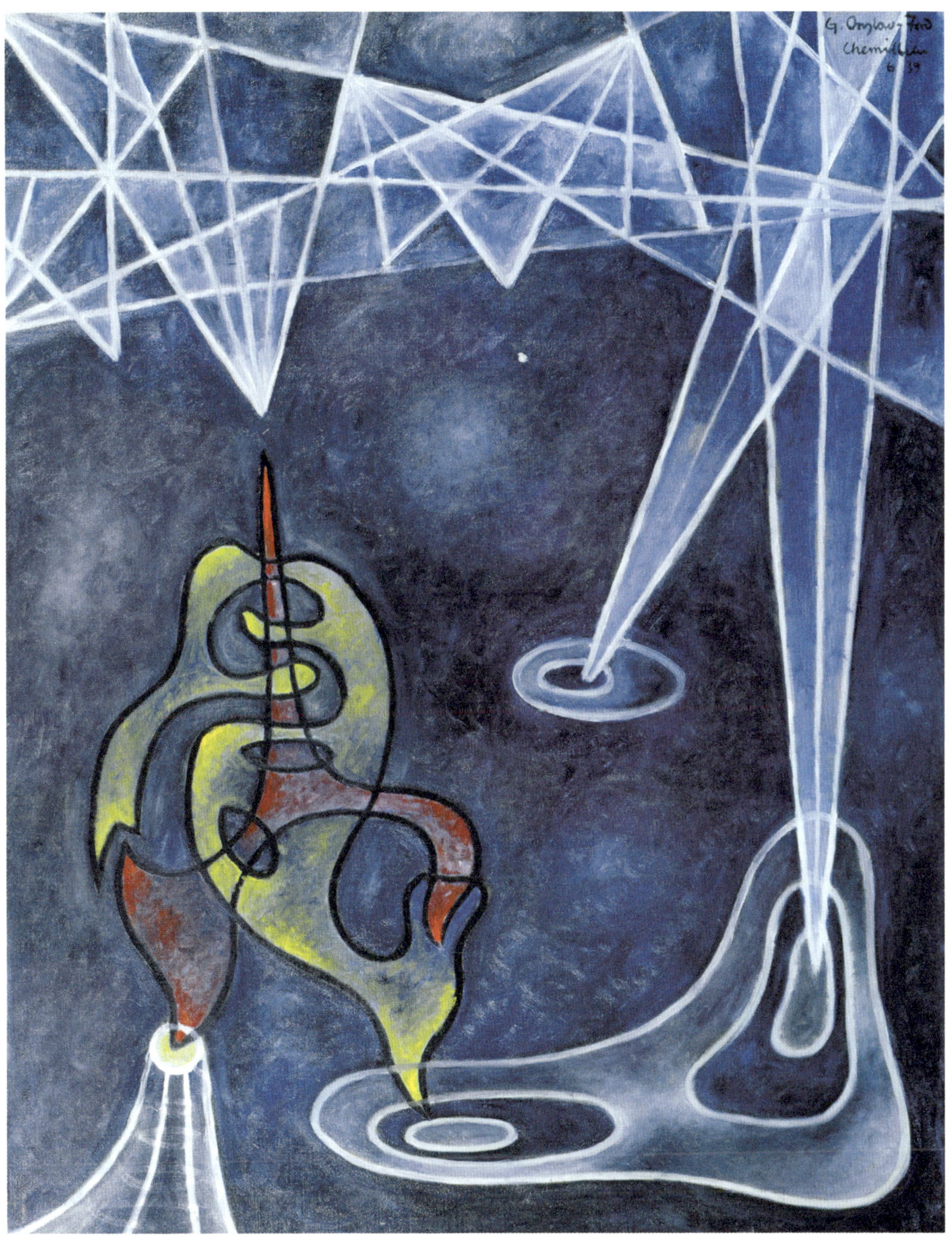

Gordon Onslow Ford, *Determination of Gender*, 1939.

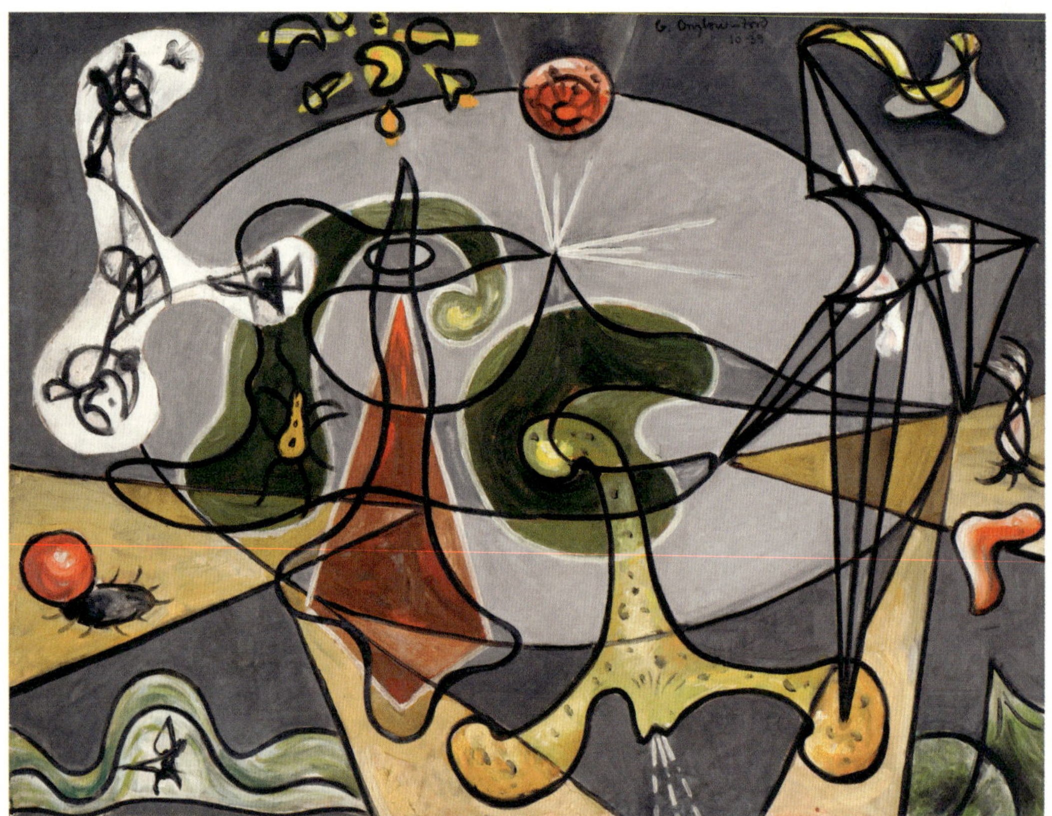

artists' colony of Sausalito, across the bay from San Francisco, converting an old ferryboat into a studio. In 1948 the San Francisco Museum of Art gave Onslow Ford a major retrospective.

Looking back at the early years, Onslow Ford made a clear distinction between the two basic types of surrealist painting: the one where the unconscious idea was realized first and was then laboriously transferred to canvas using meticulous, traditional techniques – as in the work of Dalí, Magritte and Delvaux – and the other, where the psychic automatism demanded by Breton was operating while the painting was being done, as with Masson, Miró and Matta. Onslow Ford felt strongly that the first type was bogus. He summed up his position by stating that, 'Spontaneous painting comes about

Gordon Onslow Ford, *Escape*, 1939.

through cultivating the open mind and painting just faster than rational thought, just faster than the painter's speed of consciousness, while giving full attention to what is appearing in the painting as it appears.' He gave his type of painting the title of 'Abstract Surrealism'.

In the second half of his life, he became immersed in Eastern religions and philosophies, zen and meditation, and the quality of his painting inevitably deteriorated. From his early period, when he was producing undiluted surrealist work, he now transferred his attention to what can best be described as mystical abstraction. He himself saw it as a natural progression, saying, 'We are continuing surrealism on a deeper level.' To his critics, this move felt more like surrealism on a shallower level, with his earlier complex compositions being replaced by little more than attractive patterns. This unfortunate state of affairs persisted late into his life, when all those who knew him well enough to have told him the truth were dead, and those who remained were too much in awe of his 1930s surrealist credentials to do so. It was a sad end to what had been such a promising beginning. But his early work survives to remind us of his considerable achievements. He died of a stroke at the age of ninety in 2003.

GRACE PAILTHORPE

Member of the British Surrealist Group from 1936; expelled by Mesens in 1940

BORN: 29 July 1883 in Sutton, Surrey

PARENTS: Father a stockbroker; mother a seamstress; both parents members of the Plymouth Brethren, a puritanical religious sect

LIVED: Sutton, Surrey 1883; Redhill, Surrey (childhood); Southport, Lancashire 1904; London 1908; Durham 1912; war service in France, England and Malta 1914–18; Australia & New Zealand 1919–21; Birmingham 1922; London 1930s; New York 1940; Vancouver 1941; London 1946; Dorking, Surrey 1950; Battle, East Sussex 1953; Crowborough, Sussex 1958; Ninfield, East Sussex 1962

PARTNER: Reuben Mednikoff 1935 (until her death in 1971)

DIED: 19 July 1971 in St Leonards-on-Sea, from cancer, aged 87

Grace Pailthorpe and her partner, Reuben Mednikoff, were once described as the eeriest couple in British art. Conroy Maddox called them 'the ogre and the dumpy one'. Their personal relationship was very odd. They slept together, but Pailthorpe adopted Medikoff as her son, following which he styled himself 'Ricki' and changed his name legally to Richard Pailthorpe. He called her his 'Mother Flower', and they developed a shared baby-talk language they called 'Curucuchoo'.

The pair met in 1935 at a debauched party given by a friend of the occultist Aleister Crowley, himself known as 'The Great Beast'. While the others present were engaged in satanic rituals, Pailthorpe and Mednikoff were huddled in a corner discussing how art could be used to cure mental health problems. Within a few years Pailthorpe had written an essay that summed up their approach, called 'The Scientific Aspect of Surrealism'. In it, she drew a comparison between surrealism and psychoanalysis, concluding that their final goal is the same – 'the liberation of man'. She mistakenly saw surrealist art as some new kind of visual therapy, leading to a more harmonious integration of the individual with the external world. What she overlooked was that the true goal of surrealism was the celebration of intuitive, irrational thought processes, not the curative value of those processes.

Pailthorpe was like the teacher who was telling children that the primary function of playing sport was not the excitement of the game, but to keep fit. Ironically, the significance of the paintings that she and Mednikoff produced stemmed not from their psychoanalytical value, but from their irrational visual impact. She seemed to be blissfully unaware that the application of any kind of analytical thought to surrealist works of art was alien to the basic tenets of surrealism. The couple's insistence on the scientific dissection of surrealist art began to grate on the other members of the British Surrealist Group to which they belonged. Conroy Maddox summed it up when he said that 'they reduced paintings to the level of symptoms'. Feelings against them grew so strong that, in 1940, they were formally expelled from the group by Édouard Mesens. Because they believed so strongly in the need for a scientific study of the curative value of surrealism, their expulsion from the group

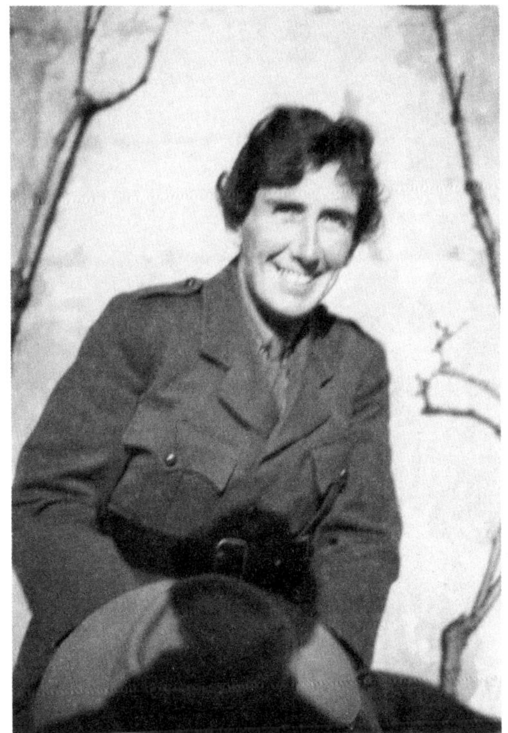

Grace Pailthorpe in World War I uniform, c. 1915.

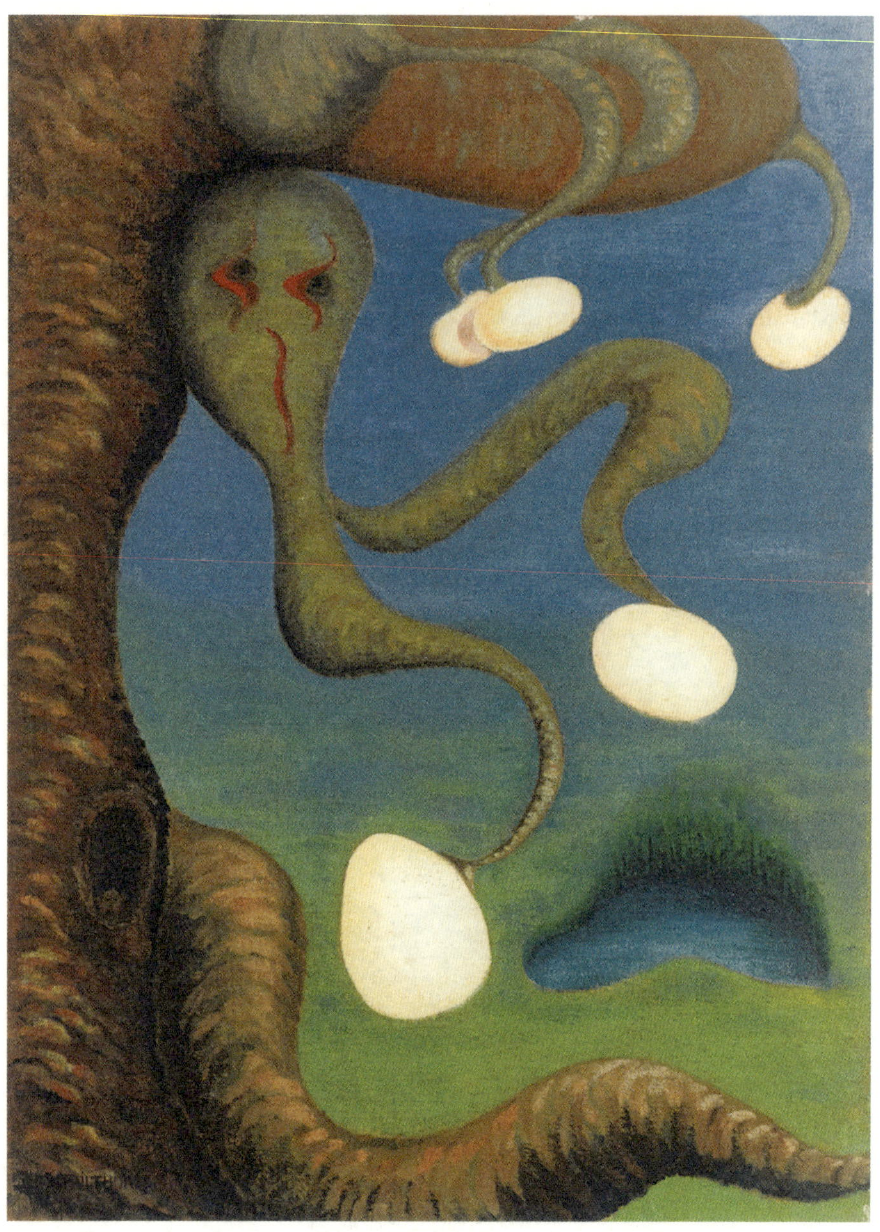

Grace Pailthorpe, *Scherzo (16 November 2.30 pm)*, 1937.

made the pair extremely angry. They felt so disgraced by their treatment that they left the country and pursued their aims in North America. After this, as surrealist artists they were largely forgotten until recently.

Pailthorpe was born in Victorian England in the year 1883, the daughter of a stockbroker. She had nine brothers but no sisters. Her parents were both members of the Plymouth Brethren, a strict religious sect. She grew up with a strong sense of serving humankind and ended up as a field surgeon in France during World War I, attending the wounded on the front lines. After the war she travelled abroad and spent three years as a medical officer in Western Australia. Returning to England in 1922, she switched her attention to psychological medicine and began studies of criminal psychology in British prisons. It was the first time that the psychological causes of criminal acts had been seriously studied, and her pioneering work made her famous in psychology circles.

In 1923 she joined the British Psychoanalytical Society and underwent analysis herself. She then embarked upon a major investigation into the causes of delinquency and its prevention. She was in private practice when she met Reuben Mednikoff at the satanic party in 1935. Mednikoff, a professional artist from a Russian Jewish family, was twenty-three years her junior, but they became an inseparable couple and remained so for the rest of their lives.

In the late 1930s Pailthorpe and Mednikoff both painted many surrealist works as part of an experimental cooperation investigating the role of the unconscious in art. Each would laboriously psychoanalyse the other's images, many of which were childishly transparent Freudian clichés. In fact, much of their work looked like surrealism done as an exercise by enthusiastic schoolchildren. Their arrogance was breathtaking: they rejected the work of Dalí, Tanguy and Miró as 'interesting but unreliable'. Nevertheless, they each had several of their paintings included in the important 1936 International Surrealist Exhibition in London, where their work was singled out for special praise by André Breton. After this they participated in a number of surrealist group shows in Europe, North America and Australia.

All was going well until Pailthorpe and Mednikoff organized the fateful meeting of the British Surrealist Group at the Barcelona Restaurant in London's Soho in 1940. Their mistake was to call the meeting themselves rather than ask Mesens to call it. He considered himself the leader of the group and felt aggrieved that they were usurping his role. Mednikoff had written a

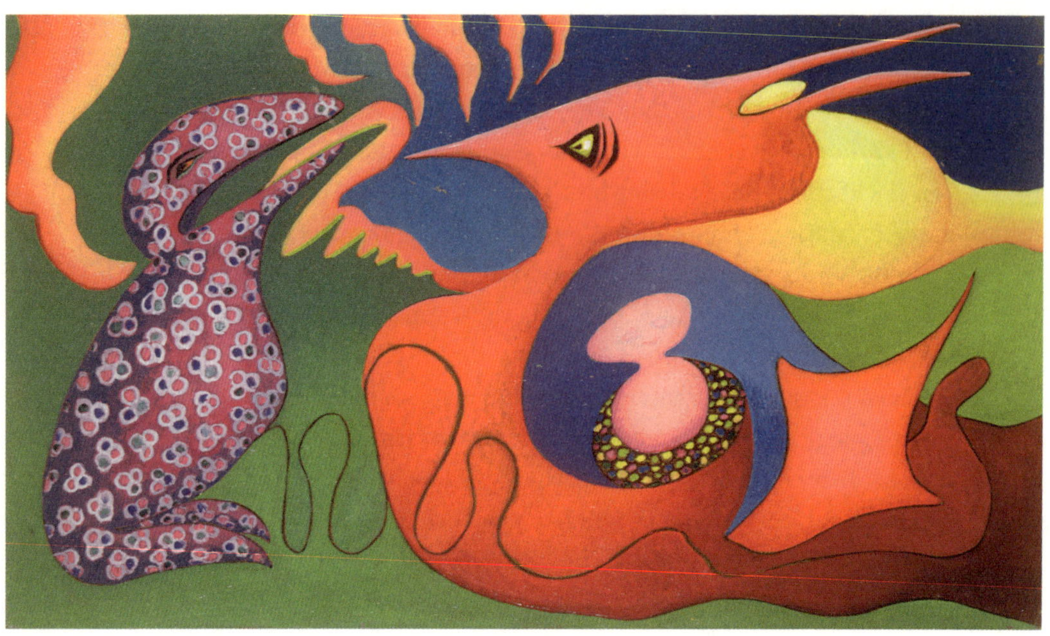

letter to each of the surrealists requesting a 'gathering of Surrealists for the purpose of planning the reformation of the Surrealist group in England'. There was to be 'a dinner, to be followed by a discussion in which all views could be made known and a constitution formulated'. To Mesens this must have looked like a take-over bid, and he set about destroying Pailthorpe and Mednikoff. He did it cleverly by reminding the group that, in Breton's original dictates, there was a requirement that no surrealist was allowed to belong to 'any group or association, professional or other ... other than the surrealist'. As a member of the British Psychoanalytical Society, this automatically ruled Pailthorpe out, and Mesens knew it. Prior to this meeting, Pailthorpe and Mednikoff probably felt themselves superior to the rest of the group and were naturally outraged suddenly to find themselves expelled from it.

A month later, they left England and travelled to New York, then California and finally to Vancouver, where Pailthorpe delivered a major lecture on the subject of surrealism and psychology. During World War II they exhibited

Grace Pailthorpe, *The Spotted Ousel*, 1942.

their work at the Vancouver Art Gallery but then returned to England in 1946. For some years Pailthorpe was a consultant psychiatrist at the Portman Clinic in London, with Mednikoff as her assistant. In the years that followed they would occasionally exhibit their paintings together and also started a School of Art Therapy, the first of its kind in Britain. In 1971 Pailthorpe died at the age of eighty-nine and within a few months Reuben also passed away, even though he was twenty-three years her junior. On their death, a great deal of their work was lost and only a small part of it survives today, a fact that caused one surrealist to whisper 'thank goodness'.

Finally, it has to be said that Pailthorpe was a contradiction. In 1939, at the height of her involvement in the surrealist movement, she made the enlightened statement that: 'One overhears many reactions to Surrealist art, but the most pathetic of all is from those who ask, "What am I supposed to see and feel from this?"' In other words, she was saying that one should experience the work but not ask questions about it. Yet it was asking these very questions to which she devoted most of her adult life.

ROLAND PENROSE

Joined surrealist group in Paris in 1928 and the British Surrealist Group in 1936

BORN: 14 October 1900 in St John's Wood, London, as Roland Algernon Penrose

PARENTS: Strict Quakers; father an Irish portrait painter;
mother the daughter of Baron Peckover, a wealthy banker

LIVED: London 1900; Oxhey Grange, Watford 1908; Italy 1918 with the Red Cross;
Cambridge 1919; Paris 1922; London 1936; East Sussex 1949

PARTNERS: Married VALENTINE BOUÉ 1925–34; divorced 1937
• PEGGY GUGGENHEIM, briefly in the 1930s
• Married LEE MILLER 1947 (until her death in 1977) (one son)
• DIANE DERIAZ 1979 (until his death in 1984); and many lovers

DIED: 23 April 1984 at Farley Farm, Chiddingly, East Sussex, aged 83

THE TRAGEDY OF ROLAND PENROSE IS THAT HE WAS A GOOD ARTIST who produced some major surrealist works, but whose paintings were overshadowed by his other high-profile activities. This came about because he happened to be an extremely good organizer, highly motivated and very rich. He bankrolled the surrealist movement to such a degree that it is probably true to say that it would have floundered without him. The humiliating image of a poverty-stricken André Breton travelling to London, cap in hand, to beg for funds from Roland sums up the importance of this polite, generous, quietly spoken, civilized Englishman.

Penrose was born when Queen Victoria was still on the throne. His mother, who had inherited a fortune from her banking ancestors, married an Irish artist, but Roland and his brothers grew up in a strict Quaker household on a large estate. It was this that gave Penrose his good manners and his kindness. It also fuelled his rebellious spirit. It was all too rigidly puritanical, too suffocatingly pious for a small boy with a lively imagination. There were daily morning prayers, evening prayers, bible readings and prayer meetings. Roland survived by daydreaming and enjoying wild, private fantasies.

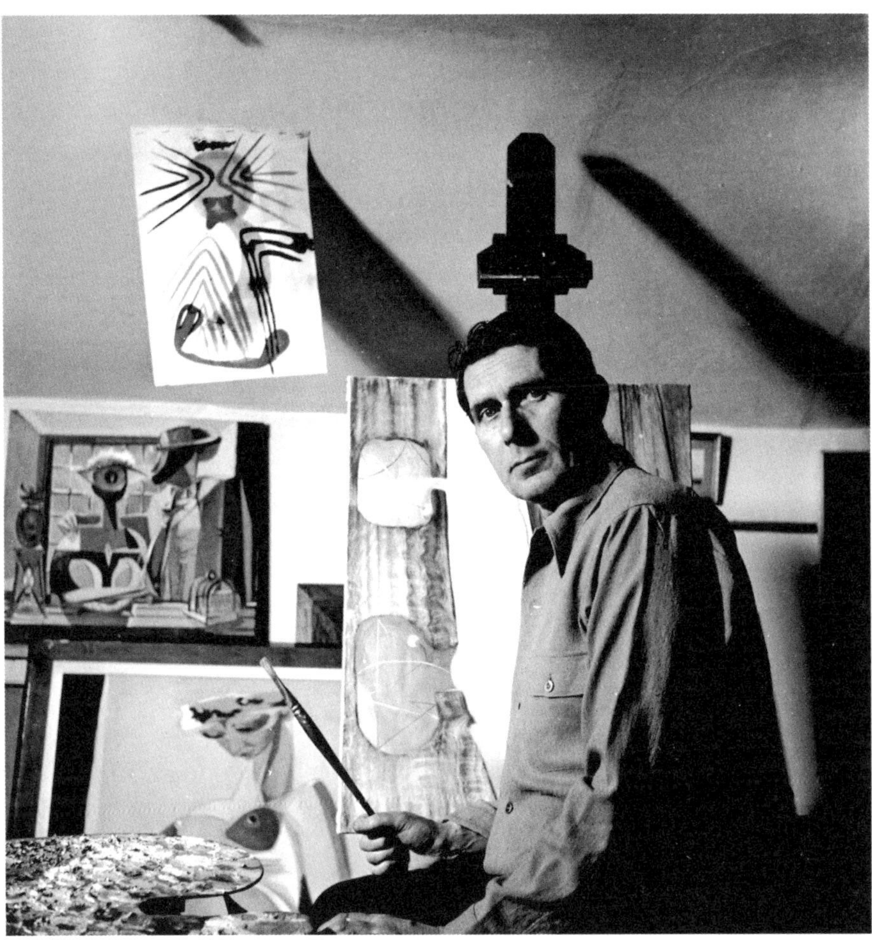

During World War I Roland lost all faith in religion; his parents' repeated prayers for peace fell on deaf ears, and the senseless slaughter continued. Towards the end of the war, he was serving with the Red Cross in the field and witnessed thousands of starving peasants and roads strewn with rotting corpses. It was a shocking experience for a teenager who had enjoyed such a sheltered upbringing and left a deep mark on him. Although he knew nothing of it, it was the same sense of shock and outrage that, elsewhere, would lead to the outbursts of the dadaists and, ultimately, the surrealist movement.

Roland Penrose, photographed by Lee Miller, Downshire Hill, Hampstead, 1949.

Studying him as a child, one would have predicted a future career as a banker or an architect, but somewhere inside the young Roland the need for rebellion was growing stronger. Socially, the first signs of it appeared when he was an undergraduate at Cambridge. There he met a handsome young actor called George Rylands and began an illegal homosexual affair with him. Today it would pass almost unnoticed, but in those days it was risky and could have seen him sent down or even sent to jail. Curiously, an interest in his own sex never resurfaced, and for the rest of his life he was a devoted heterosexual. In fact, he became what today might be called a sex addict, and was heard to describe his sharp need for endless sexual expression as

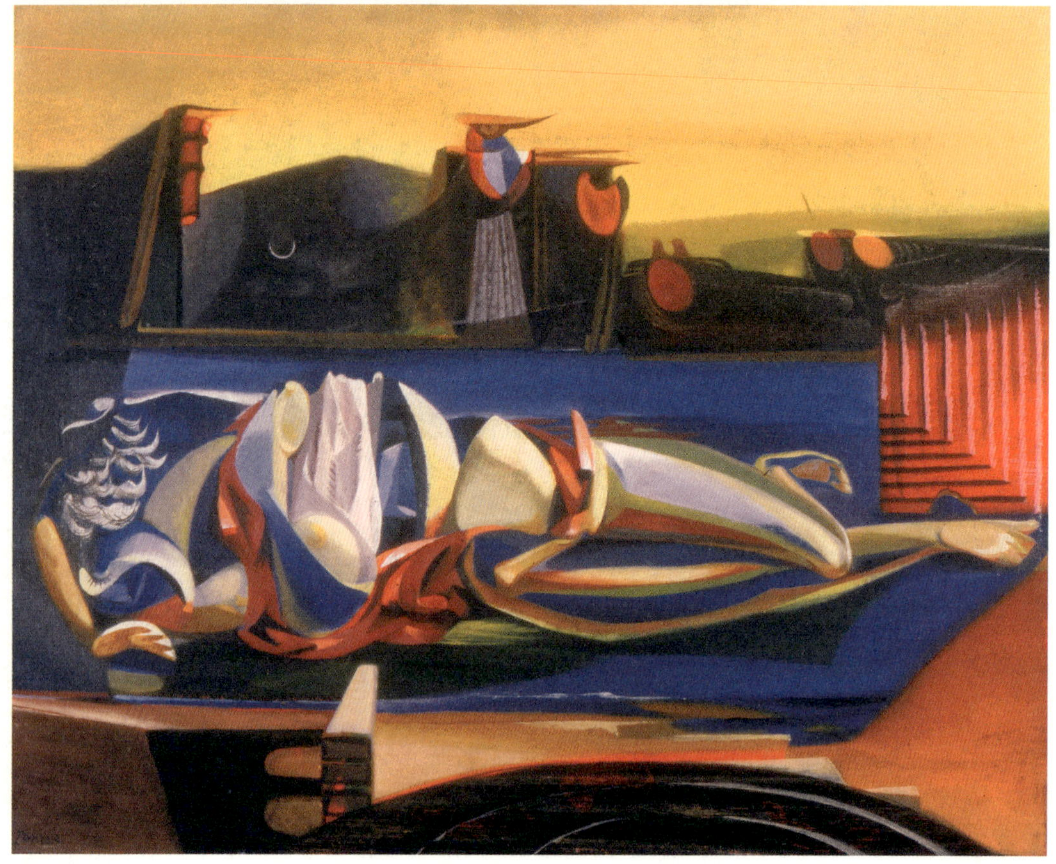

Roland Penrose, *Unsleeping Beauty*, 1946.

a curse that dogged him. After gaining a first-class degree in architecture at Cambridge, Roland upset his father by insisting on moving to Paris to study modern art. Despite his dismay, his father gave Roland a generous annual allowance and, in no time at all, the young graduate was enjoying the dubious pleasures of a Parisian brothel, where he was relieved to find that his Cambridge dalliance had not damaged his ability to enjoy the opposite sex.

Before long he had met and fallen in love with a wild surrealist poet called Valentine Boué. Their love affair was complicated by the fact that she was anatomically unable to engage in ordinary penetrative sex. Overcoming this disadvantage, their passion for one another led to creative alternative ways of making love; Roland described one instance where he tied her naked to a pine tree in a forest. They were soon married and started to move into the close circle of the surrealists that gathered around André Breton. Max Ernst was their initial contact and was very kind to Roland, generously showing him complicated techniques with painted surfaces. In return, Roland offered financial assistance and repeatedly bought Ernst's paintings to prevent him from starving. Knowledge of this must have hurt Max's pride, because he was overheard saying to Paul Éluard that Roland was a poor artist but that 'it is good to have rich friends'.

In the late 1920s Roland became a full member of the surrealist group in Paris, accepted by Breton and the others. He had found the social niche he needed to finally throw off the shackles of his strict Quaker childhood. In 1930, after receiving his family inheritance, he bought a chateau in Gascony and lived there with Valentine. They visited India together, but the relationship was beginning to falter and they eventually divorced in 1937 on the grounds that the marriage had never been consummated. Nevertheless, Roland would look after her from a distance for many years.

In Paris Penrose had met a young English surrealist poet called David Gascoyne, who persuaded him that Britain needed its own surrealist identity. Roland warmed to the idea and returned to London to set up house in Hampstead early in 1936. There he held surrealist meetings and set about organizing a major exhibition to introduce the movement to the British public. This involved roping in all the British surrealists and combining their paintings and sculptures with major works from Paris. The problem he faced was that dedicated British surrealists were rather few in number, so Roland and Herbert Read had to tour around artists' studios to see who else could, at a stretch, be classified as a surrealist and be included in the show. This annoyed some of the purists who felt that, to be involved, one had to be a fully committed member of the surrealist movement. In order to put on an impressive show, with strong British representation, Penrose and Read ignored these complaints and, in the process, revealed for the first time that there could be several categories of surrealist.

Roland's great International Surrealist Exhibition in London in 1936 was a huge success, with over 1,000 visitors every day, and established the movement firmly in the British art world and in the minds of the British public. This heightened awareness did not, however, mean that the surrealists were now widely accepted as serious artists. On the contrary, the majority of people viewed them as a ridiculous lunatic fringe. As far as the surrealists themselves were concerned, this violently negative reaction was appealing – so much better than simply being ignored.

Following his divorce from Valentine, Roland took himself off to Paris again, where he attended a fancy-dress party with Max Ernst. There he encountered Lee Miller, a blonde, blue-eyed American model and photographer who had been the lover of the American surrealist who called himself Man Ray. The couple had split up in 1932, leaving Man Ray feeling suicidal. Miller then wedded a rich Egyptian and departed to Cairo, where she enjoyed the high life but missed the Parisian surrealist scene. Still married to the Egyptian, she was now paying a visit to Paris and was soon in bed with Roland. For both of them it was more than a casual affair. Instead, it was the start of a forty-year relationship during which time they were always faithful to one another. Their definition of faithfulness, however, was not the usual one. It meant that they were both free to have as many affairs as they liked, but never secretly and always with the knowledge that their love would outlast all their dalliances – which it did. At the end of the 1930s there were surrealist house parties and social gatherings at which partner-swapping was commonplace. Roland and Lee attended these and took part in the fun and games with great abandon, but their deep love for one another never faltered.

In 1939, just before war broke out, Lee finally left her Egyptian husband and headed for England and Roland. They lived together in Hampstead, and Roland proudly showed her his recent acquisition – the London Gallery, centre of surrealist activity in England, managed for him by the Belgian surrealist Édouard Mesens. Roland and Lee could at last live together as a real couple,

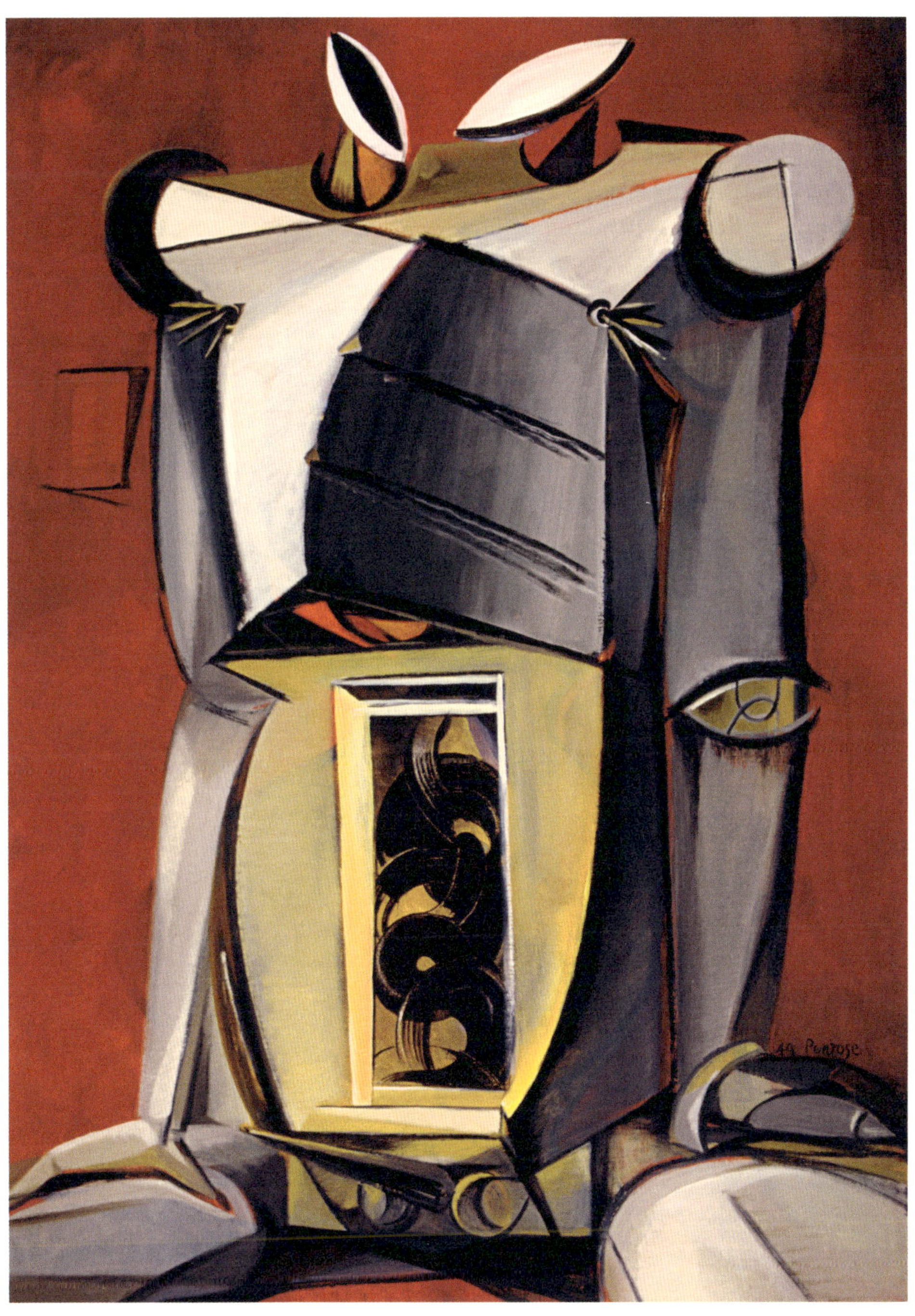

Roland Penrose, *Don't You Hate Having Two Heads? (Self-Portrait)*, 1949.

but the idyll was short-lived. In a matter of months, the war began, and before long London was being blitzed by German bombers. Roland became an air raid warden and Lee started her career as a war photographer. The London Gallery was closed, and its stock of paintings was stashed away in Pimlico. Tragically, a German bomb hit the building, and all eighty-three paintings went up in flames, including several works by Magritte, Ernst, Delvaux, Braque, de Chirico, Giacometti and Man Ray. Most of them belonged to Roland personally and were not covered by insurance.

During the war Roland moved into camouflage research and wrote a manual on the subject, explaining how animals concealed themselves and how humans could learn from their camouflage devices. Lee was sent off to the Continent in her role as a war photographer and, at the end of the war, was to capture some of her most important and unforgettable images, including the devastating scenes she encountered at the newly liberated concentration camps. Her status as an important visual recorder of the aftermath of World War II made Roland's camouflage work seem rather tame by comparison. As she recovered from her nightmare experiences, Roland busied himself with reopening the London Gallery with Mesens. He was also involved in complicated discussions about opening a Museum of Modern Art in London, to rival the one in New York. The discussions would eventually lead, in 1947, to the foundation of Roland's new baby – the Institute of Contemporary Arts (ICA) in London.

While this was going on, at home a surprise was in store for him. Lee had had several abortions over the years and had been told she would never be able to have a child. But, against the odds, she became pregnant at the start of 1947 and gave birth to their son in September of that year. Two years later Lee, Roland and their infant moved out of London to Farley Farm near Chiddingly in Sussex. This would remain their home for the rest of their lives, visited by the good and the great, including both Pablo Picasso and Joan Miró.

In 1950 Roland shut down the London Gallery, which had been losing money at an alarming rate, and poured all his energies into running the ICA. This new institute became the focus of anything novel and outrageous in the world of the fine arts and is still flourishing to this day. Roland himself continued to paint in his studio at Farley Farm and, in London, kept busy organizing huge exhibitions of the work of his close friends Picasso and Miró. His Picasso retrospective at the Tate Gallery was the most successful exhibition ever staged in Britain to date, attracting over 500,000 visitors. In recognition of this work, Roland was offered a knighthood in 1966 and, to howls of protest from other surrealists, he accepted it, saying of his critics, 'They can call me a Sir-realist.' Over the years he had poured so much of his money into surrealist coffers, repeatedly helping to keep the movement afloat, that even though he had knelt before royalty he could hardly be expelled from a movement that owed him so much.

During their Farley Farm period, Lee said that giving birth had ruined her interest in sex and she encouraged Roland to have affairs. One of these got out of hand when he fell in love with a charismatic trapeze artist called Diane Deriaz. Roland reached the stage where he wanted to marry Diane and live in Paris, while Lee would take her son to America and live with him there. Diane refused, but the tensions were acute, and Lee left for a long stay in New York. When she returned, Roland and she once again found their love for one another resurfacing, and the family stayed together at the farm.

In the early 1960s Roland and Lee visited Peggy Guggenheim's art collection in Venice and a curious incident occurred. Peggy had been unkind to Roland in her memoirs, saying that he was a bad painter and that when in the past, he had made love to her, he had tied her up with ivory bracelets. He asked her to remove the comment about him being a bad painter from any subsequent editions, which she agreed to do, and also to change her statement about the ivory bracelets, saying that he had used only ordinary police handcuffs to restrain her. Curiously, this she refused to do and insisted on retaining her reference to the ivory bracelets.

Roland's addiction to bondage sex seems to have developed at an early stage in his life, caused by the anatomical impossibility of having straightforward sex with his first wife. As an erotic ritual it helped to provide an alternative outlet. However, instead of abandoning it when he left Valentine, it appears to have become almost a necessity. Dorothy Moreland, one-time director of the ICA, said to me that 'Roland can't do it without handcuffs.' Peggy Guggenheim's memoir confirms this, saying, 'It was extremely uncomfortable to spend the night this way [shackled to a bedpost] but if you spent it with Penrose it was the only way.' Roland's son, Antony, mentions a pair of solid gold handcuffs made by Cartier that were a gift to Lee and records that, 'She wore both the handcuffs on the same wrist as a chic bracelet by day, always ready to gratify Roland's desire by snapping one on the other wrist.'

In 1976 Roland's two closest friends, Max Ernst and Man Ray, both died, and in 1977 it was Lee's turn. Roland was inconsolable. His first wife, Valentine, with whom Roland had stayed friends, had also been living at Farley Farm for several years and she too died the following year. Roland was stripped of those he loved. Even his latest girlfriend, a young Israeli called Danniella, had departed. Lonely, he again begged Diane Deriaz to marry him but she refused, although she did take him out of himself by accompanying him on long holidays to exotic locations, such as Malindi off the African coast and the Seychelles in the Indian Ocean. In 1984, a few months after returning from the Seychelles, Roland died at Farley Farm, saying 'I want to go.'

My abiding memory of Roland was his adoration of Picasso. 'Don Pablo', as Roland called him, could do no wrong. Even when the great artist had behaved particularly badly towards one of the many women in his life, Roland would always find an excuse for him. When I was the director of the ICA in London and Roland was my boss, he was always popping over to France to spend the weekend with Don Pablo, returning to the offices of the ICA in London on the following Monday clutching a barely dry oil painting by Picasso in each hand. 'Look what he gave me,' he would exclaim, with a boyish enthusiasm, holding them up for me to inspect.

During the only visit Picasso ever made to England, he stayed with Roland at Farley Farm. While he was there, Roland took him to a dinner party at the apartment of the great Irish scientist Des Bernal and, during the evening, Picasso climbed on a chair and made a large sketch on one of the whitewashed walls. Some years later, the building was about to be destroyed and the sketch was going to be lost. To Roland, the solution was obvious – he bought the wall. When I arrived at the ICA one morning, there it was at the bottom of the stairs, with Picasso's delightful sketch still safely preserved on its white surface.

PETER ROSE PULHAM

Associated with the Paris surrealists from 1936 to 1939

BORN: 26 June 1910 in Hampstead Garden Suburb, London

LIVED: London 1910; Oxford 1928; London *c.* 1931; Paris 1936; London 1939; Conives, France 1953

PARTNER: THEODORA ROSLING (later FITZGIBBON) 1938–42

DIED: 18 May 1956 in Conives, France, aged 45

SADLY, PETER ROSE PULHAM IS ONE OF THE FORGOTTEN SURREALISTS. The reason I find him fascinating is that, over seventy years ago, I walked down the stairs into the lower room of the London Gallery in Brook Street and came face to face with a group of brilliant surrealist paintings of a kind I had never seen before. Human limbs and body parts had been stretched into abstracted compositions that transmitted an intense and almost painful eroticism. I asked about the artist and was told that he was a friend of Francis Bacon's. There was apparently some debate as to whether Bacon had influenced Pulham, or whether Pulham's distorted limbs had, perhaps, influenced Bacon. The oil paintings in question had mostly been done in 1947. There was a whole suite of them, but I can only find evidence that two of them have survived. Indeed, almost all the work done by Pulham in his lifetime appears to have been lost or destroyed, which explains why he is so little known today.

Originally, Pulham had intended to become an architect and had studied at the Architectural Association School of Architecture in London. For some reason, he decided to transfer to Worcester College, Oxford, where he met Cecil Beaton and became interested in fashion. He began working for a portrait photographer and was eventually offered a position as a fashion photographer at *Harper's Bazaar* magazine in London. In 1936 they sent him to Paris to cover fashion events, but he became more interested in the great artists who were working there at the time and started photographing them in their studios. His photographs of Picasso, Ernst and other surrealists have become collector's items. He was so inspired by the atmosphere in Paris in the 1930s that he was to remain there until the outbreak of war in 1939. It was during these Paris years that, under the influence of his surrealist friends, he started to paint.

Pulham's personal life would have remained something of a mystery, were it not for the fact that his lover in Paris, who would later become known as the celebrated food expert Theodora Fitzgibbon, author of thirty cookery books, would one day write her memoirs. In them, she describes her first encounter with Pulham. She saw him sitting in the Café de Flore, where he 'was always the most interesting looking person, with the most glamorous group'. She was twenty years old and already had a lover in London, but could not stop gazing at Pulham. This went on for two weeks, until she ran out of money and had to return to London. Fortunately, she won some money on a horse and immediately returned to Paris and the Café de Flore, where she was lucky enough to find herself sitting at the table next to Pulham's. She must have been staring at him because he suddenly said: 'I wonder if you would mind sitting at my table as you distract me sitting where you are.' Later that night they became lovers, although it has to be said that Pulham seemed rather offhand. Examining her body, he commented: 'You look almost transparent in this light. Pity, I like dirty, black-haired women.' She remarked later that 'he treated me as if I was a strange little animal that he should be wary of'; but, despite this, their love affair would prove to be lasting. He took her straight into the bohemian life of Paris, where she met Picasso, Ernst, Balthus, Dalí, Breton, Cocteau and Antoine de Saint-Exupéry. It changed her life, and she found the atmosphere so exciting that she forgave Pulham for spending so much time at his easel. She did however complain that: 'He was too indolent to be a sustained lover. What energy he had went into his work.'

When war broke out in 1939, the couple were forced to abandon Paris and flee to England. Back in London, Pulham set up a studio in Old Church Street, Chelsea and worked steadily there on his surrealist paintings for two years before, in 1941, the studio was hit by a German bomb during the Blitz and almost all his surrealist work was destroyed. It was during this time that he and Theodora became friendly with Francis Bacon, Lucian Freud, Henry Moore, John Minton, John Banting, Augustus John, Dylan Thomas and the art historian David Sylvester. They had replaced the avant-garde of Paris with that of London. Theodora reports that, with the nightly bombing of the city, they often had little to eat and she had to improvise with their meals. She grew garlic in a window box and kept some hens to provide eggs for breakfast. In the evenings, they and their friends would remain stubbornly above ground, in pubs and nightclubs, rather than sitting huddled in bomb shelters.

The relationship between Peter Pulham and Theodora was a strange one. Although they had a deep bond of attachment, it was not a passionate

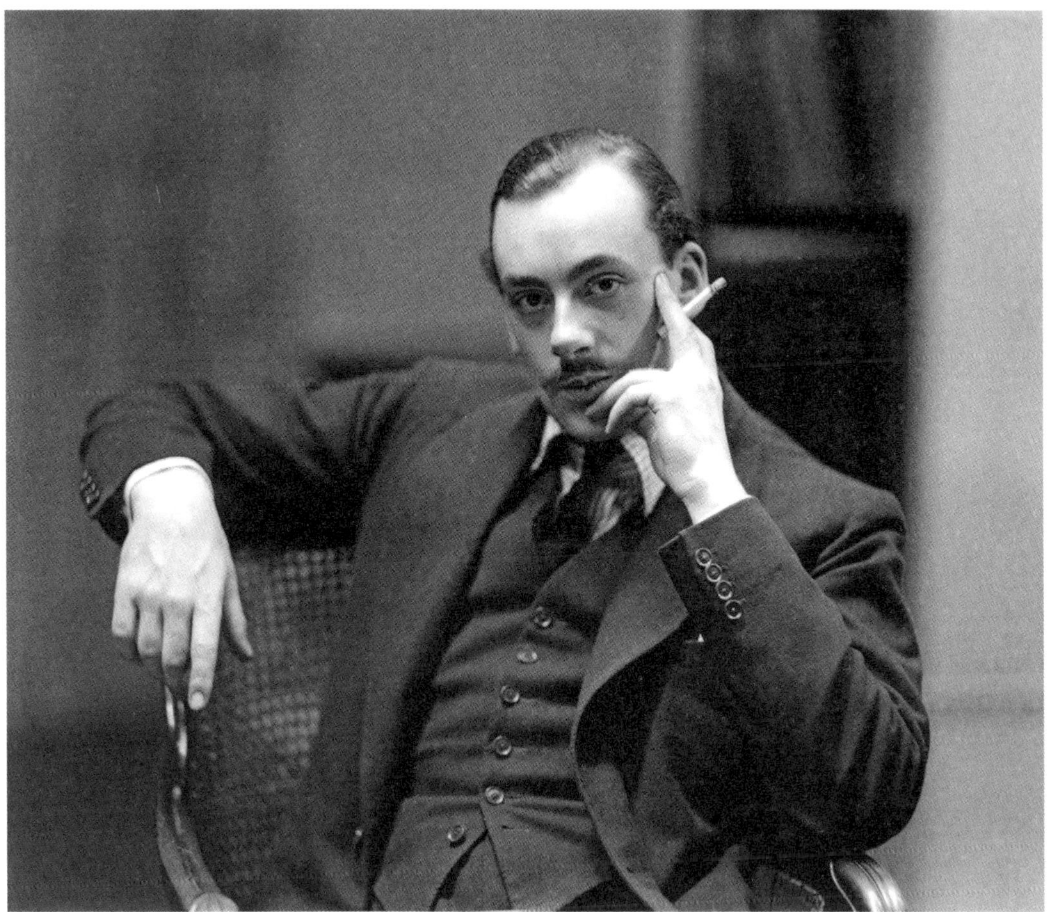

Peter Rose Pulham, photographed by Howard Coster, 1930.

relationship. So much so that when she met the Irish-American writer Constantine FitzGibbon in a local pub one night, she was ready to fall 'passionately, irrevocably in love'. Pulham's reaction was without a trace of jealousy. All he said was, 'I always thought he was just the chap for you.' After she had left him, he wrote her a letter in which he said: 'You rescued me and put me on my feet ... and I shall always be grateful to you. I'm not in love with you ... but I do love you very much.'

Pulham continued painting throughout the dark period of the war and, when it was over, held an exhibition at the Redfern Gallery in 1947. The following year he moved to the London Gallery, which was being run by Édouard Mesens as the centre of surrealist activity in London. It was there that I encountered his work for the first time and was unable to forget his haunting imagery.

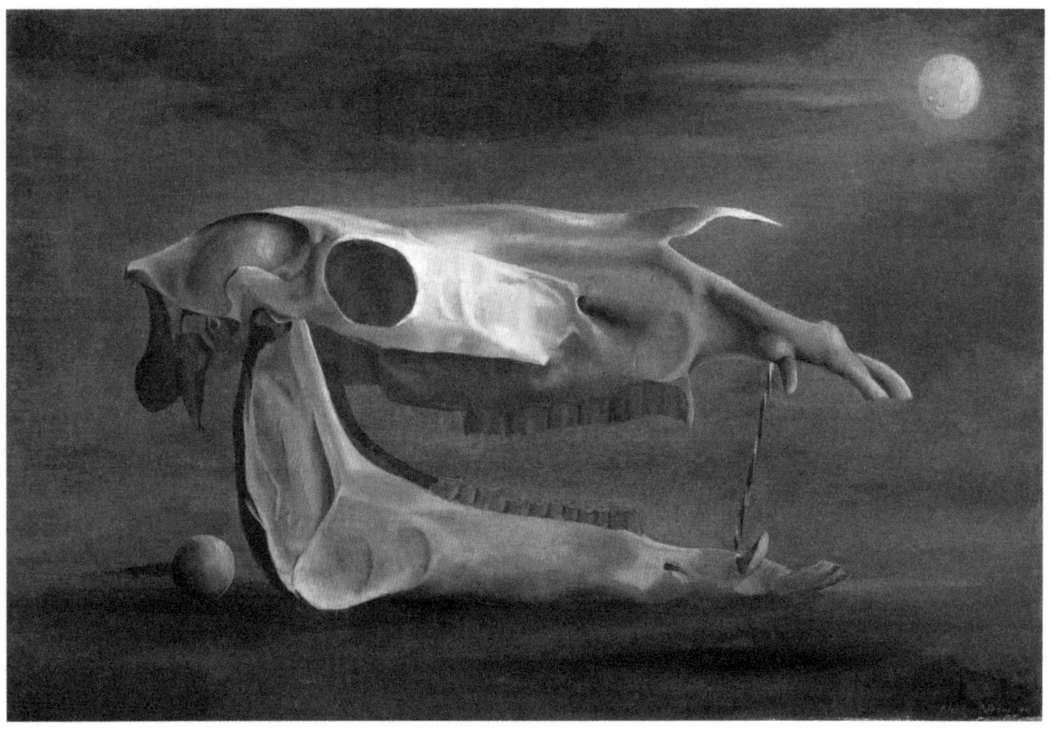

Peter Rose Pulham, *Horse's Skull, Sphere and Moon*, 1941.

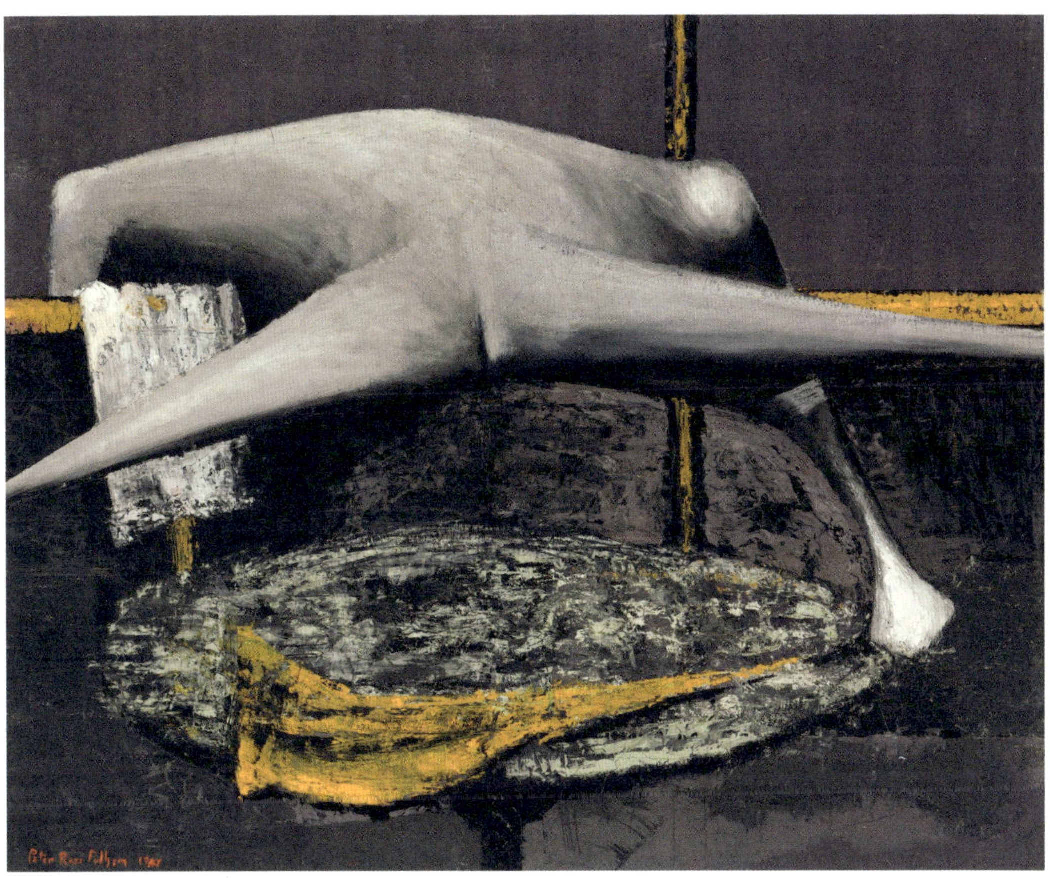

Mesens gave him another show in 1949, and this was followed by one at the Hanover Gallery in 1950, but it was extremely difficult to sell surrealist paintings in this post-war period, and this probably persuaded Pulham to return to photography until 1953. However, something happened to make him give up his life as a photographer and to destroy his negatives. He moved to Conives in central France and died there in 1956, when still only in his mid-forties.

Peter Rose Pulham, *Grisaille Figures I*, 1947.

CERI RICHARDS

Strongly influenced by the International Surrealist Exhibition in 1936

BORN: 6 June 1903 in the village of Dunvant, near Swansea

PARENTS: Father a tinplate foundry worker in Gowerton, active in the local church, wrote poetry and conducted the local choir

LIVED: Dunvant 1908; Swansea 1921; London 1924; Cardiff 1940; London 1945

PARTNER: Married FRANCES CLAYTON, a fellow artist, 1929 (two children)

DIED: 9 November 1971 in London, aged 68

CERI RICHARDS WAS A BRILLIANT WELSH ARTIST who was, perhaps, too intelligent for his own good. He knew too much and responded to too many influences, passing through one phase after another. As a result, he did not develop a single, identifiable style by which he could become widely known. He had a cubist phase, a Matisse phase, a Picasso phase, a lyrical phase, a traditional phase and even an abstract phase. He was good at all of them, but the overall impact was confusing. His most impressive phase, however, was his involvement with surrealism in the 1930s. Some of the surrealist works that he created during that decade can stand comparison with anything the genre has to offer. In 1934 he discovered Jean Arp's simplified surrealist reliefs, and these made a huge impact on him. During the following five years he developed them into much more complex and impressive constructions, and it is these that are, without question, his most memorable works.

Richards was born in a small mining village near Swansea in South Wales at the beginning of the Edwardian period. His father worked in a tinplate factory but was a cultured man who wrote poetry, directed local plays and conducted the local choir. Ceri was taught to play the piano and to appreciate the music of Bach and Handel. At school, his drawings won competitions, and at the age of eighteen he was enrolled at the Swansea School of Art. In 1924 he won a scholarship to the Royal College of Art in London. One of his contemporaries there was Edward Burra, and his teachers included Paul Nash and Henry Moore. It was Moore who was later quoted as saying that

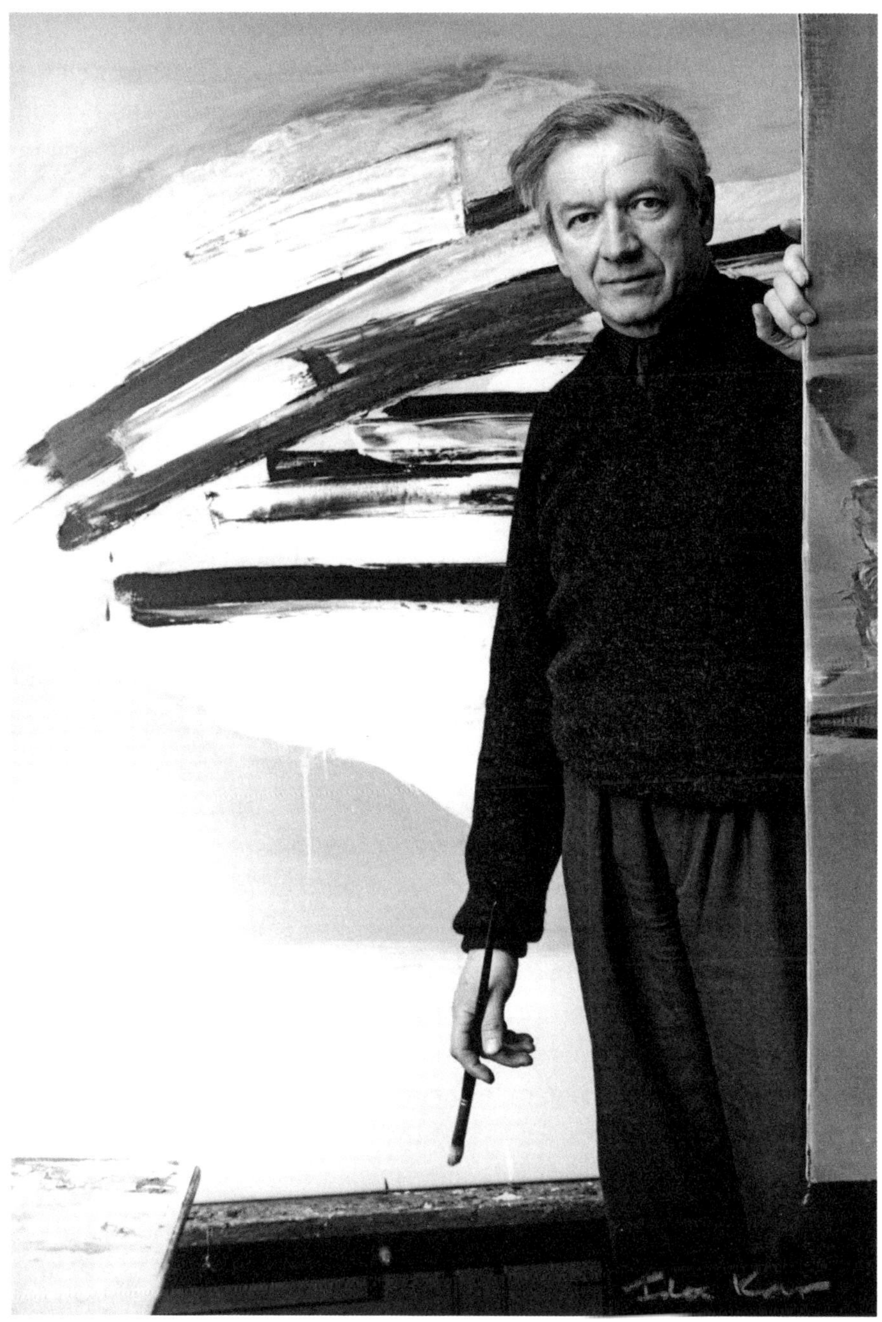

Ceri Richards, photographed by Ida Kar, 1960.

Richards was 'the finest draughtsman of his generation'.

In London Richards haunted Zwemmer's art bookshop, where he acquired all the latest publications concerning the Paris avant-garde and kept up to date with the current developments in the art world there. His son-in-law, Mel Gooding, describes how, all his life, he was always browsing in his extensive collection of art books, 'feeding his imagination as if by a kind of visual osmosis' – even during mealtimes. He rarely returned to Wales, spending most of the rest of his life in London where, in 1929, he married a fellow artist, Frances Clayton; they had two daughters. She was an honest critic of his work but was also convinced of his genius – the ideal partner for a creative artist. Among their friends were the artists Victor Pasmore and Julian Trevelyan, and a young designer called Francis Bacon who said that one day he too wanted to be a painter.

By the early 1930s Richards's work was beginning to show marked surrealist tendencies. In 1935 he acquired a copy of David Gascoyne's book *A Short Survey of Surrealism*, and it is difficult to understand why Richards was not selected for inclusion in the important International Exhibition of Surrealism in London in 1936. Some of his works dating from 1934 and 1935 would certainly have been more devoutly surrealist than some of the works put on show there. Perhaps Richards found Breton's outpourings concerning the political, philosophical and social significance of the surrealist movement distasteful. He certainly never signed any of the manifestos or declarations of the movement and was never a formal member of any of the official surrealist groups. What excited him, when he visited the 1936 exhibition, were the works of art, not the theorizing, although he did attend Breton's lecture at the exhibition and acquired a typescript transcript of it for his library. Commenting on his reaction to the exhibition, he said it 'helped me to be aware of the mystery, even the "unreality" of ordinary things ... I was not influenced by the uncontrolled subconscious element ... but the metaphysical element enthralled me.'

In the late 1930s Richards produced his best surrealist work and, in 1937, his friend Julian Trevelyan brought Jean Arp to his London studio to see his reliefs. Arp must have been rather impressed to see the impact that his own reliefs had had on Richards and the way in which his earlier simplified, embryonic reliefs had grown into much more complicated, adult forms in Richards's hands.

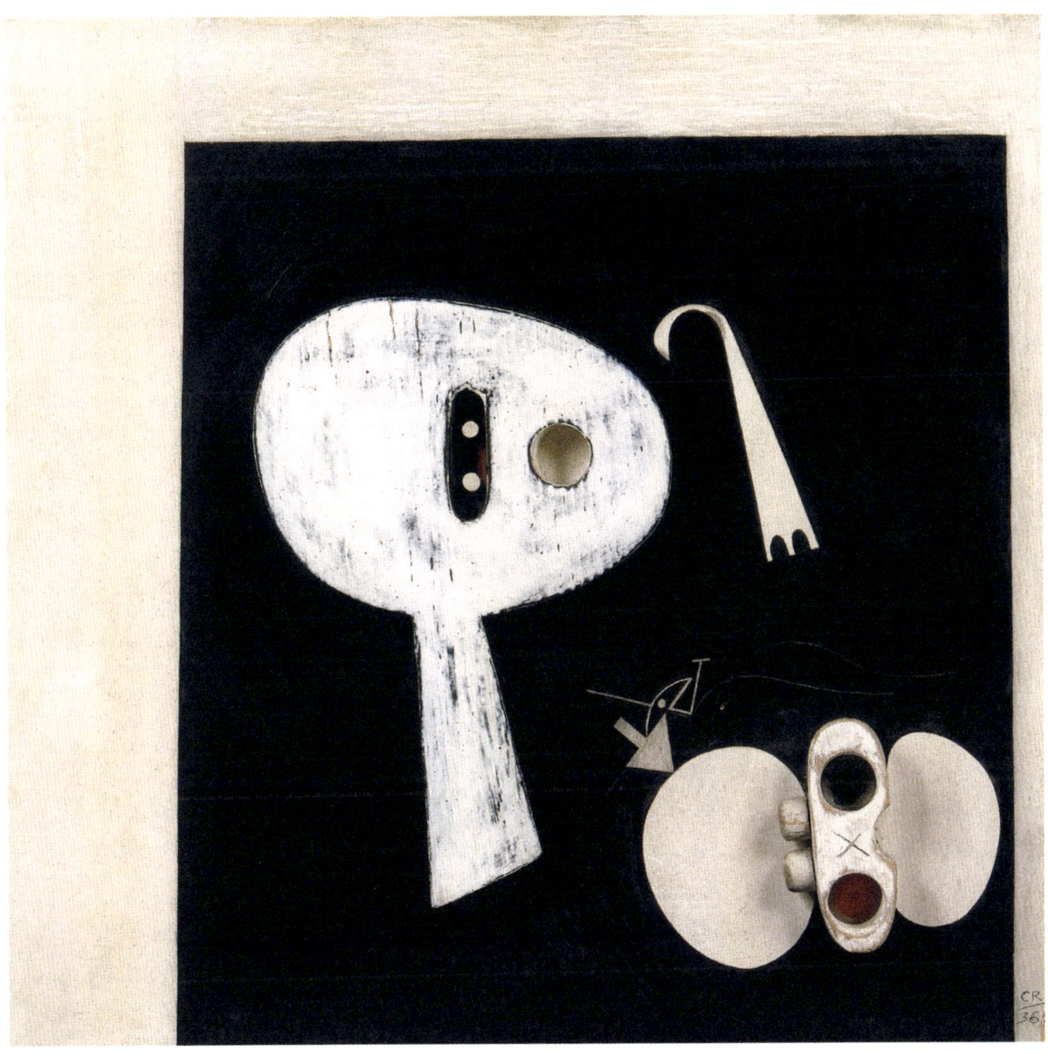

The following year, Richards visited a Max Ernst exhibition at the London Gallery and bought a major work, *The Bride of the Wind* (1926). It is a sinister, turbulent, dynamic composition, and it is noticeable that at this point Richards's own paintings also became more turbulent and restless. This matched the mood of the time as Europe was plunged into World War II. Richards and his wife fled from blitzed London to a village in the country.

Ceri Richards, *White and Dark*, 1936.

They had no income, and Richards had to become a manual labourer on the land. They lived off rabbits and rice pudding.

He was relieved when, in 1940, he was offered a post as head of painting at the Cardiff School of Art. Unfortunately, as a coastal port Cardiff, like London, suffered severe bombing. Richards ended up teaching art during the day and doing Home Guard duty at night, leaving little time for painting. The works he did manage to complete all reflected the restlessness of the period, and some of them still retained a strong surrealist quality. He remained in Cardiff for the duration of the war, returning to London when it was over, to teach at the Chelsea School of Art. At this stage, his work began to lose its surrealist feeling and became more lyrical. In the years that followed, the influences of Picasso and Matisse reasserted themselves, and his images were more figurative, although often with wildly exaggerated shapes and movements.

With the 1950s there was a return to less figurative, more chaotic compositions. Then in 1953, Richards fell seriously ill and twice underwent surgery for the removal of gallstones. Unable to paint and short of money, he had no choice but to sell his beloved Max Ernst painting. It may have been a coincidence, but the paintings he produced after this period were less turbulent, as if the hand of Ernst had been lifted. When Richards was convalescing, he made a visit to Wales to meet Dylan Thomas, and the poet and the painter felt an immediate rapport. They discussed possible joint ventures and would undoubtedly have become close friends, but the following day Thomas left for America where he died shortly afterwards. This moved Richards to make a suite of paintings as an homage to the Welsh poet.

In the 1960s his painting changed yet again, becoming superficially more abstract, although it was an organic abstraction that avoided the sterility of geometric hard-edge work. These paintings were interspersed with occasional sorties into more naturalistic subjects and other works more typical of his turbulent phases. It was as if he found it hard to settle to one form of expression and his vigorous curiosity kept challenging him to try out new ideas. This varying of styles was not attractive to the galleries who were showing his pictures. They preferred a painter's work to avoid such diversity.

To his supporters all this was a sign of his creative versatility. To his detractors it was a sign of indecision and the lack of a recognizable mature style. In 1965 one critic wrote of Richard's work that 'he wanders between

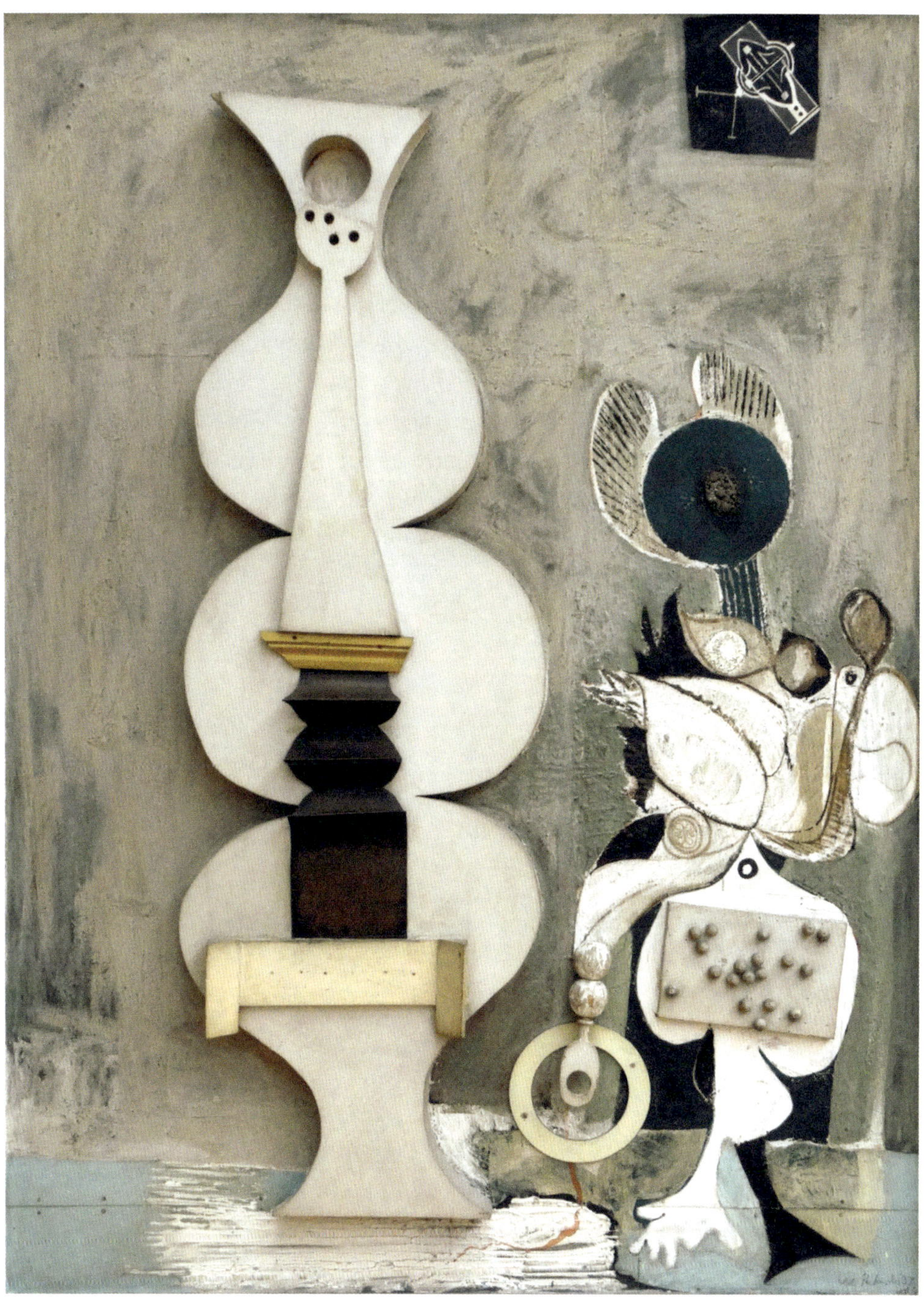

Ceri Richards, *Two Females*, 1937–38.

the worlds of figuration and abstraction with a cheerful ignoring of frontiers that few of his generation have dared to emulate'. Another described him as 'a sort of artistic jackdaw', saying that for him 'modernism was a style, a fashion to be easily donned and just as easily discarded'. The underlying suggestion was that if Richards could jump from one style to another and back again, then he was just playing and neither of them had a deeper meaning for him. This was unfair, but it did explain why his work did not become more widely appreciated. The best way to think of him is as a knowledgeable explorer with a high level of curiosity, capable of throwing himself into one visual or symbolic exploration after another.

After his death in 1971, Henry Moore wrote of him: 'More than any other British painter of his time he understood three-dimensional form and knew how to express it on a flat surface.' Coming from Moore, that was praise indeed.

EDITH RIMMINGTON

Joined the British Surrealist Group in 1940

BORN: 1902 in Leicester

LIVED: Leicester 1902; Manchester 1920s; London 1937; Bexhill-on-Sea, Sussex 1970

PARTNER: Married Robert Baxter, surrealist artist, 1920s

DIED: 1986 in Bexhill-on-Sea, Sussex, aged 84

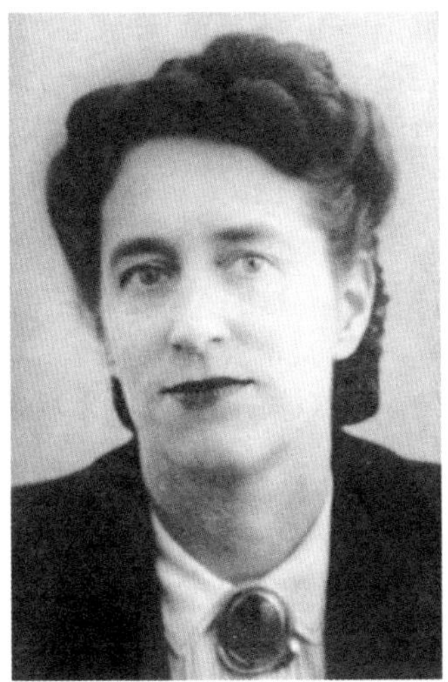

Edith Rimmington plays an important role in the history of British surrealism, but she herself remains a shadowy figure. She created some iconic surrealist images, but little is known about her personal life. Surviving works by Rimmington are extremely rare, but it is not clear whether this is because her output was limited or because much of it was lost. The quality of the works that do survive is so high that it is hard to believe that they are isolated examples.

Edith Rimmington, detail of *Untitled (Self-Portrait)*, collage, date unknown.

A preliminary search through the archives of surrealism reveals only twenty-five works by Rimmington, the earliest from 1938 and the latest from 1972. Her best work appears in the years after World War II. Her most famous painting, called *The Oneiroscopist* (or *Transcriber of Dreams*) and dating from 1947, shows a cloaked, seated figure with the feet of a giant bird, human hands, an insect head and a long, skeletal avian beak. Around its neck is a deep-sea diver's collar, and the diving helmet itself is on the ground next to the figure. This strange hybrid being, a surrealist chimera, is sitting serenely on a platform that is high above the clouds, as if waiting patiently to perform some sort of rescue operation when an emergency occurs below. Unfortunately, this can only be a disaster because its long beak will not fit into the diving helmet. So this patient creature will have to wait for eternity. Despite the minor role that Rimmington played in the history of surrealism, she has, with this one painting, created one of the most memorable images of the entire movement. One author has suggested that the diving helmet may have been included as a joke at the expense of Salvador Dalí, who almost died when he was wearing one at the opening of the International Surrealist Exhibition in London in 1936, and nearly ran out of oxygen.

Rimmington was born in Leicester at the beginning of the Edwardian period and, at the end of World War I, she attended Brighton School of Art, from 1919 until 1922. In the early 1920s she met the surrealist artist Robert Baxter, and they were married in 1926. They moved to Manchester, where Baxter had a teaching post at the art school. During this time Rimmington was concentrating on still-life paintings under the influence of the cubist Juan Gris, but she was dissatisfied with those works and subsequently destroyed them.

In 1936 she made a visit to London to see the important International Surrealist Exhibition at the New Burlington Galleries. The exhibition made a deep impression on her, and she realized that this was the form of art she felt compelled to pursue in future. In 1937 she left Manchester – and her husband – and moved to London, where she found a studio in Camden and set about making contact with the various surrealists who were gathered in the capital. That year, Rimmington's work was included in the 'Surrealist Objects and Poems' exhibition at the London Gallery. In 1939 Gordon Onslow Ford introduced her to the self-styled leader of the British surrealists, Édouard Mesens, and in 1940 she became an official member of his surrealist group,

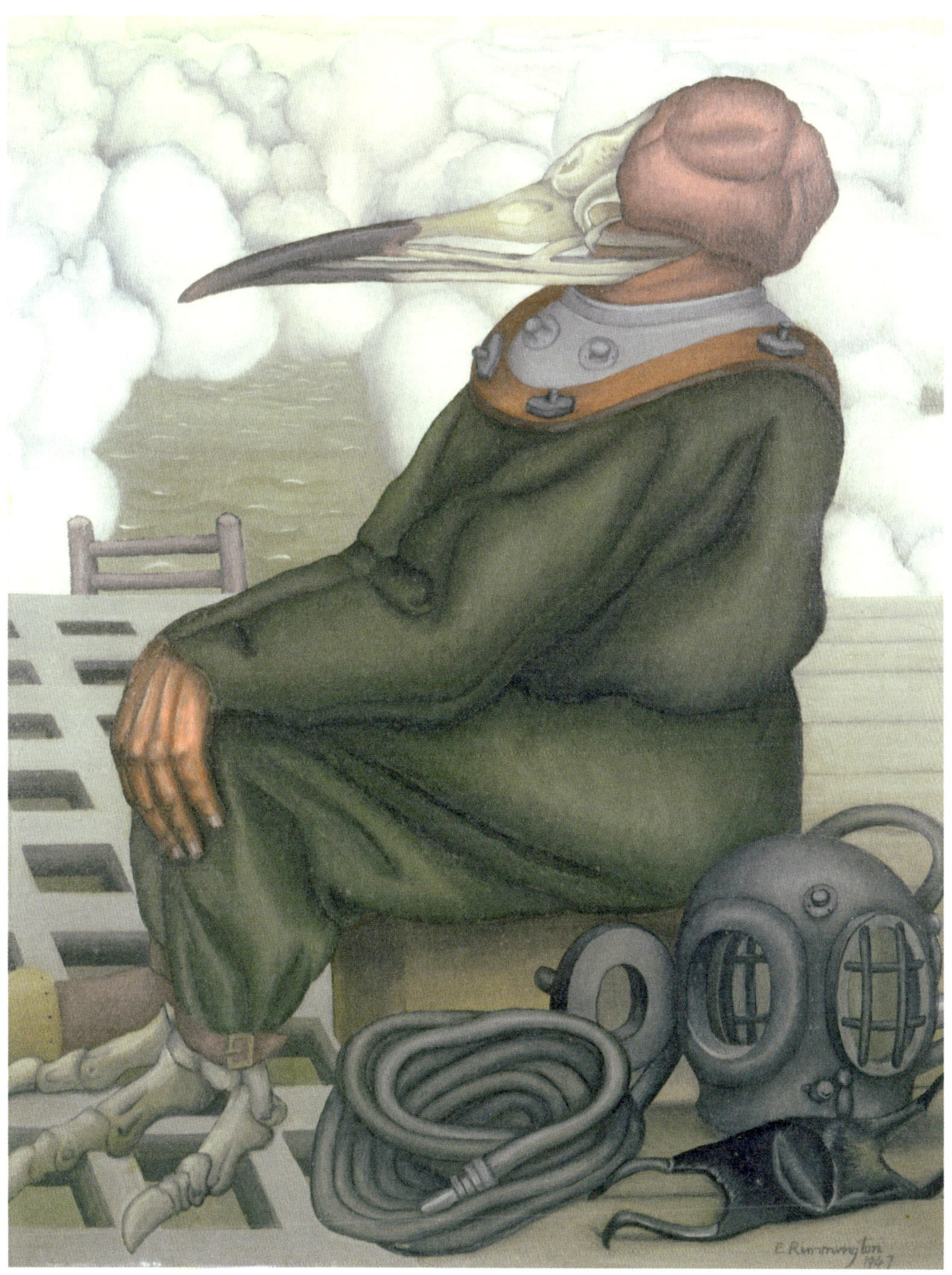

Edith Rimmington, *The Oneiroscopist*, 1947.

regularly attending their weekly meetings at the Barcelona Restaurant in Soho and the Horseshoe Pub in Tottenham Court Road.

Her closest friends during this period were Emmy Bridgwater and Conroy Maddox. She and Emmy occasionally had sessions of automatic drawing and writing in the surrealist tradition. To her credit, Rimmington never became embroiled in the spiteful battle for leadership that broke out between Mesens and Toni del Renzio and their respective factions. She maintained an impartial, balanced position by contributing to the surrealist publications of both of them.

In a letter to a friend, Rimmington complained that her wartime work as a secretary to the Latvian healer Stanley Lief was interfering with her painting activities. There may be more to it than that, however, because it is rumoured that, when her marriage to Baxter ended, either in divorce or on his death, she had an affair with Lief, the founder of the famous Champneys Spa at Tring in Hertfordshire. Although she did little painting during World War II, between 1940 and 1947 Rimmington was an active contributor to the many pamphlets and other publications produced by the surrealist group during that difficult period. Her surrealist writings during the war reveal how obsessed she had become with the violence of the period and the ever-present threat of death: 'Death is alive in rhythm at the screech of the siren like a calm box pouring out music, projecting a lifetime through endless rooms ... As death moves slowly, oh the torture of waiting for a new rhythm.'

After the war she exhibited in the major international surrealist exhibition at the Maeght Gallery in Paris in 1947 and also at Knokke-le-Zoute in Belgium in 1951. For some reason she abandoned her easel in 1967, when her focus of interest shifted from painting and drawing to photography. She spent her later years living at the seaside in Bexhill-on-Sea, in south-east England, where she died in 1986.

Michel Remy, in his study of British surrealism, has described her as 'an outstandingly powerful visionary provocateur whose images, once seen, can hardly be forgotten'.

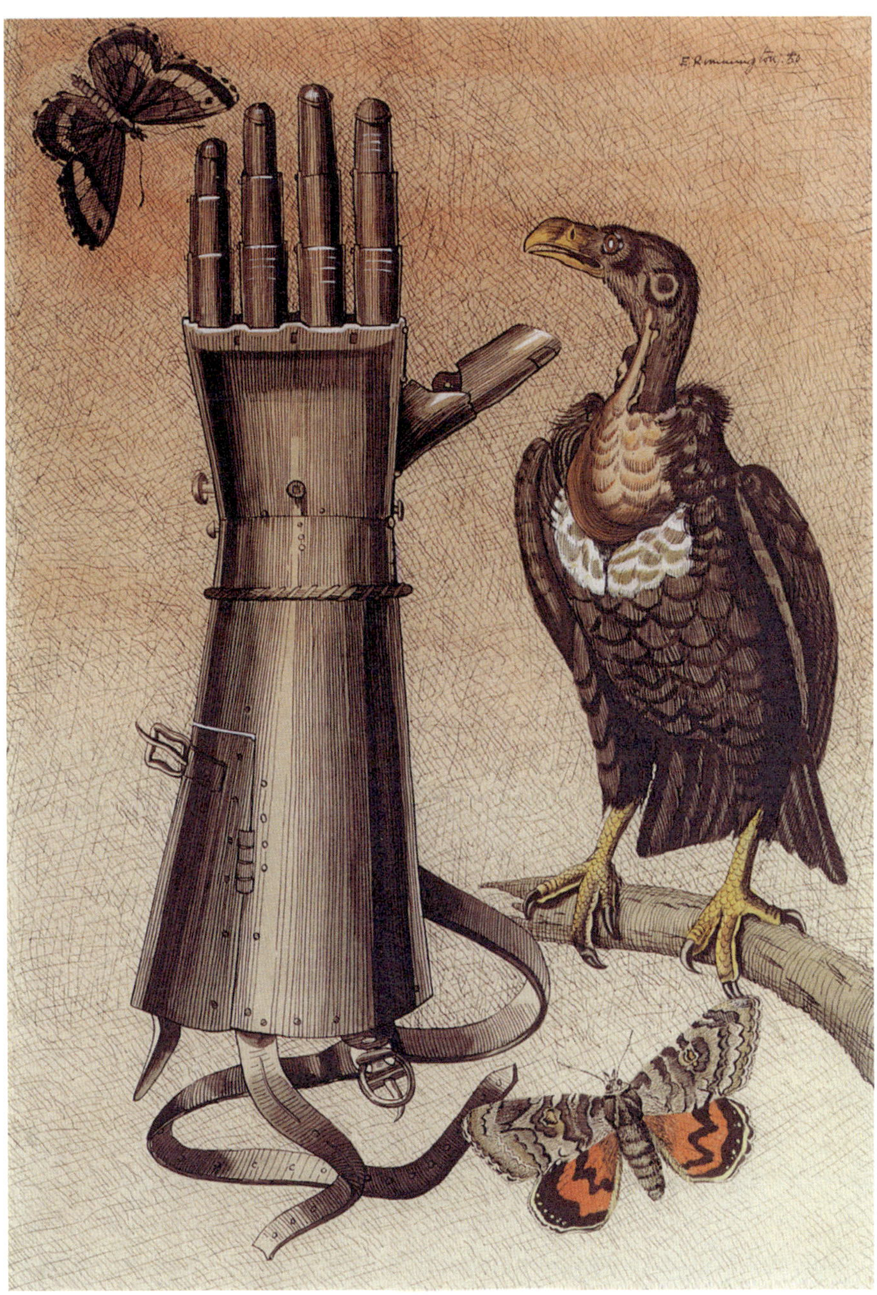

Edith Rimmington, *Relative Strength*, 1950.

GRAHAM SUTHERLAND

Exhibited with the surrealists but never a member of the group

BORN: 24 August 1903 in Streatham, London

PARENTS: Father a lawyer and civil servant

LIVED: Merton Park, Surrey 1903; Sutton, Surrey 1912; Derby 1919; London 1921; Farningham, Kent 1927; Trottiscliffe, Kent 1936; Tetbury, Gloucestershire 1939; Trottiscliffe, Kent 1940; Menton, France 1955

PARTNER: Married Kathleen Barry 1927 (until his death in 1980) (one son, died aged 3 months)

DIED: 17 February 1980 in London, aged 76

The purists were horrified to see Graham Sutherland included as an exhibitor in the great International Surrealist Exhibition in London in 1936. Here was an artist who was a brilliant landscape painter and a highly accomplished portraitist, who had never been associated with the surrealist movement in any way. Why had Roland Penrose invited him to send two works to the exhibition? Was he just trying to make up the numbers, so that British Surrealism was well represented on this special surrealist occasion? The truth is that Roland Penrose had spotted in the work of Sutherland a natural tendency to let his visual imagination take over his paintings and allow natural forms to develop into strange beings. Indeed, many of his paintings embodied a more intense surrealism than some of the works by the orthodox members of the movement. His series of 'Thorn Heads', for example, are surrealist masterpieces.

What was awkward about his inclusion in the exhibition was that he was not the least bit attracted to the surrealist movement. He was very much a solitary artist and would certainly have hated the idea of attending a surrealist meeting or engaging in the revolutionary philosophizing that would take place there. As a result, he has been written out of surrealist history. In 1944, the committed surrealist John Banting published a savage attack on Sutherland, in which he described him as a 'gentleman' who 'probably

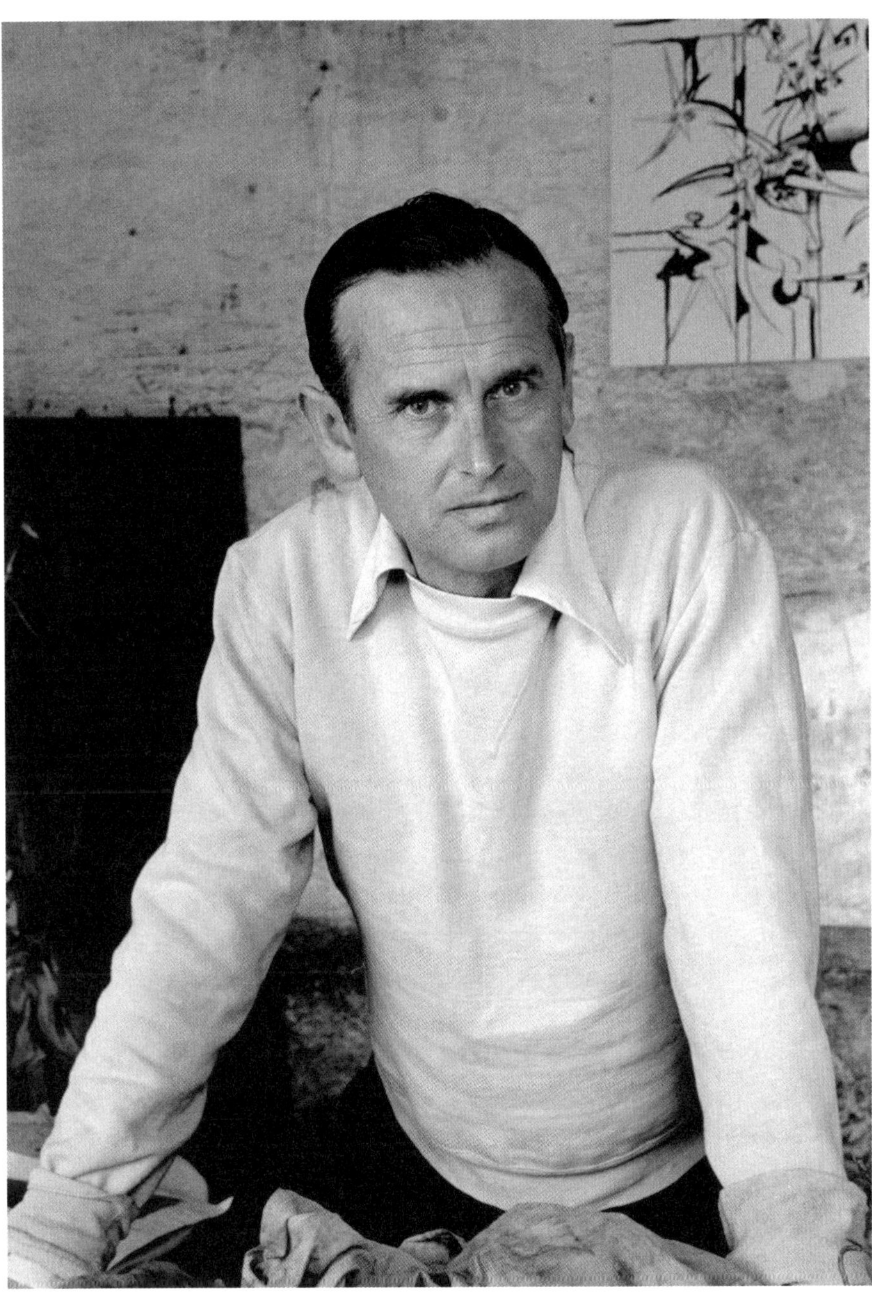

Graham Sutherland, photographed by Nat Farbman, 1953.

has no adventures, even in his sleep' and who is one of the 'Good boys of Modern Style ... the White Hope of the Gloomsbury Pinks'. More recently, in a three-volume encyclopedia of surrealism he is only mentioned once, where it says that 'his paintings were far removed from any surrealist commitment'. This is, of course, the key error about his work. It was not his paintings that were far removed, it was he himself. Like many other British artists who produced surrealist paintings, he was not a 'party member'. His surrealism occurred naturally, without any help from outside.

In a magazine interview in 1966, when asked to look back on his participation in the 1936 surrealist exhibition, Sutherland finally took his revenge on the doctrinaire surrealists who had sneered at him, saying: 'I should hate my paintings to be called surrealist.... For the most part I think surrealism far too smooth and very badly done.' He did, however, concede that surrealism had helped him to see the extraordinary in ordinary objects, and it was this, undoubtedly, that had led him to transform natural countryside features into surrealist beings. He makes the key point that 'I can't invent unless I've got something to invent from. But [thanks to surrealism] I can carry it further.'

To sum up, it was not so much that Sutherland disliked surrealism itself, but rather that he, the rural countryman, who appears on the cover of his biography wearing muddy wellington boots, disliked the intensely urban surrealist party members.

Sutherland was born in 1903 in London. When he finished school, his family sent him to Derby to work as an engineering apprentice in a railway locomotive works, but he was able to persuade them that this was not for him and, in 1921, he was enrolled at an art college in London. There he met Kathleen Barry, a sixteen-year-old Irish art student. He courted her for six years until they were finally married in 1927. The marriage lasted for over half a century until his death in 1980.

Sutherland had graduated in 1926 and, by the 1930s, was fully occupied painting his strange landscapes in which natural forms became exaggerated into often sinister shapes. When war broke out in 1939, he and Kathleen moved to live in the Gloucester countryside but, as an official war artist, he found himself visiting many industrial sites to make visual records of the damage done by the German bombing. In the post-war period he undertook some major religious commissions that would have angered the surrealists had they not already rejected him. He then went on to produce a series of

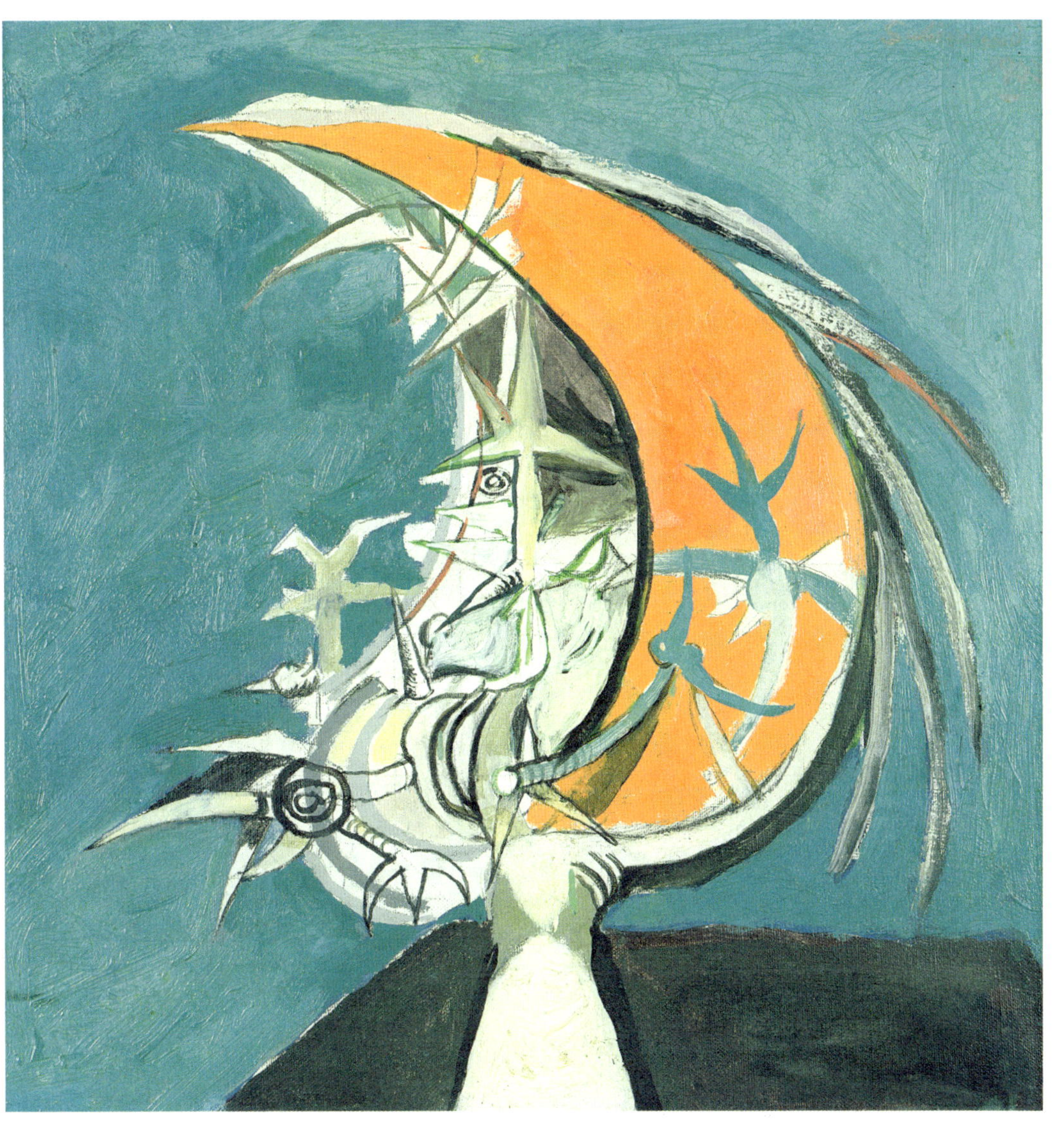

Graham Sutherland, *Thorn Head*, 1947.

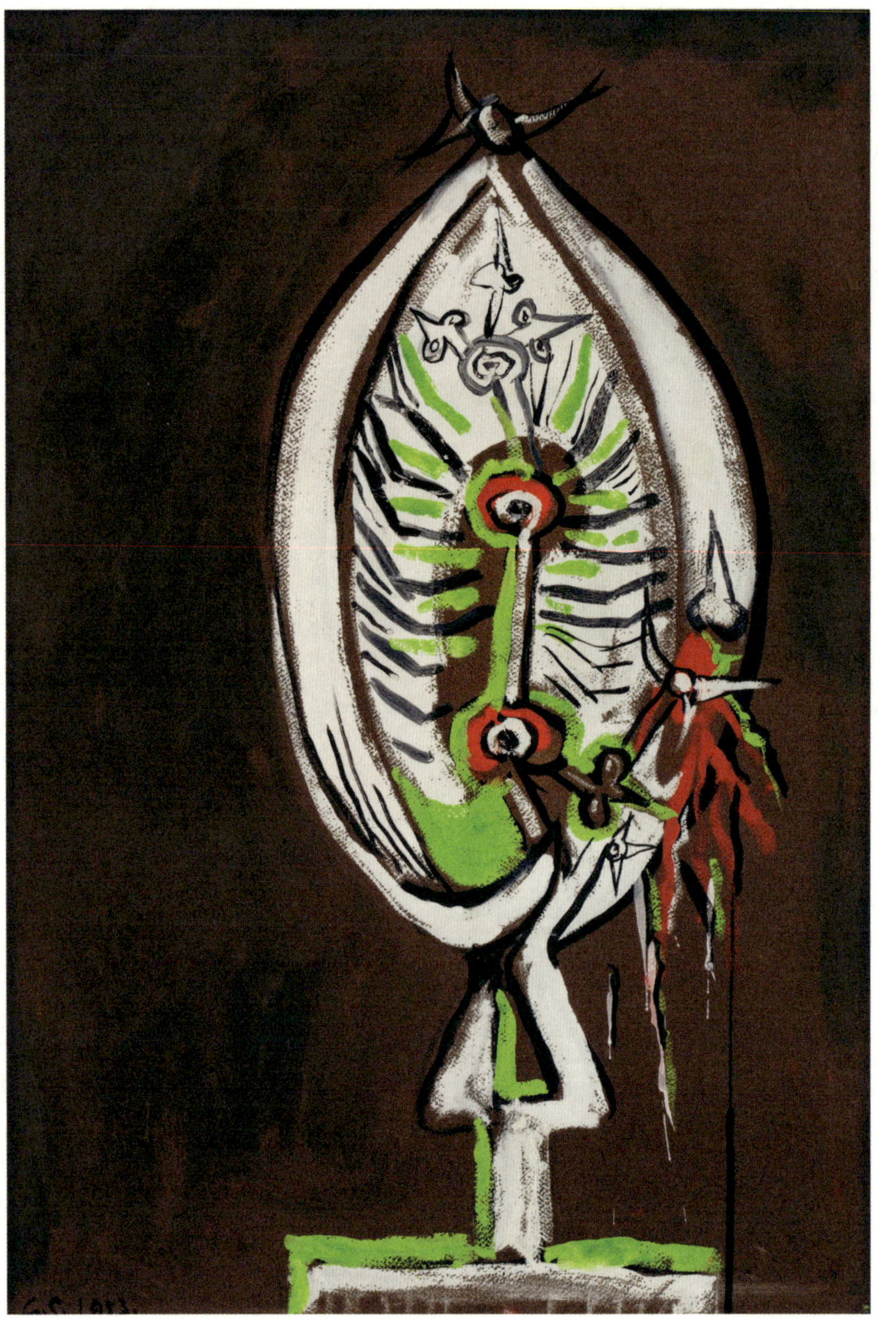

Graham Sutherland, *Thorn Head*, 1953.

masterful portraits of the rich and famous. In 1955 he and Kathleen bought a villa in the south of France and, in his later years, he enjoyed painting in the relaxed atmosphere of the French Riviera. It was more like the life of a society artist than that of a surrealist rebel, and yet his imagery, when he was away from his commissions, always retained that special inventiveness that marked him out as an artist who was susceptible to irrational exaggeration and the creation of genuinely surrealist compositions. It is not so surprising, therefore, that in the spring of 1951, fifteen years after the great Surrealist Exhibition of 1936, the godfather of British surrealism, Roland Penrose, gave Sutherland a major retrospective at his Institute of Contemporary Arts in London.

JULIAN TREVELYAN

Joined the British Surrealist Group in 1936

BORN: 20 February 1910 in Dorking, Surrey

PARENTS: Father a poet and scholar; mother a Dutch violinist

LIVED: Dorking 1910; Cambridge 1928; Paris 1931; London 1935

PARTNERS: Married URSULA DARWIN, potter, 1934 (great-granddaughter of Charles Darwin); dissolved 1950 (one child) • Married MARY FEDDEN, painter, 1951 (until his death in 1988)

DIED: 12 July 1988 in Hammersmith, London, aged 78

JULIAN TREVELYAN WAS AN IMAGINATIVE LANDSCAPE ARTIST who went through an intense surrealist phase in the mid-1930s and whose work was included in the International Surrealist Exhibition in London in 1936. Trevelyan's early life was spent in a country house near Dorking in Surrey, where his scholarly father entertained philosophers and art historians such as Bertrand Russell and Bernard Berenson. At the age of seven, young Julian was already filling sketchbooks with drawings and by eleven had invented an imaginary town, designed entirely by himself, complete with detailed street maps. By the age of fourteen he was making accomplished paintings of industrial landscapes.

From 1928 until 1931 Trevelyan read English Literature at Cambridge University. His fellow students included the infamous spies Anthony Blunt and Guy Burgess. It is said that he himself might have been recruited for espionage work, but his friendly, sociable personality meant that he would never have been capable of keeping a secret. His other fellow students included his best friend Humphrey Jennings, who was already making surrealist pictures, Tom Harrison, who later founded the Mass-Observation research project, Jacob Bronowski, who would one day present the *Ascent of Man* on television, and Kathleen Raine, the poet, who married the surrealist writer Hugh Dykes Davies.

When he was only twenty-one, Trevelyan left England and spent four formative years in Paris. It was a great release from his sheltered childhood

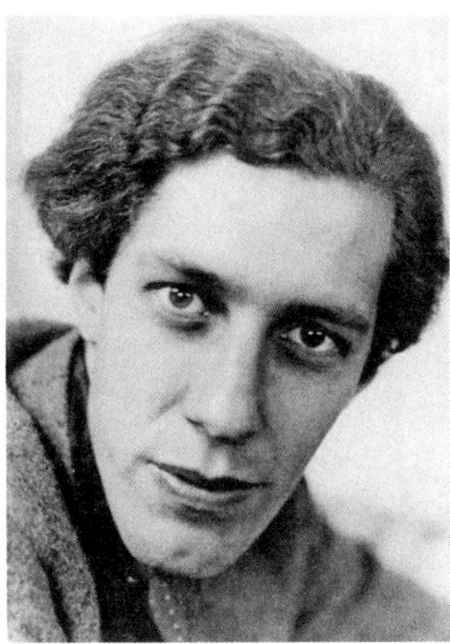

and what he called his 'tea and biscuits' days at Cambridge. Financed by his father, he took a studio in Montparnasse and, in his own words, 'Into this cauldron I flung myself avidly.' He soon found himself drinking in bars with Alberto Giacometti and other surrealists. His next door neighbour was the American Alexander Calder, who was busy making his moving sculptures, and Trevelyan bought one of the first of these.

It was during 1931, his first year in Paris, that Trevelyan made his first surrealist drawings and paintings. The following year, when he was still only twenty-one, he met the printmaker Stanley William Hayter and attended his engraving workshop, working alongside Picasso, Miró, Masson and Ernst. On one occasion Trevelyan tried to persuade Picasso to use a mirror to sign his etchings, so that the letters would appear the right way round, but Picasso refused, saying that he preferred his signature to be read backwards because that way it was 'more alive'. In 1932 Trevelyan, on a trip to Munich, saw Hitler addressing a rally of 50,000 storm troopers. He found it alarming and described it as a 'new religion'.

While he was in Paris, Trevelyan enjoyed a number of brief love affairs, but became increasingly attracted to a pottery student at the Royal College of Art in London, whom he had met on one of his occasional visits back

Julian Trevelyan, date unknown.

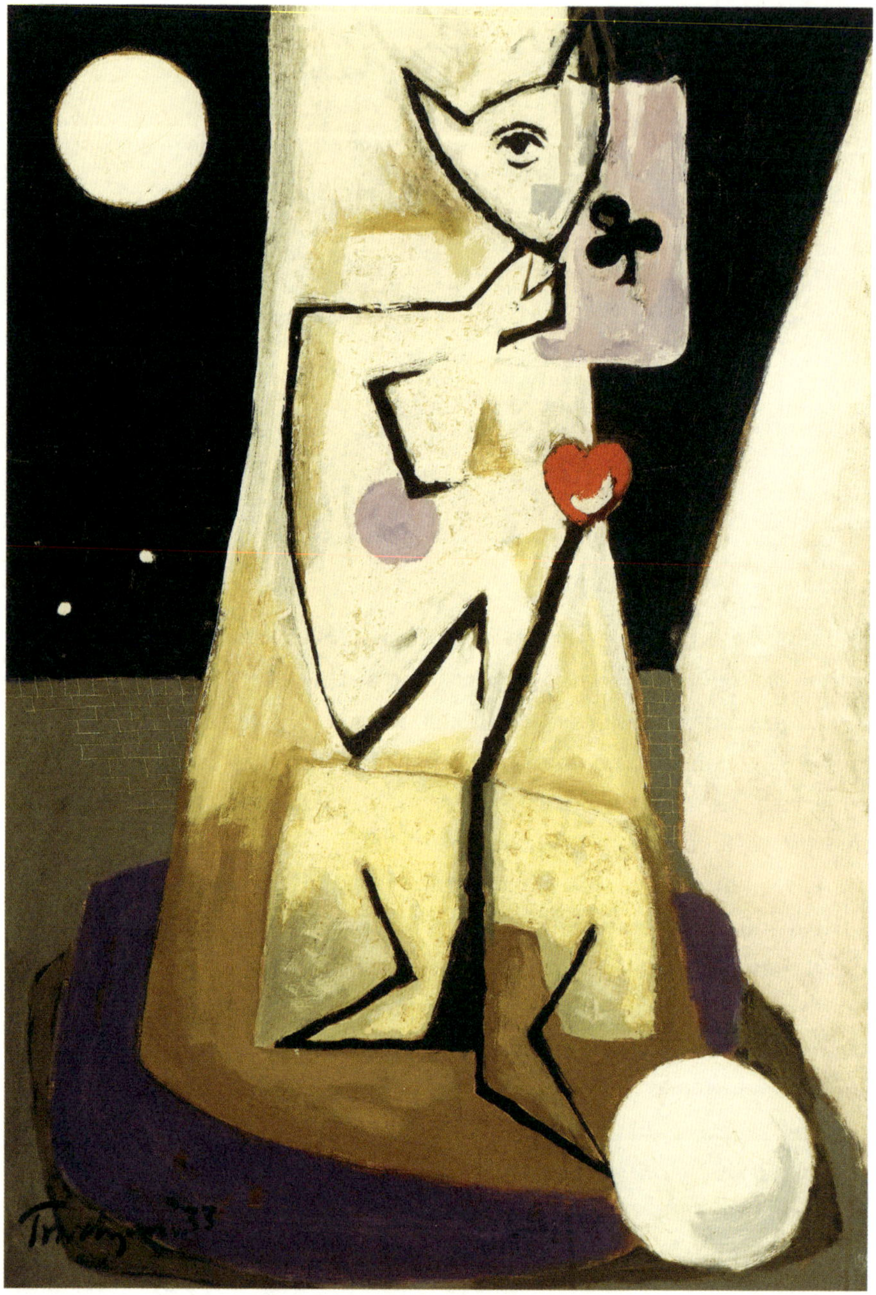

Julian Trevelyan, *Standing Figure with Ace of Clubs*, 1933.

home. Her name was Ursula Darwin, and she was the great-granddaughter of Charles Darwin. In 1933 he managed to persuade her to visit him in Paris and they were married in London in the following year. In 1935 Trevelyan abandoned Paris and bought a group of old riverside buildings on the Thames in London, called Durham Wharf. He and Ursula set up their studios there and, although she departed when their marriage ended in 1950, it would remain Julian's home for the rest of his life.

Having lost his Parisian friends, the gregarious Trevelyan now set about creating a new network of contacts in London. These included most of the British surrealists, such as Roland Penrose, Herbert Read, Ceri Richards, Cecil Collins, John Tunnard and the sculptor F. E. McWilliam. His own work now took on a new flavour, influenced by Klee, Miró, Masson and Ernst, and by 1936 he had developed a highly recognizable, personal urban world that marked the peak of his surrealist involvement. It was in this year that he was invited to contribute to the International Surrealist Exhibition, held at the New Burlington Galleries in London, where five of his works were shown. It was also in 1936 that he and several other surrealists took part in an experimental trial of the hallucinatory drug mescaline at London's Maudsley Hospital. Trevelyan made drawings under the influence of this drug and found the experience exhilarating.

At Durham Wharf, Julian now began a long series of gatherings and parties at which virtually the whole of London's avant-garde art world would turn up at one time or another. He also began to drift away from surrealism, and his paintings became more and more concerned with industrial landscapes. They still had a surrealist flavour but were increasingly based on his response to external scenes rather than internal dreams. He still felt obliged to attend surrealist meetings but finally, in 1938, he wrote to Roland Penrose and told him that he was resigning from the British Surrealist Group. This did not mean that he severed all his friendships with the other surrealists, but that he would no longer play an active part in the movement.

When war broke out in 1939, Julian and Ursula happened to be in France and had to make a wild rush to get the last ferry back to England. On board they found Roland Penrose and Lee Miller making the same trip home. The war changed Trevelyan's imagery and his style of painting, with surrealism now fading into a distant memory. He was called up and became a lieutenant in the Royal Corps of Engineers, using his visual skills to create camouflage patterns for concrete pillboxes. Like all soldiers during the war, Trevelyan had to wear an identity disc stating his name and his religion, so that, were he to be killed, he could be given an appropriate burial ceremony. On his disc he gave 'surrealist' as his religion and wondered what kind of service he might get as a result.

In 1942 he was sent to the Middle East and North Africa to inspect their camouflage defences. He narrowly escaped death and was moved to write that 'Surrealism lost much of its impetus during the war.' He felt it was absurd to make surrealist pictures when life was imitating art so violently, pointing out that, when German soldiers, carrying machine guns and dressed as nuns, were descending from the clouds in parachutes, 'life had caught up with surrealism and surrealism with life'. His experiences in the army eventually reduced him to a state of almost suicidal depression, and in 1943 he ended up in a psychiatric unit where, after treatment, he was released into civilian life as a 'psycho-neurotic'. Able to paint again, he regained his composure, and he and Ursula soon had a son who was born in a deserted maternity ward at the height of an air raid.

After the war, Trevelyan took a studio in Paris and his relationship with his wife, back in London, became increasingly remote. In 1948 both of them had become romantically involved with other people, and by 1950 their marriage was at an end. The following year he married the artist Mary Fedden, and together they revived Durham Wharf as a centre for people in the London art world, with many social gatherings and parties.

At this point Trevelyan's art became more representational and the surrealist influences of the past faded away. He was gradually absorbed into the art establishment and undertook teaching duties at the Royal College of Art. Towards the end of his life he was awarded a senior fellowship at the Royal College and was also appointed a Royal Academician. In his own work, landscape became his dominant theme, and this remained his principle preoccupation for the rest of his life. There were occasional exceptions to this general rule, however, when Trevelyan's rebellious spirit bubbled momentarily to the surface. In 1955, for example, he experimented again with working under the influence of mescaline, creating some crudely painted surrealist works that never left his studio.

In his later years he travelled a great deal, painting and sketching wherever he went. There were trips to Yugoslavia, Russia, France, Italy, Spain,

Morocco, Lanzarote, Crete, Turkey, Portugal, Uganda, the United States, India and Malta. It was in Malta in 1970 that I last encountered him. We had met many years before in London when we were involved in broadcast discussions on the nature of art at the BBC. But in 1970 I was living in Malta and was delighted to find that Julian had produced a 'Malta Suite' of prints. They had captured the spirit of that complex little island perfectly, and I acquired a complete set of them. My only sadness, knowing of his surrealist past, was that he had abandoned his earlier explorations of an internal world and was now satisfied with summarizing in paint the external world that he encountered on his travels.

He was still painting vigorously in 1988, the year of his death at the age of seventy-eight. His widow, Mary Fedden, lived on for another quarter of a century, with one of his final paintings always hanging above her bed. She eventually enjoyed great success as an artist herself, dying in 2012 at the advanced age of ninety-six.

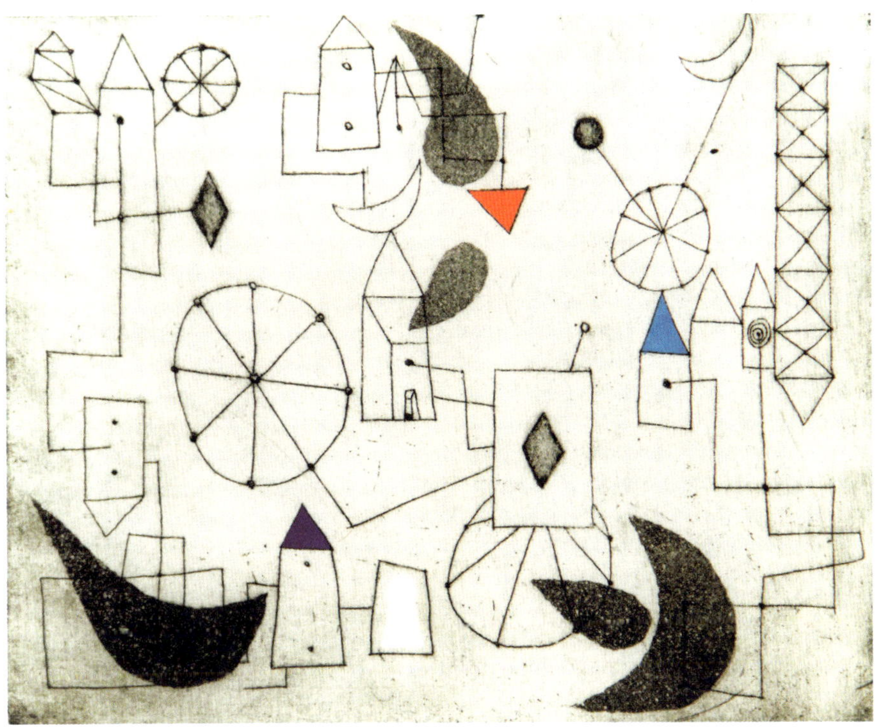

Julian Trevelyan, *Bicycle Shop*, 1937.

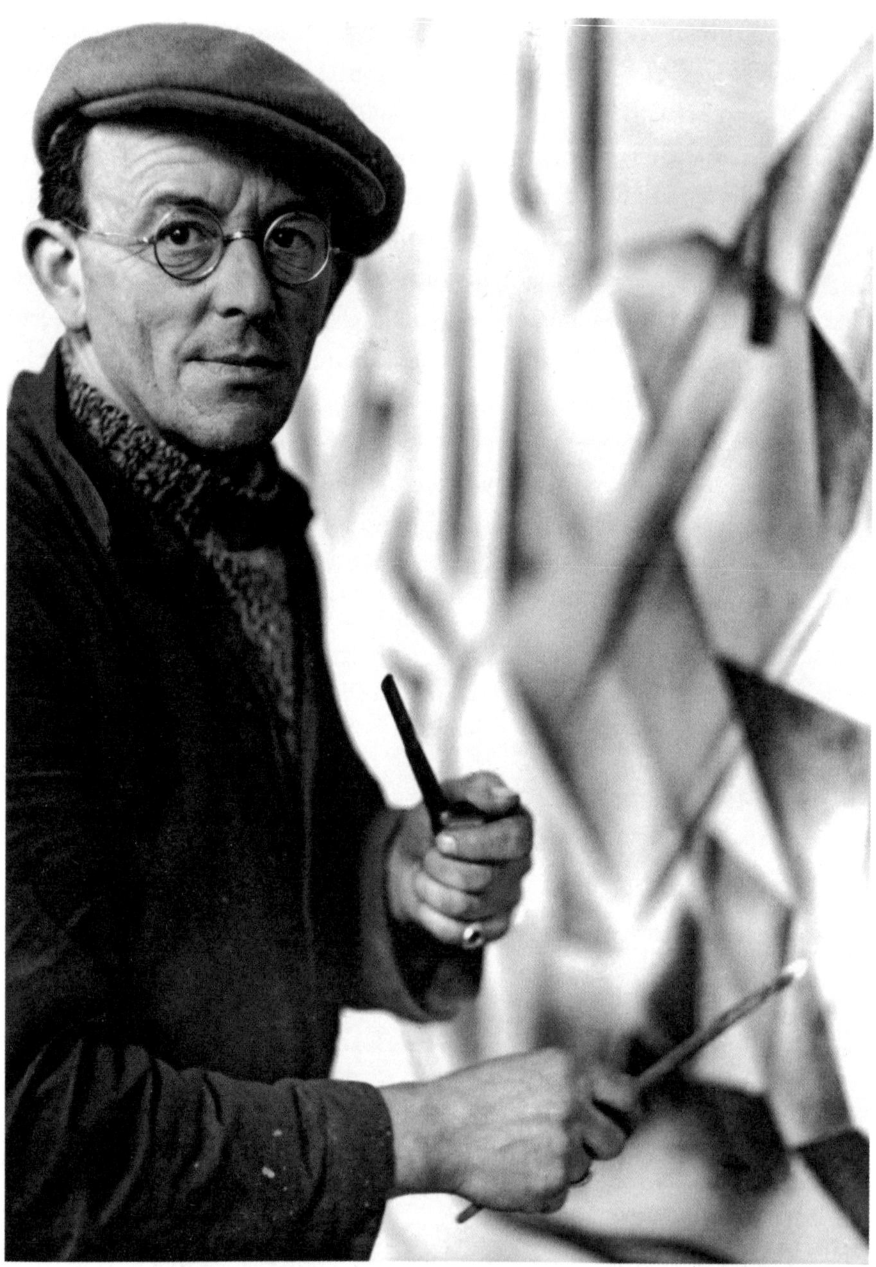

John Tunnard, 1951.

JOHN TUNNARD

Embraced British surrealism but remained outside the group

BORN: 17 May 1900 in Sandy, Bedfordshire

PARENTS: Wealthy landowners; ancestry traced to the Sheriff of Lincoln in 1440

LIVED: Sandy 1900; London 1919; Manchester 1921; Bridgnorth, Shropshire 1926; London 1928; Cadgwith, Cornwall 1933; Lamorna, Cornwall 1952; Penzance 1970

PARTNER: Married Mary May Robertson 1926 (until her death in 1970)

DIED: 12 December 1971 in Penzance, aged 71

Tunnard was described by those who knew him as a larger-than-life figure. Although his work was seen as being on the edge of surrealism, hovering dangerously close to abstraction, he himself seems to have been an out-and-out surrealist in his behaviour. Peggy Guggenheim, who gave him one of his first exhibitions at her gallery in London, commented on his bizarre costumes. He appeared at his private view wearing a blue-checked suit, a light blue pullover and a bright pink tie. Later, at another of Peggy's gallery evenings, he appeared in a peacock blue suit with a green and red scarf and a large red carnation in his buttonhole.

She also mentioned his remarkable athleticism, an attribute he demonstrated in a startling way at his private view. Overhearing a visitor asking, 'Who is John Tunnard?', he aimed himself at her from across the room and performed three somersaults, landing at her feet and declaring theatrically, 'I am John Tunnard.' An elderly gentleman, peering at his paintings, commented that the man who did them wasn't healthy; Tunnard sprang into action again, turning another somersault and landing in front of the man with an extended hand saying, 'I am perfectly healthy.'

Writing in 1939, Tunnard's friend Julian Trevelyan described him as a man whose face was a mixture 'between a fox's and a giant panda's', a man who laughs like a jackal 'so that you can hear him two blocks away', a man who is always talking about 'shipwrecks and pirates', a man who turns Cornish fishermen into jitterbugs, a man who makes musical instruments that don't make a sound. Getting into his stride, Trevelyan concluded by saying: 'Tunnard's a hot jazz-king, Tunnard's a good cook, Tunnard's the man who talks outside the performing fleas, Tunnard's a husband, Tunnard's a scream.'

He was born in Victorian England at Sandy in Bedfordshire. His family were wealthy and enjoyed rural pursuits, so that as a child the young Tunnard saw a great deal of the English countryside. He was sent away to boarding school when very young and later to Charterhouse, where his skill at drawing was noted. In the holidays he spent a great deal of time observing wildlife and also wildfowling, becoming adept at the use of a punt gun. When he left school, he moved to London where, at the end of World War I, he enrolled at the Royal College of Art. He joined a jazz band as the drummer, and his interest in music could later be traced in some of the motifs of his paintings.

After graduating, he worked with textile, carpet and fabric companies until he became a teacher in design at a London art school in 1929. By now he was married to a fellow art student and relations with his family had soured. Moving to Cornwall in 1933, he and his wife, Mary May Robertson, set up a silk-printing business to raise money. It is clear that no financial support from his wealthy family was forthcoming at this stage in his life, because he and Mary May made the journey to Cornwall in a gypsy caravan in which they lived for some months before finally renting a cottage.

In the years that followed, Tunnard divided his days between his design work and his serious painting. The hand-blocked silk business took up a lot of his time, but he was also painting scenes of the local landscape. In 1933 and 1934 these paintings were rather boringly conventional. Then, suddenly, in 1935 a transformation took place. His landscapes no longer showed houses, boats and trees, but instead were populated by strange abstract shapes. There were geometric elements present, but these were mixed with simplified, natural forms. Some people called his work abstract, but it was never entirely that. True, it had abstract features, but the overall effect was to create a private world of his own in which unidentifiable shapes filled his landscapes. In spirit, his work was much closer to that of certain of the surrealists than to the bleak geometry of artists like Piet Mondrian and Ben Nicholson. Supporting this view is a comment he made about the main influences fuelling his break away from representational art, citing Joan Miró and Paul Klee as his two most important sources of inspiration. And, in 1937, he exhibited his work in two important surrealist exhibitions.

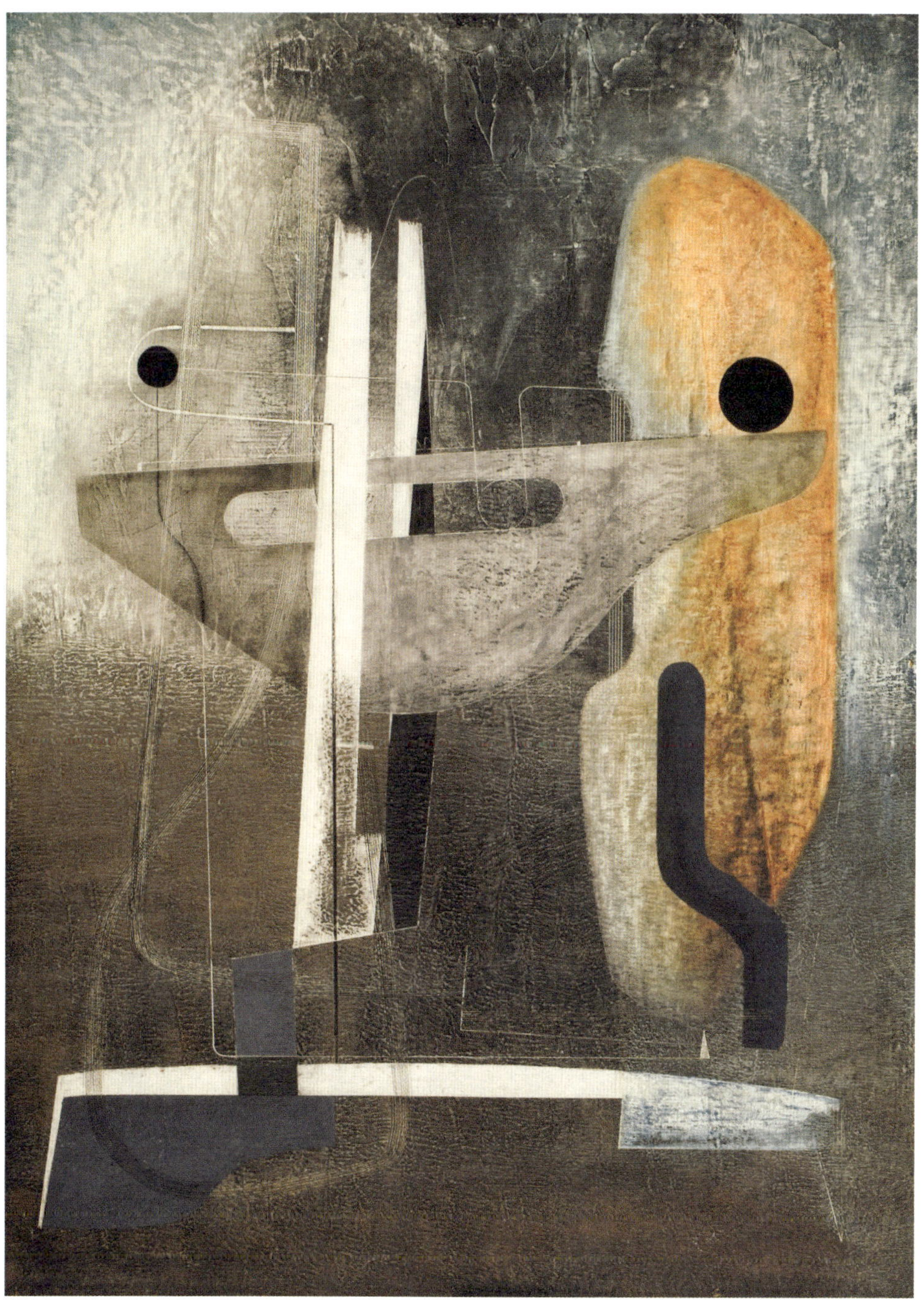

John Tunnard, *Installation*, 1942.

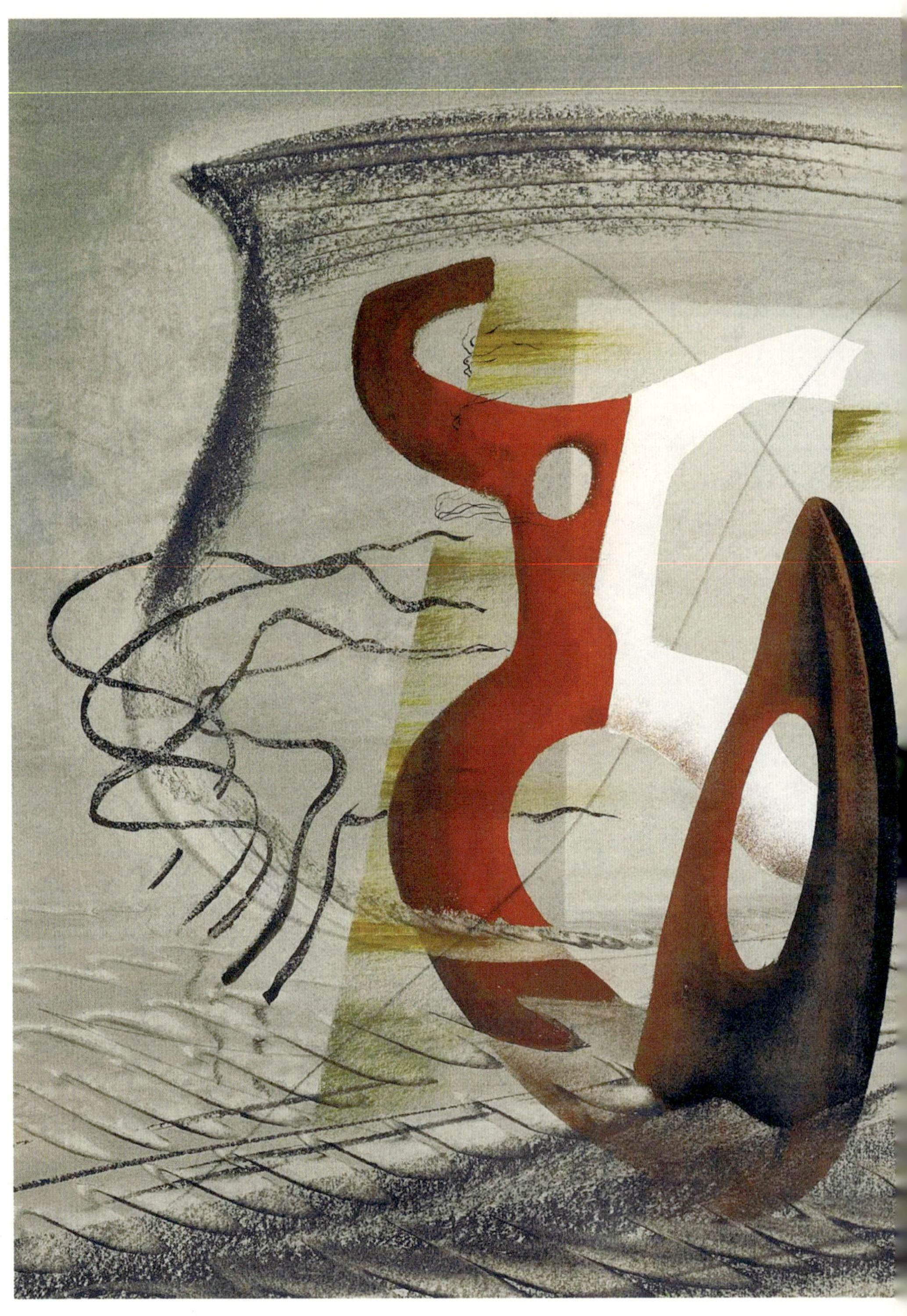

John Tunnard, *Tide Race*, 1947.

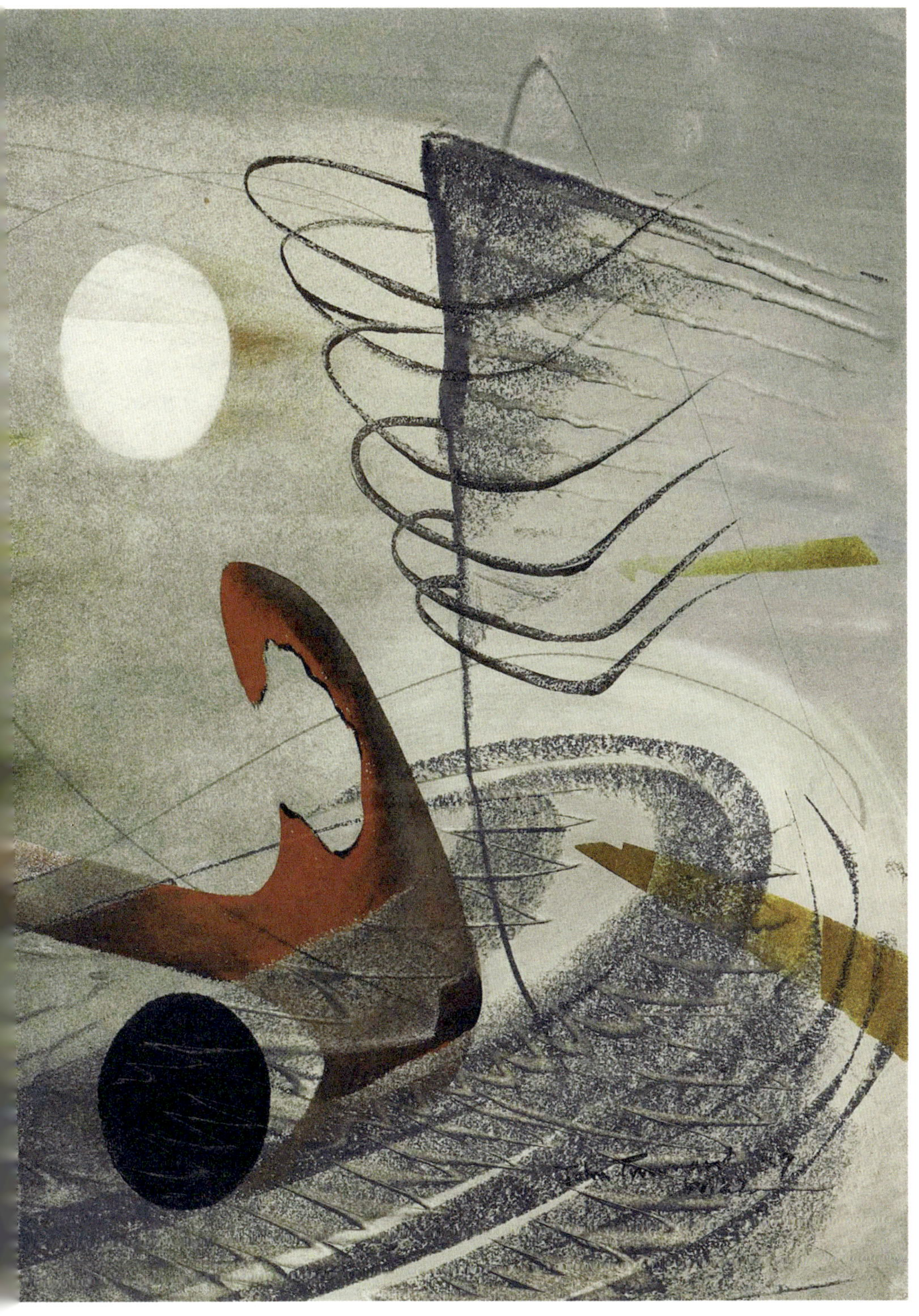

This was a time when the official surrealist group in London was laying down the law and making lists of rules that had to be obeyed by its members. This type of group activity, opposing creative individuality, had no appeal for Tunnard. He was an independent, a loner, an individualist who would have nothing to do with restrictive rules and regulations. Like a number of other British avant-garde artists, he felt a strong affiliation with surrealist art but had no time for the surrealist theorists.

When he was taken up by Peggy Guggenheim, his reputation in London art circles improved and he was able to exhibit regularly, even during World War II. Although some of his work sold, he was in serious trouble financially, and he and his wife had to take up crab-pot-making to earn enough money to survive. During the war years, when he was a conscientious objector, he acted as an auxiliary coastguard along the Cornish coast. His friend Julian Trevelyan described how Tunnard set off to work. It began with a lot of drinking in the local pub, followed by a musical session in his thatched cottage, when he danced to jazz records wearing a pink bowler hat, until he 'finally stumbled off round the cliffs to his look-out'. Once on the clifftop, Tunnard had to keep his gaze fixed on the ocean, scanning it for any sign of an invading Nazi force. Spending hours doing this, day after day, must have had an impact on his painted landscapes and given them some of their more threatening, sinister qualities.

Tunnard's relationship with his wife ran into difficulties during the war. She had given birth to a stillborn baby and was subsequently unable to have children. This put a strain on their marriage and at one point he told friends that he was thinking of leaving her. This phase passed quickly, however, and they remained together. After the war was over, they were once again desperately short of funds and he started trying to find a teaching post that would enable him to keep painting. In 1948 he managed to obtain a position at the Penzance School of Art, teaching design. This kept them in funds and lasted well into the 1960s.

It would have seemed logical for Tunnard to have become involved with the active group of artists gathered in nearby St Ives – the artistic centre of the South West. This did not happen, however, largely because he seems to have disliked the bitchy in-fighting that was going on there. When the St Ives Art Society, formed in 1949 and made up of nineteen local artists, invited thirteen more artists to join their ranks, Tunnard was the only one to refuse.

He was simply not a 'joiner'. One of the St Ives artists referred to him as a 'complete recluse' and was sad that an artist he respected was not going to join their ranks.

When Tunnard's mother died, he was at last freed from financial worries and in 1952 he bought a nearby house in which the artist Dame Laura Knight had once lived, and which was a painter's paradise. He and his wife devoted so much time to transforming the six acres they now owned that his painting output suffered as a consequence. They created a magnificent garden and, in a way, this was the new canvas on which he was expressing his aesthetic ideas. Despite his early indoctrination at the hands of a huntin', shootin' and fishin' father, his attitude to the local wildlife had changed completely, largely under the influence of his animal-loving wife. She adored badgers and foxes and angered the local farmers who saw them as pests. Tunnard himself even wrote newspaper articles about the horrors of hunting and the joys of simply observing wildlife.

As the years passed, however, his urge to paint returned, and production was soon back to its usual levels. Strangely, his obsession with natural history made few inroads into the subject matter of his paintings – apart from the inclusion of an occasional insect. Once at the easel he seemed to disappear into another, private visual world with its own rules and images and, for the whole of his life, he seldom strayed from his characteristic bio-geometric scenes.

Although never one of the best known of modern artists as far as the general public was concerned, Tunnard was respected far and wide by those within the professional art world. It comes as a surprise, for example, to find that Mark Rothko visited Cornwall in 1958 and was amazed to find that Tunnard was still actively painting, as he had for so long been a respected figure in the avant-garde scene in America. In the 1960s his painting continued unabated, and he greatly enjoyed the fact that at last he was receiving critical acclaim. A new fascination for him now was space travel, and concepts of communicating with outer space could be discerned in his later works. In 1970 his wife died, and he was quick to follow her one year later. Despite their early difficulties following the death of their child, they had grown more and more close in their final years and ultimately had become inseparable.

Critics of Tunnard's work would say that it is too geometrically abstract to be considered alongside the biomorphic work of the surrealists, and too biomorphic to be considered alongside the pure abstraction of the constructivists. In other words, it falls between two stools. Admirers of his work, however, would see it as combining the best of both worlds – the abstract and the biomorphic – and amalgamating them to create a unique personal vision. The latter view is now gaining strength, and Tunnard is being viewed as an important British surrealist who has been seriously underrated in the past.

EDWARD WADSWORTH

Influenced by surrealism in the 1920s and 1930s but not a group member

BORN: 29 October 1889 at Cleckheaton, Yorkshire

PARENTS: Father ran a worsted spinning business; left a fortune

LIVED: Cleckheaton 1899; Edinburgh 1903; Munich 1906; Bradford 1908; London 1909; Navy 1916; Liverpool and Bristol 1918; London 1919; Maresfield, Sussex 1927; Buxton, Derbyshire 1940; Maresfield, Sussex 1945

PARTNERS: Married Fanny Eveleigh, a violinist, 1912 (two children) • Kathleen Dillon, a ballet dancer, 1929–31

DIED: 21 June 1949 in London, aged 59

Wadsworth would probably be annoyed to find himself included in this book. When asked, in 1937, if he was a surrealist, he replied, 'without hesitation ... I am not. I am just interested in painting.' Despite his refusal to be called a surrealist, many of his immaculate compositions are full of surrealist elements. Many of the surrealists themselves admired his work and recognized that, although he would have nothing to do with the group or its activities, he was a natural surrealist – whether he liked it or not. Ironically, considering his views about surrealism, he was labelled as the first British surrealist by Continental commentators, back in the 1920s. What is more, his work was greatly admired by the arch-surrealist Max Ernst, as well as by Alexander Calder and Henry Moore.

I also have a personal reason for including him in this volume. When I was strolling around Georgetown, the small capital city of Bermuda, one day about forty years ago, I came to an abrupt halt on the harbour quayside when I was confronted with what appeared to me to be an exhibition of gigantic surrealist sculptures. They were, in reality, large, painted metal buoys that were standing upright, tilting sideways or lying down, in a variety of positions, some red and white, some black and brown, and others blue and white. Together, their impact on me was so powerful that I can visualize the scene vividly even today. I believe that I would not have reacted so strongly had it not been for my knowledge of Wadsworth's images, and I am grateful to him for opening my eyes to the extraordinary shapes, colours and forms that one can encounter in a dockyard or on a quayside. His compelling marine scenes have forever left a memory trace on my brain and singlehandedly converted the seafront into a rich source of surrealist imagery.

Edward Alexander Wadsworth was born in a small mill town in Yorkshire in 1889, the son of a rich industrialist. Like Roland Penrose, Kay Sage and Francis Picabia, he had none of the usual money worries that beset so many of the surrealists. Nine days after he was born, his mother, an amateur artist, died of what was known as childbed fever, and his father had to do his best to suppress the feeling that his baby son had killed his wife. Edward was sent away to boarding school in Edinburgh, where a strong work ethic was drummed into him. This may account in part for the meticulous finish that he gave to all his paintings. Nothing he ever painted could be called lazy or slapdash – just the opposite. Indeed, for some tastes, his work is a little too polished, almost too perfect, to the point where it becomes rather formal.

His father had plans for his son to take over the family firm and to become a mill owner like himself, but Edward had other ideas. He already knew that he wanted to be a painter more than anything else. He was therefore pleased when his father insisted that he go to Munich to study engineering draughtsmanship. What excited him was the thought of all the art galleries in that great German city, where he would be able to further his studies of painting.

Back in England, he managed to persuade his father to let him attend art school, first in Bradford and then in London, where he was enrolled at the Slade School of Fine Art from 1909. He was married in 1912, to a young violinist called Fanny Eveleigh, and in the same year paid a visit to Paris that enabled him to see the latest avant-garde paintings at first hand. He was open to new ideas and reacted strongly to the latest trends in art that were springing up in the French capital. At this stage, before World War I, his modernist tendencies were in the general direction of cubism, futurism, abstractionism and vorticism. This phase was interrupted by military service. His first duty was to man an anti-aircraft gun at Paddington Station in London with the aim of shooting down German zeppelins. Later, he was posted to the Aegean with Naval Intelligence, and also worked on improving camouflage techniques. After the war he produced paintings influenced by

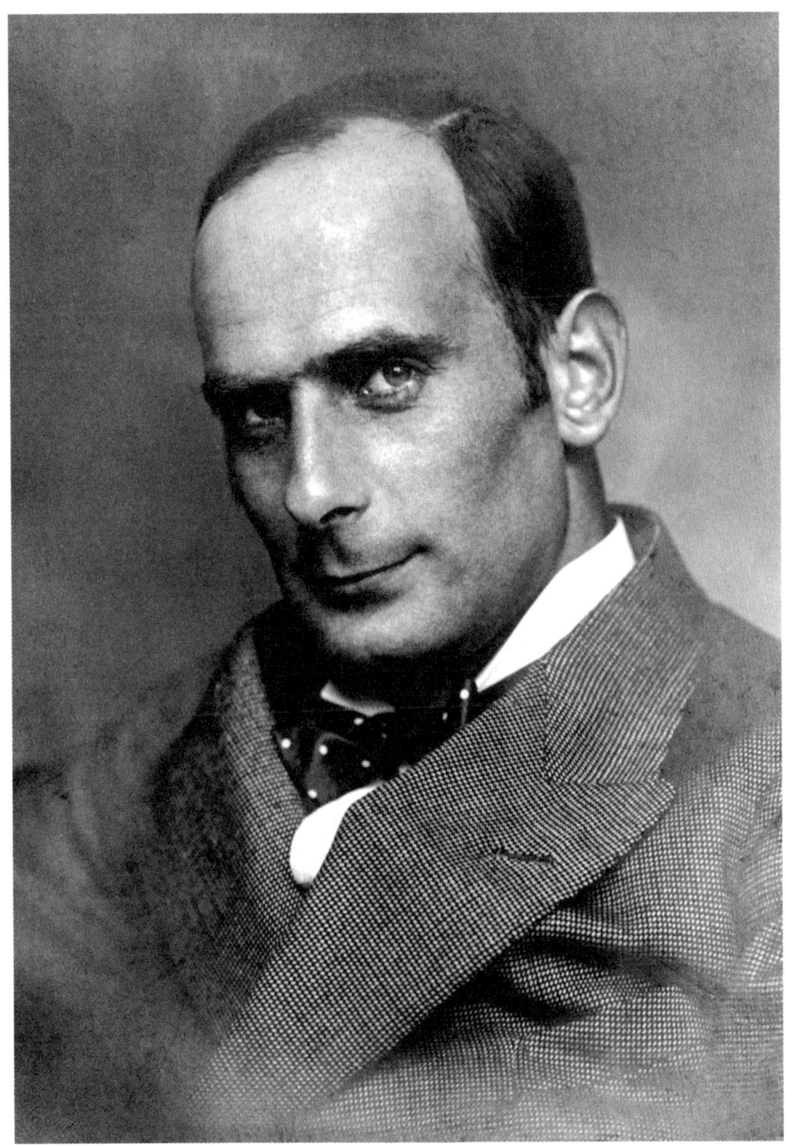

Edward Wadsworth, photographed by George C. Beresford, 1920.

the dazzle work that had been introduced on merchant vessels to confuse the German U-boats.

In 1921 Wadsworth's father died and left his only son a fortune equivalent in today's money to about £9,500,000. At the age of just thirty-two, this made him one of the richest young avant-garde artists who had ever lived. It was not in his character, however, to go wild and revel in the high life. Instead, he began painting seriously in a demanding medium – egg tempera. He said, rather drily, that tempera suited his temperament. It involved difficult, painstaking work that appealed to him, and he certainly had no financial pressure to complete paintings quickly. The downside of being so rich was that some critics falsely labelled him as a dilettante, and some of his penniless friends, such as Wyndham Lewis, found the difference in their financial status hard to bear. When Wadsworth, in what he supposed was a helpful gesture, bought a major painting by Lewis, the outcome was not as he had planned. Because the picture was too big to hang in Wadsworth's London town house, he gave it to Leeds City Art Gallery, intending this as a special favour for his friend. Lewis, however, interpreted it as a calculated insult, and their long friendship was over. There was further distress in 1922, when Wadsworth's nine-year-old daughter died of kidney failure.

As an escape from sad memories, like their daughter's dolls' house decorated with tiny paintings by Wadsworth, he and Fanny instructed their chauffeur to drive them from London to Italy and back in their splendid open touring car. They especially enjoyed their days in the primitive little fishing villages along the south coast of France, places such as Saint-Tropez, and were among the very first visitors to relish such locations, long before they became the favoured haunts of the fashionable crowd. Back in England, the Wadsworths moved out of the city and bought a house in the country, midway between London and the south coast. At this point there was a marked increase in their social life. In 1927 there were many house parties, picnics and weekend gatherings at their new home, and their friends in the art world flocked there to be entertained. Guests included Max Ernst, Pierre Roy, Henry Moore, Paul Nash and Roland Penrose.

In 1928 the Wadsworths took a house in Paris for four months, so that Edward could soak up the latest developments in modern art. A major influence at this point was the French artist Fernand Léger, who had given a lecture in which he insisted that a gas meter was as beautiful as the Venus

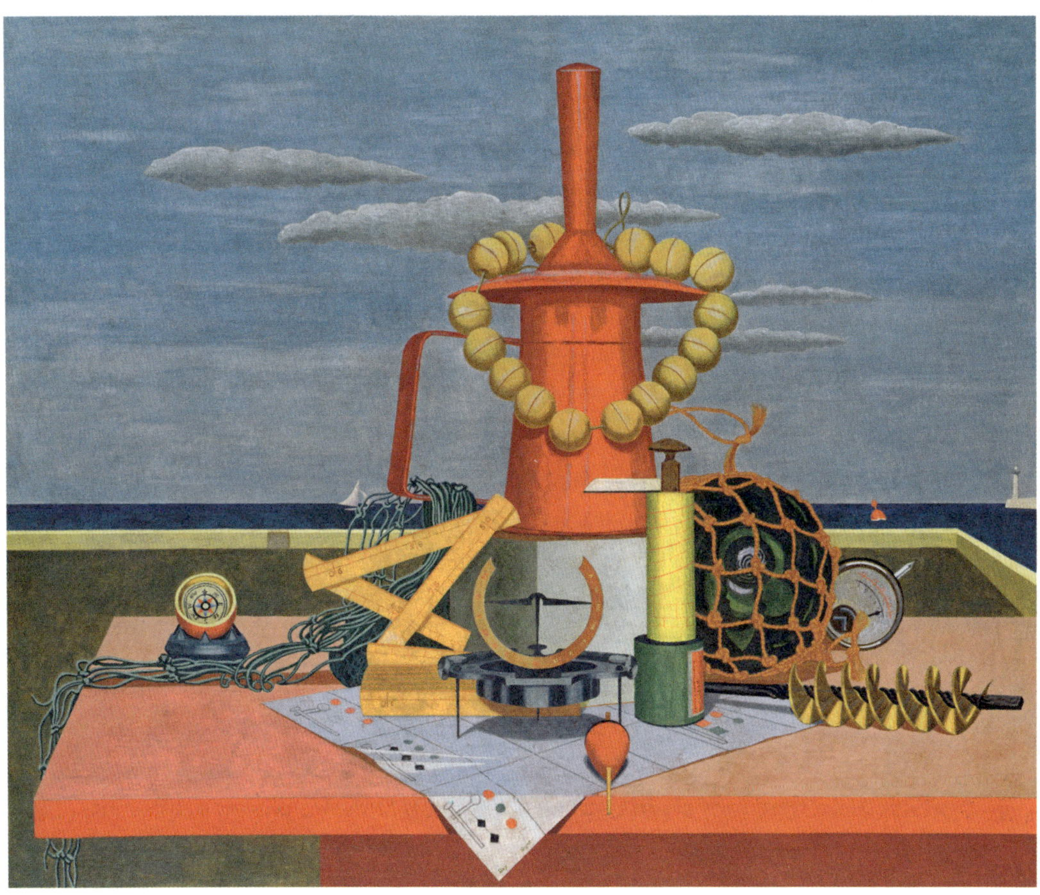

de Milo. This praise for a manufactured object struck a chord with Wadsworth, who had long been attracted to the various bits of machinery and apparatus to be found in docks and on the quayside. Léger, the mechano-cubist, gave him the courage to include manufactured objects as the central figures in many of his works. He lovingly displayed such items as compasses, floats, piping, sextants, lanterns, binoculars, barometers and set squares, as though they were objects of great beauty, laid out for us to see and to marvel at. Living things were notably absent, except for over-sized seashells, but even these were nearly always depicted long after their animal occupants had vacated them.

Edward Wadsworth, *Regalia*, 1928.

Whether he would admit to it or not, these strange assemblies of inanimate objects that dominated Wadsworth's work in the late 1920s had a strong surrealist flavour, almost as haunting as the early work of de Chirico. The surrealists themselves certainly thought so, and his work was reproduced in avant-garde magazines alongside that of Ernst, Magritte, Klee, Miró and other major names. In 1929 he was the lone Englishman in their midst. As a way of thanking the man who had inspired him, he bought some of Léger's paintings and kept them on his walls for the rest of his life. He also bought some of Henry Moore's early work, describing his friend as 'one of the very great men of our time'.

As regards his personal life during this period, his wife seems to have been remarkably tolerant of his amours, which included a two-year-long affair with Kathleen Dillon between 1929 and 1931. Dillon was a dancer who had appeared in the first English performance of Igor Stravinsky's *Pastorale*, but in 1931 she decided to marry the pianist Angus Morrison and ended their affair. Wadsworth may have lessened the pain of losing her by taking another spin in his recently acquired Rolls Royce Silver Ghost Tourer, one of the most impressive cars in existence at the time. A few years later he bought an even more impressive Rolls Royce Phantom II Continental Limousine, of which there were only six in the world. This car, however, played a different role in his life. Instead of giving him great pleasure it was the cause of great agony when he accidentally killed a man in a road accident in 1934. He faced a possible manslaughter conviction that would have seen him jailed but, in the end, it was decided that the tragedy was not his fault and he was let off.

During this anxious time his paintings started to change, returning to the style that had attracted the surrealists back in the period between 1926 and 1929. From 1934, on and off for about ten years, he produced a stream of his dreamlike still-life paintings in which the assembled nautical objects took centre stage. He was so obsessed with these themes that, when he was asked by Cunard to paint two large pictures to decorate public rooms on the new *Queen Mary* ocean liner, he presented them with a pair of compositions that they found too strange for their taste. They accepted one of them but demanded a straightforward painting of a ship for the other. He obliged but was unhappy about it.

Wadsworth's working methods were described by the French-American artist Louis Bouché, who visited his studio in the mid-1930s: he kept strict

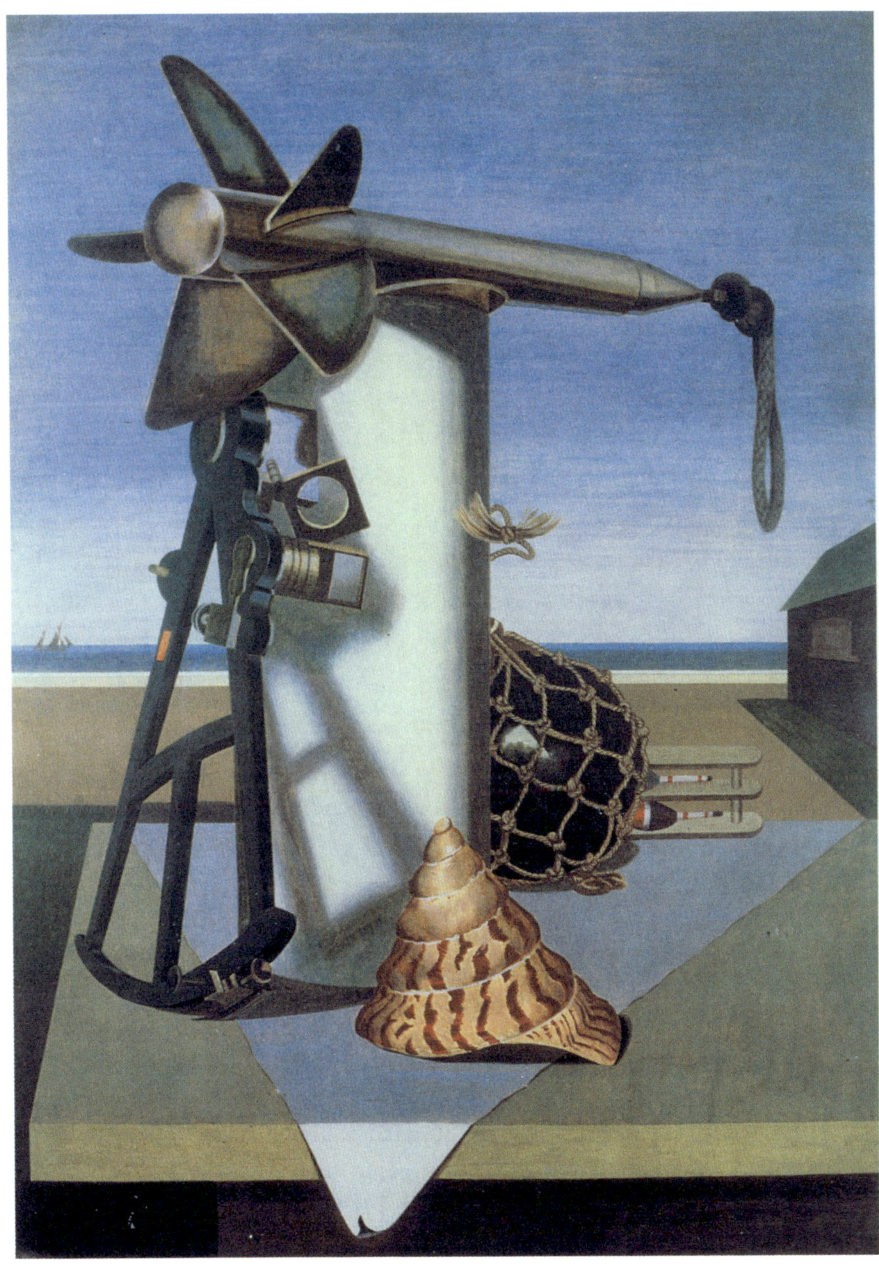

Edward Wadsworth, *North Sea*, 1928.

office hours, painting from 9.30 a.m. to 1.00 p.m. and again from 2.30 p.m. to 6.00 p.m. His studio was said to look more like a laboratory than an artist's den. The walls were all painted white, and along one of them there was a large glass display case full of nautical instruments and beach combings. Along another wall was a long table covered in jars of powdered colours awaiting mixing. The floor was strewn with cigarette ends, and an English sheepdog wandered this way and that. Very loud jazz music was playing on the radio. The artist himself had the brisk air of 'an American go-getter'.

When World War II broke out Wadsworth was soon to lose his splendid studio because his house was in a zone that was to be cleared of all civilians. He and his family had to retreat to Buxton in Derbyshire, where he had to paint in a tiny garret room that measured only five by six feet. Worse still, egg rationing meant that his painting technique using egg tempera was at risk. He was forced to save his one-egg-per-week allowance solely to mix with his pigments. On top of that he was made a sergeant in the Home Guard, with his duties taking up a lot of his time. Despite these difficulties, he managed to produce some memorable paintings during the war period, including several with the strongest surrealist flavour of all.

After the family returned to their home in the south of England at the end of the war, Wadsworth's work became increasingly abstract and remained so until he died in 1949. His early death at the age of only fifty-nine was his own fault. All through the war he had suffered from a leaking appendix but had done nothing about it. It had been slowly poisoning his system but, like many Englishmen, he avoided seeking or taking medical advice. In a cavalier way he was just starting a new love affair and was driving a sporty new car when he collapsed, was rushed to hospital in London and within a few days was dead.

Although, to surrealist eyes, Wadsworth's later abstract works now seem rather dated and shallow, his compositions of irrationally assembled inanimate objects, endowed with a powerful mystery and a haunting presence, will always remain an important body of surrealist works, regardless of his dismissal of the term.

SCOTTIE WILSON

Associated with the surrealists in London in 1945 but not an official member of the group

BORN: 6 June 1888 in Glasgow, as Louis Freeman

PARENTS: Lithuanian; father a furrier

LIVED: Glasgow 1888; India and South Africa (in the army) 1906; Glasgow 1911; France (in war) 1914; Toronto 1918; Glasgow and London 1922; Toronto 1932; Vancouver 1938; London 1945

PARTNERS: none (solitary life)

DIED: 26 March 1972 in London, of cancer, aged 83

Scottie Wilson was unique, being influenced by no other artist and, for that matter, influencing nobody. He stood alone, creating his own private dream world, a self-styled primitive and the only 'outsider artist' to be accepted by Breton as a surrealist. His work was so admired by the surrealists that, although Scottie himself had nothing to do with the movement, they included his work in the major International Surrealist Exhibition in Paris in 1947.

Scottie was born of Jewish Lithuanian parents in the Gorbals district of Glasgow in 1888. In those days, the Gorbals region of the city was described as 'a dangerous slum associated with the problems of drunkenness and crime', and Scottie endured a tough childhood there. A few years earlier, his immigrant parents had arrived in England seeking employment. We will never know Scottie's real name, because the immigration clerk could not pronounce or spell it, and wrote it down in a simplified form as 'Freeman'. Though he was born Louis Freeman, he later changed his name to Scottie Wilson to make it sound more Scottish and less Jewish.

He left school at the age of nine and, for the rest of his life, would be unable to read or write. He once said, 'My mind is reading all the time. I don't need papers or books. My mind is full of books.' His first job was as a barefoot paper-boy. The shame of having no shoes must have left a mark on his memory because in later life he became obsessed with polishing and

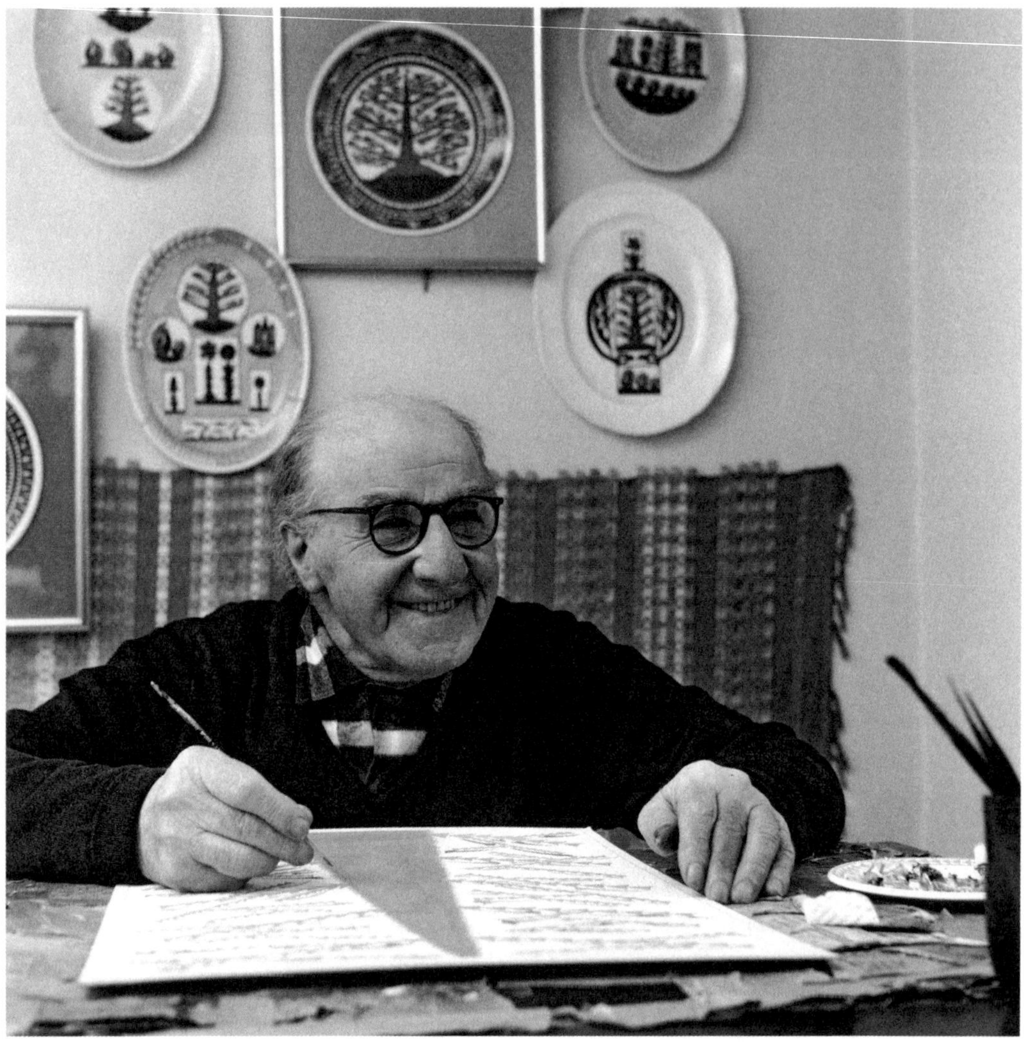

wearing expensive boots, even when the rest of his clothing was rather shabby. After this, he graduated to helping with his brother's market stall. Together they sold a dubious herbal mixture that claimed to make you stronger. His only pleasures were visits to the zoo and the circus, where he became fascinated by the animals, and it was of course animals that would play a major role in his compositions. His one luxury seems to have been boiled sweets,

Scottie Wilson, photographed by Arthur Sidey, 1967.

a weakness that lasted all his life, and he would sometimes pull some from his pocket and offer them to a surprised visitor at one of his exhibitions.

After a poverty-stricken childhood, Scottie joined the army in 1906. He was posted to India and then to South Africa, but finally could take no more of it and bought himself out with the money he had saved. Unfortunately, this left him unable to pay for his fare home, so he had to work his passage as a stoker in the sweltering heat of a ship's boiler room.

When war broke out in 1914 Scottie joined up again and served on the Western Front. After the war he eventually deserted and escaped to Canada. There he travelled around selling tinned meat, jam and second-hand furniture. After a while he settled down in Toronto, where he opened a junk shop selling scent bottles and old fountain pens. Business was slow, and he passed the time using one of the pens to doodle on a large piece of cardboard that lay on the table in his back room. This doodle got bigger and bigger and more and more complicated, and Scottie suddenly became fascinated by the images he was making. He began to create more and more drawings and eventually took to hanging them up in the window of his little shop for people to see. Local collectors and academics noticed them as they passed by and started buying them.

This was happening at the end of the 1920s. Scottie now had a new source of income, and he loved the process of making the drawings – so much more interesting than all the boring jobs he had been forced to do in the past – so he paid more and more attention to it. By the early 1940s he was exhibiting his work in Toronto, Winnipeg and Vancouver. One of his collectors now owned twenty-five of his works.

When World War II ended in 1945, Scottie decided to return to Britain and settled in London. He then began a campaign to market his work, using methods hitherto unknown to the world of modern art. The wording of a poster he had made in November 1945 sums up the flavour of his unique approach to making money out of his art. It informed you that, at the Music Hall in Aberdeen, for one week only, you could see Scottie at work. You were also promised an 'Exhibition of 300 of the most Amazing Dream Pictures ever shown to the public', and there was an offer of £1,000 to any person creating similar work. To heighten the mystique of the event, there was a warning: 'No person with a camera admitted.' Admission was one shilling, sixpence for children.

Scottie organized many such events and, quite by chance, Roland Penrose wandered into one of them. It was being held in a deserted wallpaper shop on the seafront in Scarborough and, stunned by what he saw, Penrose bought the entire show. He then contacted Édouard Mesens, who arranged a London exhibition for Scottie. On his next trip to Paris, Mesens showed his work to André Breton, who immediately decided to include Scottie in the big surrealist show he was organizing at the Maeght Gallery in 1947.

Scottie now found himself being regarded as an honorary surrealist, but this did not stop him from stubbornly continuing with his own, preferred method of marketing, namely his touring shows. Apart from Aberdeen, he also travelled in his small van to Blackpool, Cardiff and Devon. If he could not manage to hire a venue for his displays, he would park, open up the back of his van, pin up some of his pictures, put out a collecting plate, turn on his gramophone to attract attention and then, using a loudspeaker, would announce that his drawings were on sale at good prices. When he could afford to do so, he would not put them on sale but simply exhibit them and ask for silver donations when people inspected them. When someone said they liked his work, he replied, 'I do myself – you know, if I had any money I'd buy the lot.' Sadly, he rarely did have any money.

A drink in a pub was an essential part of Scottie's daily routine and, if he found himself running short of cash, he would go into a local shop and beg them to give him the price of a pint of beer in exchange for one of his works. Sometimes they took pity on him and, after he had left, would then pin the drawing up in their shop window, priced at a few shillings. By luck, I was travelling down through Devon shortly after Scottie's tour there in 1949 and was able to start my collection of his work by tracking down the shops where he had been lucky.

Because of the extraordinary originality of his compositions, a major London gallery started giving him solo exhibitions, with all his work beautifully framed. Inevitably, they put professional prices on the pictures and, when some of them were sold, Scottie immediately demanded money from the gallery. They explained that payment would be made at the end of the show, but this was not good enough for Scottie, who needed a drink and was not prepared to wait. So he went round the corner and into a pub, where he offered examples of his work for the price of a pint. Needless to say, this upset the owners of the gallery and Scottie found himself in trouble.

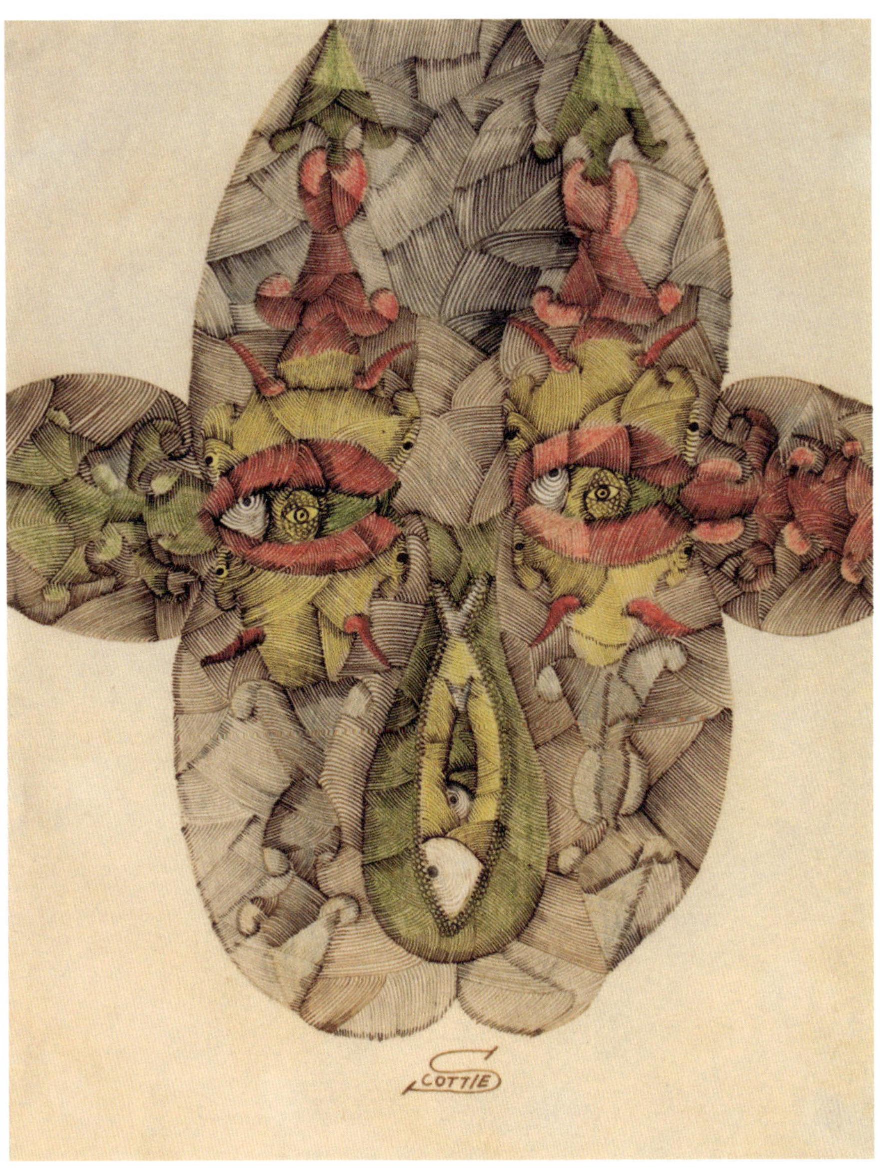

Scottie Wilson, *Self-Portrait Head*, c. 1938.

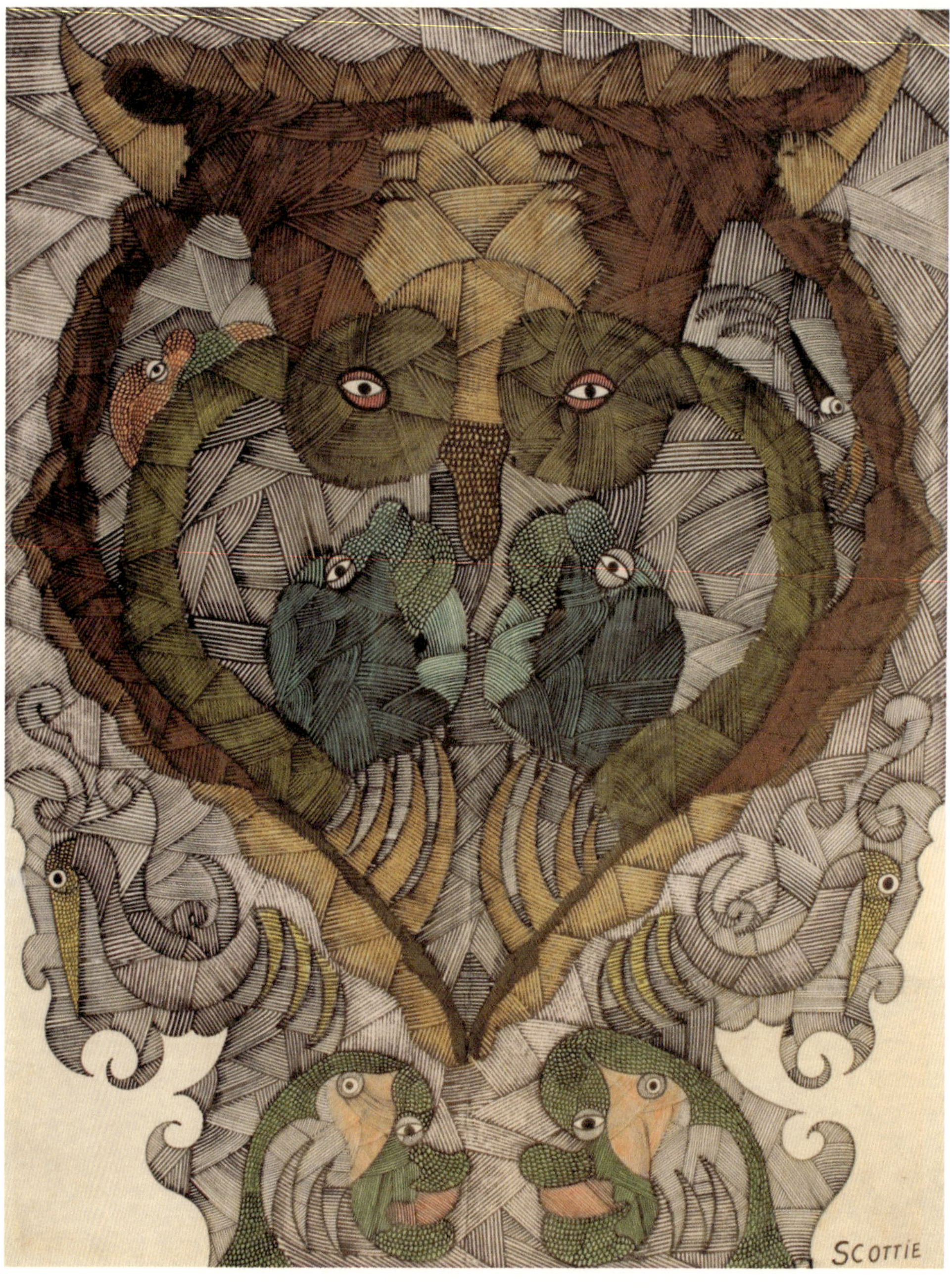

Scottie Wilson, *Untitled*, c. 1940.

He also had to face another hazard at the private views of his exhibitions. The alcohol was free, and Scottie usually over-indulged. In his published diaries, Christopher Isherwood vividly describes one such occasion. Scottie had arrived with Lucian Freud who had then vanished, leaving Isherwood to see to it that the drunken Scottie got home safely. He and a friend did their best, but it was not easy. They had to 'cart him around north London in a taxi, maudlin drunk and occasionally vomiting, but refusing to give us his address.... Finally we took him to a police station where the police sergeant sympathetically but firmly insisted on the truth. I think Scottie had been ashamed because it was a very poor street.'

Despite his problems with alcohol, Scottie was now making wonderfully complex coloured drawings, using his obsessional cross-hatching technique. Tiny parallel ink lines would be drawn over each coloured shape, creating a unique style that nobody else has ever tried to imitate. The images he employed were limited in their range. I analysed a random selection of one hundred of his works and found that there was a total of only seventeen images employed, as follows: bulbous faces (390); large birds (212); small birds (534); fish (615); butterflies (18); flowers (132); trees (22); houses (63); smoking chimneys (33); grasses (26); sun or moon (29); sea monsters (40); snakes or eels (11); goblins (13); insects (7); turtles (5); and unidentified animals (10).

There were two distinct phases to his work. The first phase – which ran from 1930 to 1950 – saw his pictures signed with a large 'S' that enclosed the other, smaller letters 'cottie'. The second phase – which overlapped with the first, running from 1945 to 1970 – saw the 'S' reduced to the same size as the other letters. Some motifs appeared throughout his work, but others were limited to either the first or second phase. For example, the 534 small birds all appeared in the second phase. Also, the butterflies, trees, houses, grasses, suns and moons almost all appeared in that second phase. The turtles, insects, snakes, eels and sea monsters were nearly all confined to the first phase.

Towards the end of Scottie's life, in the 1960s, Mervyn Levy, a friend of mine, persuaded Royal Worcester to market a set of crockery covered in Scottie Wilson designs. Mervyn's motive was to help Scottie survive financially. He had loved Scottie's work for many years and wanted to help the old man, who was living in very frugal circumstances, in a single room in London. Scottie was delighted with the commission and worked hard at the designs. Mervyn had been concerned about Scottie's welfare because he lived such a solitary existence. He had never had a wife or a partner and made few friends. He was suspicious of everyone and trusted nobody. He lived in a single rented room that acted as a bedroom, living room and studio, doing his own very simple cooking. He disliked gallery people, saying his work was 'too truthful for those mouthpieces', and showed little interest in the work of other artists. There were only two exceptions – William Blake, because he would have understood Scottie's pictures – and René Magritte, because his paintings made Scottie laugh. He found Magritte's visual jokes very funny, especially the one in which a musical instrument had burst into flames.

I visited him shortly before his death and asked if there was anything I could do for him. He said, 'Get me a little bird in a cage, to keep me company.' I agreed, but Mervyn warned me not to do so, because Scottie would not be able to look after it. When I was leaving, Scottie saw that I was concerned about him, and his last words to me, spoken with a wry smile, were 'Don't you go feeling sorry for old Scottie.'

After his death, it turned out that his final words to me had more significance than I had realized, for underneath his humble bed was discovered a suitcase stuffed full with banknotes. Scottie the super-tramp had managed to salt away enough money to see him through any dire emergency that might have occurred. It must have given him the strength to maintain his stubborn independence of action, right to the very end.

FURTHER RESOURCES

BRITISH ARTISTS INCLUDED IN THE INTERNATIONAL SURREALIST EXHIBITION IN LONDON IN 1936

Eileen Agar: 3 oils; 5 objects
John Banting: 2 oils; 2 watercolours; 1 object
John Selby Bigge: 2 oils
Edward Burra: 6 oils
Cecil Collins: 1 oil; 1 drawing
Merlyn Evans: 3 oils; 2 drawings; 2 collages
Stanley William Hayter: 2 oils; 8 etchings; 1 object
Humphrey Jennings: 1 oil; 2 collages; 3 image-objects
Reuben Mednikoff: 1 oil; 1 watercolour; 2 drawings
Henry Moore: 4 sculptures; 3 drawings
Paul Nash: 4 oils; 5 collages; 3 objects
Grace Pailthorpe: 1 watercolour; 2 drawings
Roland Penrose: 4 oils; 2 objects
Graham Sutherland: 2 oils
Julian Trevelyan: 3 oils; 2 etchings

SURREALIST GROUP EXHIBITIONS IN BRITAIN

1936 International Surrealist Exhibition, New Burlington Galleries, London

1937 'Surrealist Objects and Poems', London Gallery, London

1971 'Britain's Contribution to Surrealism', Hamet Gallery, London

1976 'The Edward James Collection: Dalí, Magritte and other Surrealists', Scottish National Gallery of Modern Art, Edinburgh

1978 'Dada and Surrealism Reviewed', Hayward Gallery, London

1978 'Surrealism Unlimited', Camden Arts Centre, London

1986 'British Surrealism Fifty Years On', Mayor Gallery, London

1986 'Surrealism in England', Herbert Read Gallery, Canterbury

1986 'Surrealism in Britain in the Thirties', Leeds City Art Galleries

1986 'Contrariwise: Surrealism and Britain, 1930–1986', British Council touring exhibition, first shown as part of the Swansea Festival

1989 'Surrealism in Hull: British Surrealist Art from the Ferens Art Gallery, Hull and the University of Hull Art Collection', Middleton Hall, University of Hull

1997 'Surrealism and After', Scottish National Gallery of Modern Art, Edinburgh

2001 'Surrealism: Desire Unbound', Tate Modern, London

2007 'Surreal Things: Surrealism and Design', Victoria & Albert Museum, London

2008 'British Surrealism and Other Realities', Modern Art, Middlesbrough

2009 'British Surrealism in Context: The Sherwin Collection', Leeds Art Gallery

2009 'Subversive Spaces: Surrealism & Contemporary Art, Whitworth Art Gallery, Manchester

2009 'Angels of Anarchy: Women Artists and Surrealism', Manchester Art Gallery

2020 'British Surrealism', Dulwich Picture Gallery, London

FURTHER READING ON BRITISH SURREALISM

Bernasconi, John, et al., *Surrealism in Hull: British Surrealist Art*, University of Hull, 1989

Fleiss, Marcel, *Peinture Surrealiste en Angleterre 1930–1960*, Galerie 1900–2000, Paris, 1982

Haycock, David Boyd, *British Surrealism*, Dulwich Picture Gallery, London, 2020

Levy, Silvano, *Surrealism in Birmingham 1935–1955*, Birmingham Art Gallery, 2001

Melly, George, *Surrealism is Dead, Long Live Surrealism*, Crawshaw Gallery, London, 1988

Ray, Paul C., *The Surrealist Movement in England*, Cornell University Press, Ithaca, New York, 1971

Remy, Michel, *Towards a Dictionary of Surrealism in England*, Groupe-Édition Marges, Nancy, 1978

Remy, Michel, *Le Mouvement Surréaliste en Angleterre*, doctoral thesis, Paris, 1985

Remy, Michel, *British Surrealism Fifty Years On*, Mayor Gallery, London, 1986

Remy, Michel, *Surrealism in Britain*, Ashgate Publishing, Aldershot, 1999; paperback edition 2001

Renzio, Tony del and Duncan Scott, *Surrealism in England: 1936 and After*, Canterbury College of Art, 1986

Robertson, Alexander, et al., *Surrealism in Britain in the Thirties*, Leeds City Art Galleries, 1986

Rull, Liza, *Real Surreal: British and European Surrealism*, Wolverhampton Art Gallery and Museum, 1995

Sherwin, Jeffrey, *British Surrealism in Context*, Leeds Museums and Galleries, 2009

Sherwin, Jeffrey, *British Surrealism Opened Up*, Northern Artists Gallery, Bradford, 2014

Wilson, Andrew, *British Surrealism and Other Realities*, Middlesborough Institute of Modern Art, 2008

FURTHER READING ON INDIVIDUAL BRITISH ARTISTS

EILEEN AGAR

Agar, Eileen, *A Look at My Life*, Methuen, London, 1988

Byatt. A. S., *Eileen Agar 1899–1991: An Imaginative Playfulness*, Redfern Gallery, London, 2005

Lambirth, Andrew, *Eileen Agar: A Retrospective*, Birch & Conran, London, 1987

Simpson, Ann, *Eileen Agar 1899–1991*, National Galleries of Scotland, Edinburgh, 1999

JOHN ARMSTRONG

Lambirth, Andrew, *John Armstrong: The Paintings*, Philip Wilson, London, 2009

FRANCIS BACON

Adès, Dawn, and Andrew Forge, *Francis Bacon*, Tate Gallery, London, 1985

Alley, Ronald, *Francis Bacon*, Thames & Hudson, London, 1964

Archimbaud, Michel, *Francis Bacon in Conversation*, Phaidon Press, London, 1993

Brighton, Andrew, *Francis Bacon*, Tate Publishing, London, 2001

Cappock, Margarita, *Francis Bacon's Studio*, Merrell, London, 2005

Davies, Hugh, *Francis Bacon: The Papal Portraits of 1953*, Museum of Contemporary Art, San Diego, 2001

Davies, Hugh, and Sally Yard, *Francis Bacon*, Abbeville Press, New York, 1986

Edwards, John, *7 Reece Mews: Francis Bacon's Studio*, Thames & Hudson, London, 2001

Farson, Daniel, *The Gilded Gutter Life of Francis Bacon*, Vintage, London, 1994

Ficacci, Luigi, *Francis Bacon 1909–1992*, Taschen, Cologne, 2003

Hammer, Martin, *Bacon and Sutherland*, Yale University Press, New Haven, CT, 2005

Hammer, Martin, *Francis Bacon and Nazi Propaganda*, Tate Publishing, London, 2012

Harrison, Martin, *In Camera: Francis Bacon*, Thames & Hudson, London, 2005
Harrison, Martin, *Francis Bacon: Catalogue Raisonné* (5 vols), The Estate of Francis Bacon, London, 2016
Leiris, Michel, *Francis Bacon*, Rizzoli, New York, 1983
Peppiatt, Michael, *Francis Bacon: Anatomy of an Enigma*, Weidenfeld and Nicolson, London, 1996
Sinclair, Andrew, *Francis Bacon, His Life and Violent Times*, Crown, New York, 1993
Sylvester, David, *Interviews with Francis Bacon*, Thames & Hudson, London, 1975
Sylvester, David, *Looking Back at Francis Bacon*, Thames & Hudson, London, 2000

JOHN BANTING

Banting, John, *A Blue Book of Conversation*, Nicholson and Watson, London, 1946
Melly, George, *John Banting*, Hamet Gallery, London, 1971

JOHN BIGGE

Neill, Roger, 'An Oxfordshire Artist and Two World Wars', *Oxford Times: Oxfordshire Limited Edition* supplement, May 2014, pp. 63–65

EDWARD BURRA

Causey, Andrew, *Edward Burra: Complete Catalogue*, Phaidon Press, London, 1985
Chappel, William (ed.), *Well, Dearie! The Letters of Edward Burra*, Gordon Fraser, London, 1985
Drew, Joanna, et al., *Edward Burra*, Hayward Gallery, London, 1985
Rothenstein, John, *Edward Burra*, Penguin, London, 1945
Rothenstein, John, *Edward Burra*, Tate Gallery, London, 1973
Stevenson, Jane, *Edward Burra: Twentieth-Century Eye*, Jonathan Cape, London, 2007

LEONORA CARRINGTON

Aberth, Susan, *Leonora Carrington: Surrealism, Alchemy, and Art*, Lund Humphries, Aldershot, 2004
Carrington, Leonora, *The Hearing Trumpet*, Penguin, London, 1976
Chadwick, Whitney, *Leonora Carrington*, Consejo Nacional para la Cultura y las Artes, Mexico City, 1994
Moorhead, Joanna, *The Surreal Life of Leonora Carrington*, Virago Press, London, 2017

CECIL COLLINS

Anderson, William, *Cecil Collins: The Quest for the Great Happiness*, Barrie & Jenkins, London, 1988
Collins, Judith, *Cecil Collins: A Retrospective Exhibition*, Tate Gallery, London, 1989
Comfort, Alex, and Conrad Senat, *Cecil Collins: Paintings and Drawings (1935–1945)*, Counterpoint Publications, Oxford, 1946

ITHELL COLQUHOUN

Hale, Amy, *The Supersensual Life of Ithell Colquhoun*, Francis Boutle, London, 2011
Levy, Silvano, 'The del Renzio Affair: A leadership struggle in wartime surrealism', *Papers of Surrealism*, issue 3, spring 2005
Ratcliffe, Eric, *Ithell Colquhoun, Pioneer Surrealist*, Mandrake, Oxford, 2007
Shillitoe, Richard, *Ithell Colquhoun, Magician Born of Nature*, Lulu Press, Morrisville, 2010

MERLYN EVANS

Gooding, Mel, *Merlyn Evans*, Cameron & Hollis, Moffat, Dumfrieshire, 2010
Murray, Andrew, et al., *Merlyn Evans: 1910–1973*, Mayor & Redfern Galleries, London, 1988

SAM HAILE

Remy, Michel, et al., *Sam Haile*, Birch & Conran, London, 1987

S. W. HAYTER

Hayter, S. W., *About Prints*, Oxford University Press, 1962
Hayter, S. W., *New Ways of Gravure*, Oxford University Press, 1962
S. W. Hayter: Colour Engravings, Day and Bird, 1991

TRISTRAM HILLIER

Hillier, Tristram, *Leda and the Goose*, Longmans, London, 1954

Pery, Jenny, *Painter Pilgrim: The Art and Life of Tristram Hillier*, Royal Academy Publications, London, 2008

Usherwood, Nicholas, *A Timeless Journey*, Bradford Art Galleries, 1983

HUMPHREY JENNINGS

Coombs, Neil, *The Communicating Village: Humphrey Jennings and Surrealism*, Ph.D. thesis, John Moores University, Liverpool, 2014

Jackson, Kevin, *The Humphrey Jennings Film Reader*, Carcanet, Manchester, 1993

Jackson, Kevin, *Humphrey Jennings*, Picador, London, 2004

CONROY MADDOX

Levy, Silvano, *Conroy Maddox: Surreal Enigmas*, Keele University Press, 1995

Levy, Silvano, *The Scandalous Eye: The Surrealism of Conroy Maddox*, Liverpool University Press, 2003

Rosemont, Penelope, and Paul Garon, *Conroy Maddox: Letters to Surrealists in the USA*, Black Swan Press, Chicago, 2019

Short, Robert, *Conroy Maddox: Surrealism Unlimited*, Camden Arts Centre, London, 1978

F. E. McWILLIAM

Ferran, Denise, *F. E. McWilliam at Banbridge*, F. E. McWilliam Gallery, Banbridge, County Down, 2008

Ferran, Denise, and Valerie Holman, *The Sculpture of F. E. McWilliam*, Lund Humphries, London, 2012

Gooding, Mel, *F. E. McWilliam: Sculpture 1932–1989*, Tate Gallery, London, 1989

Marle, Judy, and T. P. Flanagan, *F. E. McWilliam*, The Arts Council of Northern Ireland and the Arts Council of the Republic of Ireland, 1981

REUBEN MEDNIKOFF

Remy, Michel, et al., *Sluice-Gates of the Mind: The Collaborative Work of Pailthorpe and Mednikoff*, Leeds Museum and Art Gallery, 1998

OSCAR MELLOR

Mellor, Phoebe, *The Paintings of Oscar Mellor*, Taurus Gallery, Oxford, 2008

HENRY MOORE

Berthoud, Roger, *The Life of Henry Moore*, Faber & Faber, London, 1987

Bowness, Alan, *Henry Moore: Complete Sculpture* (6 vols), Lund Humphries, London, 1944–88

Compton, Susan, *Henry Moore*, Weidenfeld and Nicolson, London, 1988

Garrould, Ann, *Henry Moore: The Complete Drawings* (7 vols), Lund Humphries, London, 1996–2003

Grigson, Geoffrey, *Henry Moore*, Penguin, Harmondsworth, 1943

Hedgecoe, John, *Henry Moore: My Ideas, Inspiration, and Life as an Artist*, Ebury Press, London, 1986

Strachan, W. J., *Henry Moore Animals*, Aurum Press, London, 1983

Sweeney, James Johnson, *Henry Moore*, Museum of Modern Art, New York, 1946

Sylvester, David (ed.), *Henry Moore: Sculpture and Drawings* (6 vols), Lund Humphreys, London, 1957

Wilkinson, Alan, *Henry Moore Writings and Conversations*, Lund Humphries, London, 2002

PAUL NASH

Cardinal, Roger, *The Landscape Vision of Paul Nash*, Reaktion Books, London, 1989

Causey, Andrew, *Paul Nash*, Oxford University Press, 1980

Causey, Andrew, *Paul Nash: Writings on Art*, Oxford University Press, 2000

Causey, Andrew, *Paul Nash: Landscape and the Life of Objects*, Lund Humphries, Farnham, 2013

Eates, Margot, *Paul Nash, Master of the Image*, John Murray, London, 1973

Fraser Jenkins, David, *Paul Nash; The Elements*, Dulwich Picture Gallery, London, 2010

Montagu, Jemima, *Paul Nash: Modern Artist, Ancient Landscape*, Tate Publishing, London, 2003

Read, Herbert, *Paul Nash*, Penguin, London, 1944

GORDON ONSLOW FORD

Sawin, Martica, *Gordon Onslow Ford: Paintings and Works on Paper 1939–1951*, Francis M. Naumann Fine Art, New York, 2010

Selz, Peter, *Gordon Onslow Ford: Exploring the Open Mind*, Weinstein Gallery, San Francisco, 2003

Weinstein, Rowland, *Gordon Onslow Ford: Centennial Celebration*, Weinstein Gallery, San Francisco, 2013

GRACE PAILTHORPE

Remy, Michel, et al., *Sluice-Gates of the Mind: The Collaborative Work of Pailthorpe and Mednikoff*, Leeds Museum and Art Gallery, 1998

ROLAND PENROSE

Penrose, Antony, *Roland Penrose: The Friendly Surrealist*, Prestel, Munich, 2001

Penrose, Roland, *The Road is Wider than Long*, London Gallery, London, 1939

Penrose, Roland, *Scrap Book: 1900–1981*, Thames & Hudson, London, 1981

Roland Penrose and Lee Miller: The Surrealist and the Photographer, Scottish National Gallery of Modern Art, Edinburgh, 2001

Slusher, Katherine, *Lee Miller, Roland Penrose: The Green Memories of Desire*, Prestel, New York, 2007

CERI RICHARDS

Ceri Richards, Tate Publishing, London, 1981

Gooding, Mel, *Ceri Richards*, Cameron & Hollis, Moffat, Dumfriesshire, 2002

GRAHAM SUTHERLAND

Alley, Ronald, *Graham Sutherland*, Tate Gallery, London, 1982

Berthoud, Roger, *Graham Sutherland: A Biography*, Faber & Faber, London, 1982

Cooper, Douglas, *The Work of Graham Sutherland*, Lund Humphries, London, 1961

Hammer, Martin, *Graham Sutherland: Landscapes, War Scenes, Portraits 1924–1950*, Scala Publishers, London, 2005

Hayes, John, *The Art of Graham Sutherland*, Alpine Fine Arts, New York, 1980

Sackville-West, Edward, *Graham Sutherland*, Penguin, London, 1944

Tassi, Roberto, *Graham Sutherland: Complete Graphic Work*, Ediciones Poligrafa, Barcelona, 1988

JULIAN TREVELYAN

Raine, Kathleen, *A Place, A State*, Enitharmon Press, London, 1974

Trevelyan, Philip, *Julian Trevelyan: Picture Language*, Lund Humphries, Farnham, 2013

JOHN TUNNARD

Martin, Simon, et al., *John Tunnard: Inner Space to Outer Space*, Pallant House Gallery, Chichester, 2010

Peat, Alan, and Brian Whitten, *John Tunnard, His Life and Work*, Scolar Press, Aldershot, 1997

EDWARD WADSWORTH

Black, Jonathan, *Edward Wadsworth: Form, Feeling and Calculation*, Philip Wilson, London, 2005

Edward Wadsworth: Paintings from the 1920s, Mayor Gallery, London, 1982

Glazebrook, Mark, *Edward Wadsworth: Paintings, Drawings and Prints*, Lund Humphries, London, 1974

Lewison, Jeremy, et al., *A Genius of Industrial England: Edward Wadsworth*, Arkwright Arts Trust, London, 1990

SCOTTIE WILSON

Melly, George, *It's All Writ Out for You: The Life and Work of Scottie Wilson*, Thames & Hudson, London, 1986

Petullo, Anthony J. and Katherine M. Murrell, *Scottie Wilson: Peddlar Turned Painter*, Petullo Publishing, Milwaukee, 2004

ART CRITICISM BY DESMOND MORRIS AND WRITINGS ON HIS ART

Levy, Silvano, *Desmond Morris: 50 Years of Surrealism*, Barrie and Jenkins, London, 1997

Levy, Silvano, *Desmond Morris: Naked Surrealism*, Pandora, Antwerp, 1999

Levy, Silvano, *Desmond Morris: Catalogue Raisonné, 1944–2000*, Pandora, Antwerp, 2001

Levy, Silvano, *Lines of Thought: The Drawings of Desmond Morris*, Kettlestone Press, Norfolk, 2008

Levy, Silvano, *Desmond Morris: Catalogue Raisonné, 2000–2012*, Sansom & Co., Bristol, 2012

Levy, Silvano, *Desmond Morris: Catalogue Raisonné, 2012–2020*, Sansom & Co., Bristol, 2020

Morris, Desmond, *The Biology of Art*, Methuen, London, 1962

Morris, Desmond, *The Art of Ancient Cyprus*, Phaidon, Oxford, 1985

Morris, Desmond, *Dark Inside My Head*, Belgrave Gallery, London, 2007

Morris, Desmond, *The Artistic Ape: Three Million Years of Art*, Red Lemon Press, London, 2013

Morris, Desmond, *Headworks: Collected Poems 1945–2014*, Dark Windows Press, Rhos-On-Sea, 2014

Morris, Desmond, *The Boats of Malta: The Art of the Fishermen*, Faraxa, Malta, 2016

Morris, Desmond, *Cats in Art*, Reaktion Books, London, 2017

Morris, Desmond, *Sixty-Nine Surrealists*, Dark Windows Press, Rhos-On-Sea, 2017

Morris, Desmond, *The Lives of the Surrealists*, Thames & Hudson, London, 2018

Morris, Desmond, *Bodyworks*, Dark Windows Press, Rhos-On-Sea, 2019

Morris, Desmond, *Postures: Body Language in Art*, Thames & Hudson, London, 2019

Morris, Desmond, *Congo: Catalogue Raisonné*, Mayor Gallery, London, 2019

Morris, Desmond, *A Tue-Tête: Headworks*, Le Grand Tamanoir, Paris, 2020

Morris, Desmond, *Creatures of the Mind: A 21st Century Bestiary*, Dark Windows Press, Rhos-On-Sea, 2020

Morris, Desmond, *The Surrealist Art of the Kuna*, Dark Windows Press, Rhos-On-Sea, 2020

Morris, Desmond, *Surrealist Familiars: Obscure Objects in the Artist's Studio*, Dark Windows Press, Rhos-On-Sea, 2020

Morris, Desmond, *Wordworks: Painting with Words, 1948–1920*, Dark Windows Press, Rhos-On-Sea, 2020

Oakes, Philip, and Desmond Morris, *The Secret Surrealist: The Paintings of Desmond Morris*, Phaidon, Oxford, 1987

Remy, Michel, *The Surrealist World of Desmond Morris*, Johnathan Cape, London, 1991

ACKNOWLEDGMENTS

I would like to acknowledge the help I have received with the subject of this book. In particular I am extremely grateful to Silvano Levy, Andrew Murray, Michel Remy and Tor Scott, with whom I have had many valuable discussions over the years. I would also like to express my debt to my late wife, Ramona, for her tireless assistance in researching the elusive details of the lives of many of the surrealists.

I would also like to thank all those at Thames & Hudson who have worked so hard to bring this book to life: editorial director Roger Thorp, editor Michela Parkin, associate editor Mohara Gill, designer Karolina Prymaka, cover designer Aman Phull, picture researcher Maria Ranauro and production controller Ginny Liggitt.

Sadly, all the British artists that I have known who were active in the surrealist movement between the wars are now dead, but I would like to record my sincere thanks for all the stimulating ideas and amusing anecdotes they shared with me in earlier days. Those that I was fortunate enough to know personally included Eileen Agar, Francis Bacon, Conroy Maddox, F. E. McWilliam, Oscar Mellor, Henry Moore, Roland Penrose, Julian Trevelyan and Scottie Wilson.

LIST OF ILLUSTRATIONS

Dimensions of works are given in centimetres and inches, height before width before depth.

36 Francis Bacon, *The Crucifixion*, 1933. Oil on canvas, 111.5 × 86.5 (44 × 34⅛). © The Estate of Francis Bacon. All rights reserved. DACS/Artimage 2022. Photo Prudence Cuming Associates Ltd
39 Francis Bacon, *Composition (Figure)*, 1933. Gouache, pastel and ink on paper, 53.5 × 40 (21⅛ × 15¾). Private collection. © The Estate of Francis Bacon. All rights reserved. DACS/Artimage 2022. Photo Prudence Cuming Associates Ltd
42 John Banting, photographed by Humphrey Spender, 1930s. © National Portrait Gallery, London
43 John Banting, *Guardian Bust*, 1936. Oil on board, 48.3 × 41.3 (19 × 16¼). The Murray Family Collection, UK and USA. Photo Chris Harrison Photography. © The Estate of John Banting/Bridgeman Images
44 John Banting, *The Yellow Harpist*, 1946. Pencil, gouache and black ink, 56 × 75 (22⅛ × 29⅝). Photo Christie's Images, London/Scala, Florence. © The Estate of John Banting/Bridgeman Images
47 John Selby Bigge, photographed by Bassano Ltd., London, 1933. © National Portrait Gallery, London
48 John Selby Bigge, *Dieppe*, 1931. Oil on wood, 44.8 × 60.6 (17¾ × 23⅞). Tate. © The Estate of John Bigge
49 John Selby Bigge, *Surrealist Landscape*, 1942. Oil on wood, 45 × 60.5 (17¾ × 25¾). The Murray Family Collection, UK and USA. Photo Chris Harrison Photography. © The Estate of John Bigge
52 Emmy Bridgwater, 1940. Photo Bridgeman Images
53 Emmy Bridgwater, *Night Work is about to Commence*, 1940–43. Oil on board, 46 × 61 (18⅛ × 24⅛). Birmingham Museums and Art Gallery. Purchased with the assistance of the Friends of Birmingham Museums & Art Gallery and the Victoria & Albert Purchase Grant Fund, 2001/Bridgeman Images. © The Estate of Emmy Bridgwater
54 Emmy Bridgwater, *Brave Morning*, *c.* 1942. Oil on canvas, 61 × 80 (24⅛ × 31½). The Sherwin Collection, Leeds/Bridgeman Images. © The Estate of Emmy Bridgwater
56 Edward Burra in London, undated. Photo © Lefevre Fine Art Ltd., London/ Bridgeman Images
57 Edward Burra, *Bal des Pendus*, 1937. Watercolour on board, 155.3 × 114 (61⅛ × 44⅞). Museum of Modern Art, New York (233.1948). Photo digital image, The Museum of Modern Art, New York/Scala, Florence, 2022. © Estate of the Artist c/o Lefevre Fine Art Ltd., London
58–59 Edward Burra, *Soldiers at Rye*, 1941. Gouache, watercolour and ink on paper, 102.2 × 207 (40¼ × 81½). © Tate
63 Leonora Carrington in her Greenwich Village apartment, photographed by Hermann Landshoff, *c.* 1942. Münchner Stadtmuseum, Munich (FM-2012/200.223). Photo Scala, Florence/bpk, Bildagentur für Kunst, Kultur und Geschichte, Berlin
64 Leonora Carrington, *And Then We Saw the Daughter of the Minotaur*, 1953. Oil on canvas, 60 × 70 (23½ × 27½). Museum of Modern Art, New York. Gift of Joan H. Tisch, by exchange, (146.2019). Photo private collection. © Estate of Leonora Carrington/ARS, NY and DACS, London 2022
67 Leonora Carrington, *Are You Really Syrious?*, 1953. Oil on three-ply, 53.5 × 91.5 (21 × 36). Collection of Miguel S. Scobedo. © Estate of Leonora Carrington/ARS, NY and DACS, London 2022
69 Cecil Collins, *c.* 1965. Photo Tony Evans/Getty Images
70 Cecil Collins, *The Promise*, 1936. Oil on plywood, 50.8 × 61 (20 × 24⅛). © Tate
73 Cecil Collins, *Hymn*, 1953. Oil on board, 122.6 × 153 (48⅜ × 60¼). © Tate
76 Ithell Colquhoun, 1949. Photo Reg Speller/Fox Photos/Hulton Archive/Getty Images

Private collection. Kind permission given by the artist's daughter, Lee Saunders

119 F. E. McWilliam, 1948. Photo © The estate of F. E. McWilliam

120 F. E. McWilliam, *Carving*, 1936. Walnut on marble base, 30 (11⅞) high. The Sherwin Collection, Leeds/Bridgeman Images. © The estate of F. E. McWilliam

123 F. E. McWilliam, *Spanish Head*, 1939. Hoptonwood stone, 120 × 61 × 23 (47¼ × 24⅛ × 9⅛). The Sherwin Collection, Leeds/Bridgeman Images. © The estate of F. E. McWilliam

125 Reuben Mednikoff, 1938. Scottish National Gallery of Modern Art Archive. Purchased with the assistance of the Friends of the National Libraries, 1999; Birth Trauma and Toe Dance series purchased 2001 (GMA A62/3/20/1)

126 Reuben Mednikoff, *The Anatomy of Space (21 January)*, 1936. Oil on canvas, 110.5 × 85.8 (43⅝ × 33⅞). Private collection

127 Reuben Mednikoff, *The Stairway to Paradise (20 March – 1)*, 1936. Pen, ink and watercolour on paper, 26 × 34.5 (10¼ × 13⅝). The Murray Family Collection, UK and USA

130 Oscar Mellor, early 1950s. Courtesy of the family of Oscar Mellor. © The Estate of Oscar Mellor

131 Oscar Mellor, *A Small Bunch of Eyes*, 1948. Oil on canvas, 57 × 36.5 (22½ × 14⅜). Arts Council Collection, Southbank Centre, London. © The Estate of Oscar Mellor

132 Oscar Mellor, *The Green Child*, 1950. Oil on canvas, 30 × 20 (11¾ × 7⅞). The Murray Family Collection, UK and USA. Photo Chris Harrison Photography. © The Estate of Oscar Mellor

135 John Melville, date unknown. Photo previously reproduced in Andrew Murray, *British Surrealism Fifty Years On* (March–April 1986), the Major Gallery, London

136 John Melville, *Dancers No. 3*, *c.* 1934. Oil on canvas, 76.3 × 64.3 (30 × 25⅜). Photo Christie's Images, London/Scala, Florence, 2022

137 John Melville, *Natural History Museum of the Child*, 1937. Oil on canvas, 71.1 × 100.3 (28 × 39½). Leeds Museums and Galleries (Leeds Art Gallery)/Bridgeman Images

141 Henry Moore, 1945. Photo Hulton-Deutsch Collection/Corbis via Getty Images

142 Henry Moore, *Two Forms*, 1934, cast 1967. Bronze, 22.2 × 17.1 × 8.9 (8¾ × 6¾ × 3½). Private collection, UK. Photo A. C. Cooper. Reproduced by permission of The Henry Moore Foundation

145 Henry Moore, *The Helmet*, 1939–40. Bronze, 29.2 (11½) high. The Henry Moore Foundation, gift of Irina Moore 1977. Photo Menor. Reproduced by permission of The Henry Moore Foundation

149 Paul Nash, 1944. Photo Hulton-Deutsch Collection/Corbis via Getty Images

151 Paul Nash, *Mineral Objects*, 1935. Oil on canvas, 50.2 × 60.3 (19¾ × 23¾). Yale Center for British Art, Paul Mellon Fund (B1998.21.1)

152 Paul Nash, *Nocturnal Landscape*, 1938. Oil on canvas, 76.5 × 101.5 (30⅛ × 40). Manchester Art Gallery/Bridgeman Images

154 Gordon Onslow Ford, Switzerland, *c.* 1938. © Courtesy the Lucid Art Foundation, Gordon Onslow Ford Collection and Archive

157 Gordon Onslow Ford, *Determination of Gender*, 1939. Oil on canvas, 92.1 × 72.7 (36⅜ × 28⅝). Tate. © Courtesy the Lucid Art Foundation, Gordon Onslow Ford Collection and Archive

158 Gordon Onslow Ford, *Escape*, 1939. Oil on canvas, 76.2 × 101.6 (30 × 40). Courtesy Weinstein Gallery. © Courtesy the Lucid Art Foundation, Gordon Onslow Ford Collection and Archive

of Bohun Gallery, Henley-on-Thames/ Bridgeman Images. © The Estate of Julian Trevelyan/Bridgeman Images

204 John Tunnard, 1951. Photo The National Archives/SSPL/Getty Images

207 John Tunnard, *Installation*, 1942. Tempera on gesso-prepared board, 75.6 × 55.9 (29⅞ × 22⅛). The Ingram Collection of Modern British and Contemporary Art/Bridgeman Images. © The Estate of John Tunnard. All rights reserved. DACS 2022

208–9 John Tunnard, *Tide Race*, 1947. Watercolour, gouache and chalk on paper, 56 × 73.6 (22⅛ × 29). Jerwood Collection/Bridgeman Images. © The Estate of John Tunnard. All rights reserved. DACS 2022

215 Edward Wadsworth, 1920. Photo George C. Beresford/Hulton Archive/Getty Images

217 Edward Wadsworth, *Regalia*, 1928. Tempera and oil on canvas on board, 76.3 × 91.7 (30⅛ × 36⅛). Tate. Photo Mayor Gallery, London/Bridgeman Images

219 Edward Wadsworth, *North Sea*, 1928. Tempera on wood, 86.4 × 60.9 (34⅛ × 24). Private collection

222 Scottie Wilson, 1967. Photo Arthur Sidey/Mirrorpix/Getty Images

225 Scottie Wilson, *Self-Portrait Head*, *c.* 1938. Crayon and ink, 38.1 × 25.4 (15 × 10). Courtesy Henry Boxer Gallery

226 Scottie Wilson, *Untitled*, *c.* 1940. Crayon and ink, 45.7 × 33 (18 × 13). Courtesy Henry Boxer Gallery

INDEX

Page references in *italics* refer to illustrations.

First published in the United Kingdom in 2022 by
Thames & Hudson Ltd, 181A High Holborn, London WC1V 7QX

First published in the United States of America in 2022 by
Thames & Hudson Inc., 500 Fifth Avenue, New York, New York 10110

The chapters titled Eileen Agar; Francis Bacon; Leonora Carrington; Conroy Maddox; Henry Moore; Roland Penrose are based on text from *The Lives of the Surrealists* by Desmond Morris, first published by Thames & Hudson, 2018.

British Library Cataloguing-in-Publication Data
A catalogue record for this book is available from the British Library

Library of Congress Control Number 2021945522

ISBN 978-0-500-02488-1

Printed and bound in China by C&C Offset Printing Co, Ltd

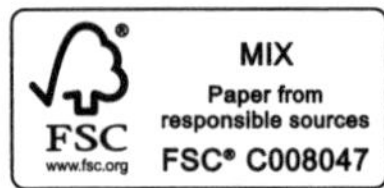